Home Cooks'
EASY RECIPES

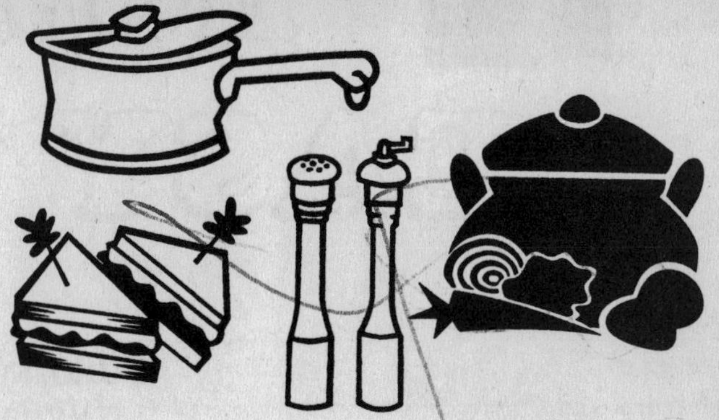

THE COMPLETE COOKBOOK FOR HOME COOKS LIKE YOU!

CONTENTS

PAGE

OVER 600 EASY TO MAKE RECIPES

Paradise Press, Inc.

HOME COOKS' EASY RECIPES

Editorial Director
Vivian Rothe
Associate Editors
Ramona Lehrman
Judi K. Merkel
Peggy Moss
Production
Carol Dailey
Cathy Reef
Sandra Ridgway
Photography
Rhonda Davis
Nora Elsesser

ISBN #1-884907-52-0
30428
Exclusive Distribution by Paradise Press, Inc.

Appetizers

APPEALING

Turtle Ice Cream Treat

- Ice cream sandwich wafer, chocolate or vanilla
- Vanilla ice cream
- 6 pecan halves
- Prepared caramel sauce

You will need: ice cream scoop, spoon, plate.

Put ice cream wafer on plate. Put a large scoop of ice cream in center. Use 1 large pecan for head, 4 for feet and a small piece for the tail. Spoon caramel sauce over top of ice cream. Serve and eat. Serves 1.

Funny Face Pizza

- 1 English muffin, split in half
- 2 tablespoons prepared pizza sauce
- 10 thin slices pepperoni *or* salami
- 2 slices mozzarella cheese
- 2 slices ripe olive

You will need: toaster, measuring spoons, knife, cutting board, cookie sheet, hot pads, timer, wide metal spatula and oven.

Turn on oven. Set at 375 degrees. Toast English muffin halves in toaster. Carefully remove and put on a cookie sheet. Spread each with 1 tablespoon pizza sauce. Top each with 5 slices of pepperoni. Cut a face out of each slice of cheese. Use an olive slice for the nose. Put cheese over pepperoni.

Put pizzas in oven and bake 8–10 minutes, or until cheese is melted. Carefully remove from oven with hot pads. Lift off cookie sheet with spatula. Serve and eat. Serves 2.

Nacho Cheese Tortillas

- 2 tablespoons mild *or* hot Mexican cheese spread
- 1 flour tortilla
- Salsa

You will need: measuring spoons, knife, paper plate, microwave oven, small bowl.

Spread cheese over tortilla; roll up. Put on paper plate. Microwave on HIGH 1 minute. Cut into 4 pieces. Put some salsa in bowl. Dip in salsa as you eat. Serves 1.

Frozen Fruit Pops

- 3 cups grape juice *or* fruit punch
- 1 (14-ounce) can sweetened condensed milk
- 1/4 cup lemon juice
- 12 (3-ounce) paper cups
- 12 wooden sticks

You will need: measuring cups, large mixing bowl, wire whisk, measuring cup with spout (for pouring mixture into paper cups), 8-inch square pan, freezer, timer.

Mix juices and sweetened condensed milk in bowl using wire whisk. Carefully pour some of mixture into measuring cup with a pouring spout. Put paper cups into square pan. Fill paper cups almost to the top. Put in freezer for 1 hour. Remove from freezer and put wooden stick in center of each "pop."

Return to freezer for 5 hours. To serve, carefully peel off paper cup. (To keep, put frozen pops in a plastic bag and freeze up to 2 weeks.) Makes 12.

Taco Corn

- 8 cups plain popped corn *or* microwavable popcorn *or* buy it already popped
- 1/4 cup (1/2 stick) butter
- 2 teaspoons taco seasoning mix

You will need: large mixing bowl, 1-cup glass measuring cup, measuring spoons, spoon.

Put popped corn in mixing bowl. Put butter in glass measuring cup. Microwave it on HIGH 40–50 seconds, or until melted. Carefully remove from the microwave oven. Stir taco seasoning mix into butter. (Save remainder of package for another use.) Pour over popped corn; mix well. Makes 8 cups.

Winter's Eve Fondue

- 1 envelope onion soup mix
- 2 cups dry white wine
- 4 cups shredded Swiss cheese (about 1 pound)
- 2 tablespoons cornstarch
- 2 tablespoons kirsch (optional)
- French bread, cut into bite-size cubes

In medium saucepan, heat onion soup mix blended with wine. When wine begins to simmer, gradually add cheese mixed with cornstarch, stirring after each addition, until completely melted. Stir in kirsch.

Pour into fondue pot or chafing dish. Serve by dipping speared bread cubes into fondue.

Variation: Use 2 1/4 cups apple juice for wine and kirsch.

Christmas Dip

- 2 single-serving envelopes onion soup mix
- 1 cup (8 ounces) sour cream
- 1 medium avocado, mashed
- 1/4 cup diced green pepper
- 1/4 cup finely chopped pimiento
- 1 teaspoon lemon juice
- 1/4 teaspoon garlic powder

In medium bowl, blend all ingredients; chill. Makes about 2 1/2 cups dip.

Greek Cucumber Dip

- 2 large cucumbers, peeled and coarsely grated
- 1 cup plain yogurt
- 1 cup sour cream
- 1 small garlic clove, finely minced
- 1 teaspoon salt
- 1/4 teaspoon pepper
- Raw vegetables *or* Pita Crisps (recipe follows)

Enclose 1/4 of grated cucumber in a dish towel and wring out as much moisture as possible. Repeat with remaining cucumber. Combine all ingredients and mix well. Refrigerate until ready to serve. Serve with raw vegetables or Pita Crisps. Makes 2 1/2 cups.

Pita Crisps

Split a pita bread in half, forming 2 thin rounds. Cut rounds into quarters; place on cookie sheet and bake 7–10 minutes at 325 degrees until crisp and very lightly browned.

Cheese-Artichoke Spread

- 2 (14-ounce) cans artichoke hearts, drained
- 1 cup grated Parmesan cheese
- 1 cup mayonnaise
- 8 ounces shredded mozzarella cheese
- Pinch garlic powder
- Dash freshly ground pepper
- Parsley sprigs

Cut each artichoke heart into 6–8 pieces. Combine with remaining ingredients, except parsley. Spread in quiche dish or other flat pan. Bake at 350 degrees for 25–30 minutes. Garnish with parsley. Serve with wheat crackers.

Braunschweiger Ball

- 1 1/2 pounds braunschweiger
- 2 (3-ounce) packages cream cheese
- 2 tablespoons mayonnaise
- 2 tablespoons blue cheese dip
- 1/4 teaspoon garlic salt
- 1 tablespoon chili powder
- 1 (3-ounce) package cream cheese, softened
- Green olives, sliced

Mix all ingredients, except the last 3-ounce package cream cheese and green olives; chill and form into ball. Frost with reserved package softened cream cheese and sliced green olives. Very good served on crackers.

Marinated Shrimp

- 1 pound medium shrimp
- 1/4 cup fresh orange juice
- 3 tablespoons fresh lemon juice
- 1 tablespoon olive oil
- 1 medium clove garlic, minced
- 1 medium shallot, minced
- 1 teaspoon minced fresh rosemary
- Ground black pepper to taste

Peel and devein shrimp. Bring a medium-size pan of water to boil, add shrimp and simmer for 3 minutes. The shrimp should be pink, cooked and curled. If not, cook a little longer. Drain and rinse with cold water. Drain thoroughly. Combine remaining ingredients, except pepper. Place shrimp in bowl and pour marinade over. Sprinkle with pepper. Cover and marinate in refrigerator for 2 hours. To serve, remove from marinade with slotted spoon. Spoon onto lettuce leaves to serve. Sprinkle marinade over shrimp.

Fruit Cheese Ball

- 2 (8-ounce) packages cream cheese, softened
- 1 large can fruit cocktail, well-drained
- 2 small packages instant vanilla pudding

Mix all ingredients together; roll in ground pecans. Serve with cinnamon graham crackers.

Deviled Crab Toastettes

- 1 pound crabmeat
- 1 cup mayonnaise
- 2 teaspoons fresh lemon juice
- 1 1/2 teaspoons Worcestershire sauce
- 1 teaspoon Dijon-style mustard
- 2 tablespoons grated Parmesan cheese
- 1 cup plus 2 tablespoons grated Gruyère cheese
- 8 slices thin white bread
- 4 tablespoons unsalted butter, softened
- Salt and pepper

Preheat broiler; remove any pieces of shell or cartilage from crabmeat. In food processor fitted with metal blade, blend mayonnaise, lemon juice, Worcestershire sauce, mustard, 1 teaspoon salt, 1/2 teaspoon pepper, Parmesan cheese and 2 tablespoons Gruyère cheese. Add crabmeat; process briefly until mixture is thoroughly blended.

Trim crusts from bread. Toast bread lightly under broiler; spread each slice with 1/2 tablespoon butter. Spread crabmeat mixture over toast; top with remaining Gruyere cheese and place under broiler for 2–3 minutes, until cheese melts and begins to brown. Remove toast from broiler; cut into quarters and serve. Makes 32 canapés.

Stuffed Cherry Tomatoes

- 1 (10-ounce) package frozen chopped spinach
- 2 cups low-fat cottage cheese
- 2 tablespoons fresh parsley, chopped
- 1/2 teaspoon salt
- 1 pound cherry tomatoes

Thaw and thoroughly drain spinach. Combine with cottage cheese, parsley and salt. Cover and refrigerate 2 hours or overnight. Cut tops off tomatoes and hollow out. Fill each tomato with spinach mixture, rounding at the top. Serve immediately or refrigerate until ready to use. Makes 12–15. (22 calories per tomato)

Pistachio Crescents

1¾ cups (9 ounces) shelled, unsalted pistachio nuts, blanched, divided*
¾ cup sugar, divided
1 cup (2 sticks) butter, softened**
1 egg
2 teaspoons vanilla extract
2 cups all-purpose flour
Dash salt
4–6 drops green food color, if desired

Place ¾ cup nuts and ¼ cup sugar in food processor or blender; cover. Process until nuts are finely chopped; set aside. Cream butter in large mixer bowl. Gradually add remaining ½ cup sugar; beat until light and fluffy. Mix in egg and vanilla. Gradually stir in flour, salt and nut mixture; mix well. Stir in food color. Wrap dough in plastic wrap and refrigerate 1–2 hours, or until firm.

Preheat oven to 375 degrees. Coarsely chop remaining nuts; spread on waxed paper. Work with half of the dough at a time; leave remaining dough wrapped and refrigerated. Roll tablespoonfuls of dough to form a 3-inch log. Roll in chopped nuts. Place on unbuttered cookie sheets, 1 inch apart. Shape into crescents.

Bake 10–12 minutes, or until golden. Cool on cookie sheets a few minutes. Remove from cookie sheets and cool completely on wire racks. Store in airtight metal containers in cool place up to 3 weeks. Freeze up to 6 months. Makes 4 dozen.

*Roasted, unsalted cashew nut pieces may be substituted for the pistachio nuts. Omit green food color.

Sausage-Stuffed Mushrooms

1 pound hot pork sausage
1 pound large fresh mushrooms
½ pound mozzarella cheese

Clean mushrooms and pull out stems. Fill mushrooms with raw sausage; pat until sausage is mounded and secure. Bake on an ungreased cookie sheet at 350 degrees for 30 minutes, or until sausage looks well-browned. The last 5 minutes of baking time, top the mushrooms with shredded mozzarella cheese.

Tex-Mex Dip

3 medium-size ripe avocados
2 tablespoons lemon juice
½ teaspoon salt
¼ teaspoon pepper
8 ounces sour cream
2 (10½-ounce) cans jalapeño bean dip
1 large bunch green onions, chopped (include tops)
3 medium tomatoes, cored, seeded and chopped
½ cup salad dressing
1 package taco seasoning
2 (3½-ounce) cans pitted ripe olives, chopped
8 ounces sharp cheddar cheese, shredded

Peel avocados and mix in bowl with lemon juice, salt and pepper. Mix sour cream, taco seasoning and salad dressing. Put in second bowl. Spread bean dip in large flat dish; top with avocado mixture. Cover with taco seasoning mixture; layer with chopped onion, olives and tomatoes. Cover with cheese.

Chipped Beef Dip

2 cups sour cream
2 (8-ounce) packages cream cheese, softened
3 packages chipped beef, cut up
3 bunches green onion and tops, minced
1 large green pepper, minced

Combine all ingredients; mix well. Place in 1-quart baking dish. Bake in a 325-degree oven for 30 minutes. Serve this dip warm with fresh vegetables or crackers.

Party Pita Chips

4 pita bread pockets
⅓ cup Italian salad dressing
2 tablespoons grated Parmesan cheese
1 teaspoon Italian herb seasoning

Preheat oven to 400 degrees. Split pita bread into 2 rounds each. Cut each round into wedges. Brush wedges with dressing. Arrange on baking sheet. Sprinkle with Parmesan cheese and Italian seasoning. Bake for 10 minutes. Great as a snack chip or for dips.

Easy Clam or Shrimp Dip

1 (10-ounce) package frozen chopped spinach, thawed and well-drained
1 cup cream cheese
1 cup mayonnaise
1 package dry vegetable soup mix
1 (5-ounce) can baby clams or shrimp, drained and rinsed

Mix together all ingredients and refrigerate for a few hours to allow flavors to blend. Serve as a dip for raw vegetables or with assorted crackers.

Cheddar-Bacon Spread

4 slices bacon
1 (10-ounce) package extra-sharp cheddar cheese, shredded (2½ cups)
½ cup milk
¼ cup mayonnaise
1 teaspoon Worcestershire sauce
⅛ teaspoon ground red pepper
Party rye bread slices

In skillet, cook bacon until crisp. Remove to paper towel to drain. Crumble bacon; set aside. In blender, blend cheddar cheese and next 4 ingredients until smooth. Stir in crumbled bacon. Serve on party rye bread.

Crab Dip

6 ounces crabmeat
1 tablespoon milk
¼ teaspoon salt
1 tablespoon horseradish
1 (8-ounce) package cream cheese, softened
2 tablespoons finely chopped onion
Dash pepper
Sliced almonds

If you use frozen or canned crabmeat, press out as much of the liquid as possible. Combine ingredients, except the nuts, in an attractive oven-safe dish. Sprinkle almonds over top and bake at 375 degrees for 15 minutes, or until hot and almonds start to turn golden. Serve with snack crackers.

Party-Pleasing Marinated Shrimp

- 4 tablespoons cooking oil
- 2 tablespoons lemon juice
- 1 tablespoon vinegar
- 1 tablespoon prepared mustard
- 1 stalk celery, diced
- 2 green onions, sliced
- 1 can shrimp

Combine all ingredients; mix well. Marinate for 6 hours, or overnight. Serve with wafers. Serves 4. Double, triple or quadruple the recipe according to party size.

Hot Soft Italian Pretzels

- 4 purchased soft pretzels
- Prepared mustard
- 1 teaspoon Italian seasoning
- 1/4 cup (1 ounce) finely shredded provolone cheese

Place pretzels on microwavable plate. Squeeze or spread mustard evenly over top of each pretzel. Sprinkle each with 1/4 teaspoon Italian seasoning. Divide cheese evenly over pretzels. Press cheese gently so it adheres to pretzel. Microwave at MEDIUM-HIGH (70 percent) for 1 1/2–2 1/2 minutes, or until cheese is melted and pretzels are warm.

Cheese Fondue Party

- 2 (8-ounce) packages Swiss cheese, shredded
- 2 1/2 tablespoons flour
- 1/4 teaspoon salt
- 1/4 teaspoon pepper
- 1/2 teaspoon paprika
- 2 small cloves garlic, finely mashed
- 1 (12-ounce) can beer
- 1/2 teaspoon liquid hot pepper sauce
- 1 loaf French bread, cut into 1-inch cubes

In a large bowl mix cheese, flour, salt, pepper, paprika and mashed garlic. Pour into fondue casserole, heavy skillet or blazer pan of chafing dish; pour in beer. Gradually stir in cheese mixture, 1 cup at a time; stir after each addition until cheese is melted and smooth; add hot pepper sauce. Spear bread cube with long-handled fork; dip into fondue; twirl cheese around the bread. Serves 6.

Party Shrimp Pâté

- 1 envelope unflavored gelatin
- 1/4 cup lemon juice
- 1/4 cup water
- 2 cups (16 ounces) sour cream
- 3/4 cup chili sauce
- 2 tablespoons horseradish
- 1 1/2 cups chopped cooked shrimp (about 1/2 pound)
- Assorted crackers and party-size bread

In medium saucepan, sprinkle unflavored gelatin over lemon juice and water; let stand 1 minute. Stir over low heat until gelatin is completely dissolved, about 5 minutes; cool. Blend in sour cream, chili sauce and horseradish; fold in shrimp. Turn into 3 1/2-cup mold or bowl; chill until firm. Serve with crackers and party-size bread. Makes about 3 1/2 cups pâté.

Foldover Cornmeal Cheese Biscuits

- 1 1/2 cups all-purpose flour
- 1/2 cup white cornmeal, stone-ground
- 1 1/4 tablespoons sugar
- 2 teaspoons baking powder
- 1/4 teaspoon salt
- 1/2 teaspoon baking soda
- 1/4 cup shortening
- 1/4 cup butter
- 1 egg, lightly beaten
- 1 cup sour cream
- 1 1/2 cups American cheese, grated

Sift together first 6 ingredients; add shortening and butter; cut in thoroughly. Stir in egg and sour cream; do not overmix. Knead dough gently until no longer sticky. Roll dough 1/4 inch thick; use a 2 1/2-inch biscuit cutter; reroll dough trimmings.

Sprinkle circle with small amount of grated cheese; fold circle over just slightly off-center (Parkerhouse-roll-style); press down lightly. Place folded biscuits on a lightly greased baking sheet. Bake at 400 degrees for 12–15 minutes. Makes 2 dozen.

Pizza Bread

- 1 teaspoon honey
- 1/4 cup warm water
- 1 package dry yeast
- 3 1/2 cups flour
- 1 teaspoon salt
- 2 tablespoons dried oregano
- 1 tablespoon sugar
- 1 cup sliced scallions, both white and green parts
- 1 cup sliced pepperoni
- 1 cup milk
- 2 tablespoons olive oil
- 1/4 cup tomato pizza sauce, heated
- 1/3 cup grated mozzarella cheese

Dissolve honey in warm water. Add yeast and set aside until mixture bubbles. Mix flour, salt, oregano, sugar, scallions and pepperoni together. Add milk, yeast mixture and olive oil. Blend, then turn out onto a floured board and knead until dough is smooth, about 8 minutes.

Place dough in a greased bowl, turning it so that the top of the dough is lightly covered with oil. Cover with a towel and let rise in a warm place until doubled in bulk, about 1 hour. Punch dough down. Knead for 1 minute, then transfer to an oiled 9 x 5 x 3-inch loaf pan. Cover with a towel and let rise again in warm place until doubled in bulk, about 1 hour. Preheat oven to 375 degrees. Bake bread for 35 minutes, or until bread sounds hollow when tapped. Brush loaf with pizza sauce and sprinkle cheese in strip down center of bread. Return loaf to oven and bake until cheese melts, about 3 minutes.

Italian Alpine Caps

- 24 mushrooms (about 1 pound)
- 1/4 cup Italian *or* Caesar dressing
- 1 cup soft bread crumbs
- 1/4 cup grated Parmesan cheese
- 1 tablespoon finely chopped parsley

Preheat oven to 350 degrees. Remove and finely chop mushroom stems.

In medium bowl, combine Italian dressing, bread crumbs, cheese, parsley and chopped stems. Fill caps with bread crumb mixture; place in shallow baking dish. Add water to barely cover bottom and bake 20 minutes. Makes 24 stuffed mushrooms.

Beverages

REFRESHING

Spirit of the Season Punch

- 1 quart boiling water
- 8 tea bags
- 1 gallon apple cider
- 1 cup lemon juice
- 2 1/4 cups brown sugar
- 12 whole allspice
- 12 whole cloves
- 4 cinnamon sticks, broken
- 1 bottle (4/5-quart) burgundy wine
- Apple slices

In large saucepan, pour boiling water over tea bags; cover and brew 5 minutes. Remove tea bags. Add cider, lemon juice, sugar and spices. Simmer 10 minutes, stirring occasionally. Remove spices; add wine and heat through. Garnish with apple slices. Makes about 35 (5-ounce) servings.

Holiday Toddy

- 3 cups boiling water
- 5 tea bags
- 2 whole cloves
- 1/8 teaspoon ground nutmeg
- 1/4 cup sugar
- 1 (12-ounce) can ginger ale

In teapot, pour boiling water over tea bags, cloves and nutmeg; cover and brew 5 minutes. Remove tea bags and cloves; stir in sugar.

Serve in cups or mugs and top with splash of ginger ale. If desired, stir in additional sugar. Serves 6.

A party favorite.

Rosy Wassail Cheer

- 1/2 cup brown sugar
- 1/4 cup instant tea powder
- 3 whole allspice
- 3 whole cloves
- 1 cinnamon stick
- 1 (1-quart) bottle cranberry juice cocktail
- 2 cups water
- 1/4 cup lemon juice

In large saucepan, combine all ingredients. Bring to a boil, then simmer 10 minutes; remove spices. Serve in cups or mugs and garnish, if desired, with additional cinnamon sticks. Makes about 10 (5-ounce) servings.

Lemonade

- 1 tablespoon fresh-grated lemon peel
- 1 1/2 cups sugar
- 1 1/2 cups fresh-squeezed lemon juice
- 1/2 cup boiling water

Combine sugar and boiling water to dissolve sugar. Add lemon juice and lemon peel. Store, covered, in refrigerator. Makes 2 2/3 cups base, enough for 8–10 servings.

Lemonade by the glass: Pour 1/4–1/2 cup syrup base into tall glasses. Add 3/4 cup cold water; stir. Add ice cubes and enjoy.

Lemonade by the pitcher: Combine full recipe of syrup base with 6 cups cold water; stir. Add ice cubes. Makes about 2 quarts.

Irish Mocha Mint Float

- 3 tablespoons Irish mocha mint coffee
- 2 quarts boiling water
- Vanilla ice cream

Dissolve coffee powder in boiling water and chill. Pour into tall cold glasses and add a large scoop of vanilla ice cream.

Melon Shake

- 1/2 cup watermelon, cantaloupe *or* honeydew
- 2 large scoops (1 cup) vanilla ice cream
- 1/4 cup milk

Cut melon of your choice in half. Using a melon baller, scoop enough melon to measure 1/2 cup. Place in blender. Add ice cream and milk. Cover and blend until smooth. Serve immediately.

Santa's Pleasure Punch

- 1/2 cup lemon-flavored iced tea mix
- 2 (12-ounce) cans apricot nectar
- 2 cups pineapple juice
- 2 (7-ounce) bottles ginger ale, chilled

In large pitcher, combine all ingredients except ginger ale. Just before serving, add ginger ale. Serve in tall ice-filled glasses. Serves 6.

Breads

TO MAKE

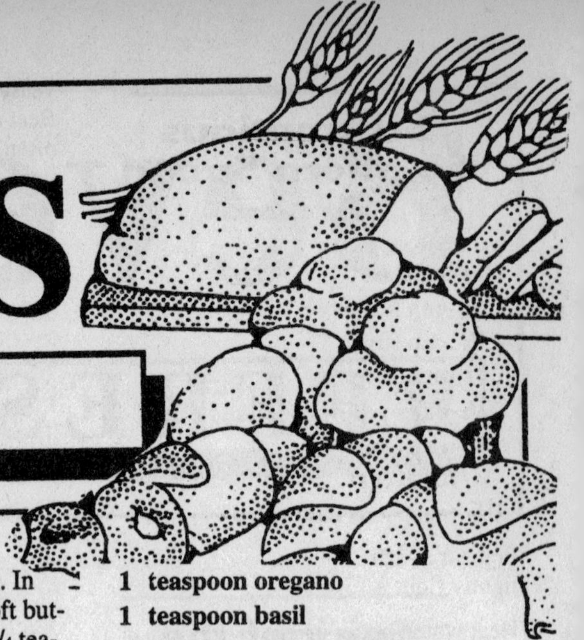

Three-Way Refrigerator Dough

- 3 cups bread flour, divided
- 3 tablespoons sugar
- 1 teaspoon salt
- 1 (1/4-ounce) package regular dry yeast
- 1 cup hottest tap water
- 2 tablespoons shortening
- 1 large egg

Into a large bowl measure 1 1/2 cups flour, sugar, salt and yeast. Mix briefly with dry beaters on low speed.

Measure 1 cup hottest tap water in pint pitcher; add shortening; whisk vigorously until smooth. Slowly pour into dry ingredients while beating on low speed; beat 2 minutes on low. Add egg; beat 1 minute on high. Mix in enough flour to make a firm dough, about 1 1/4 cups. (I do this with a sturdy spatula.) When thoroughly mixed, cover and let rest 10–15 minutes.

Sprinkle the remaining 1/4 cup flour on pastry cloth; knead dough 5–10 minutes. For the best-quality bread, knead in as little additional flour as possible.

Spray a medium bowl with pan release or grease; drop in ball of dough; turn to coat; cover; refrigerate. After 2 hours, punch down by turning dough over in bowl and gently pressing out bubbles. Cover; store in refrigerator 2 hours to several days; use in the following recipes.

Sticky Cinnamon Buns

Half of refrigerator dough makes 10 rolls.

Grease custard cups or muffin tins. In bottom of each, mix 1 teaspoon soft butter, 2 teaspoons brown sugar and 1/4 teaspoon water. Sprinkle in 1 teaspoon chopped pecans.

To make cinnamon buns, flatten dough as for Dinner Rolls; spread generously with melted butter; sprinkle with cinnamon and brown or granulated sugar and chopped pecans, if desired. Fold dough over to enclose filling and make a 4-inch-wide rectangle; cut into strips about 3/4-inch wide; twist; coil into prepared cups. Cover; let rise to double, about 1 hour. Bake at 400 degrees until brown, about 15 minutes. Set cooling rack over plate; turn out buns on rack carefully so sticky glaze coats sides of buns. Serve warm with plenty of butter.

Pizza Dinner for Two

Prepare Tomato Sauce given below. Preheat oven to 475 degrees.

Pat a scant half of refrigerated dough evenly in a greased 12- or 13-inch pizza pan. Rub crust lightly with oil—olive oil is a flavorful choice. Spoon on 1 cup of tomato sauce. I top it with lots of lightly sautéed onion slices, crumbled crisply cooked bacon and shredded mozzarella cheese. Use whatever topping items you like. No rising is necessary. Bake on lowest oven rack at 475 degrees until crust is brown at edge, 15–20 minutes.

Tomato Sauce

- 1 tablespoon bacon drippings *or* margarine *or* olive oil
- 1 medium onion, chopped
- 1 clove garlic, mashed
- 1 (8-ounce) can tomato sauce
- 1 teaspoon oregano
- 1 teaspoon basil

In small saucepan heat bacon drippings or other fat. Add onion and garlic; cook on low until soft; stir in tomato sauce, oregano and basil. Cook gently, stirring often, until it thickens a bit. Makes 1 cup.

Dinner Rolls

Half of refrigerator dough makes 10 rolls.

To make rolls I lightly roll part of the dough into a rectangle 8 inches wide. It should be somewhat thick, about 1/2 inch. Spread generously with melted butter. With pastry shell or knife, cut strips about 3/4 inch wide. Twist and coil into well-greased muffin cups. I use tall tulip-shaped custard cups. (Sprinkle with poppy or sesame seed if desired.)

Cover; let rise until double, about 1 hour. Bake in preheated 400-degree oven until nicely brown, about 15 minutes. Turn out onto a rack to cool. While still hot I rub tops with real butter.

Mildred's Beer Bread

- 4 cups biscuit mix
- 4 ounces cheddar cheese, grated
- 3 tablespoons sugar
- 1 can beer, room temperature

Combine all ingredients and mix until well-blended. Place in greased loaf pan and bake at 400 degrees for 20 minutes, or until top is golden brown.

Scrumptious Southern Spoon Bread

2½ cups water
½ cup butter *or* margarine
¼ cup sugar
1 teaspoon salt
1½ cups yellow cornmeal
1½ cups milk
6 large eggs
1½ teaspoons baking powder

Preheat oven to 350 degrees. Grease and lightly flour a 13 x 9-inch pan; set aside.

Heat water, butter or margarine, sugar and salt to boiling in large saucepan over medium heat. Whisk in yellow cornmeal and cook, stirring constantly until mixture is thickened, approximately 2 minutes. Remove from heat and place in large bowl. Whisk in milk until smooth. Add eggs; then add baking powder.

Pour into prepared pan. Bake 35–40 minutes, until puffed and golden brown. Serve very warm.

This is a lighter-than-air sensation that is delicious served at breakfast, lunch or dinner. Serves 12.

Holiday Oatmeal Bread With Honey Butter

1 cup quick-cooking oats
⅓ cup butter
2 cups boiling water
½ cup honey
1 tablespoon salt
2 (¼-ounce) packages active dry yeast
2 eggs
6¼ to 7¼ cups all-purpose flour
1 egg, slightly beaten
1 tablespoon water
3 tablespoons quick-cooking oats

Honey Butter

½ cup butter, softened
2 tablespoons honey

In large mixer bowl combine 1 cup oats, butter, boiling water, honey and salt. Cool to warm (105–115 degrees). Stir in yeast. Add 2 eggs and 2½ cups flour. Beat at medium speed, scraping bowl often, until smooth (1–2 minutes). Stir in enough remaining flour to make dough easy to handle.

Turn dough onto lightly floured surface; knead until smooth and elastic (about 10 minutes). Add more flour as needed until dough no longer sticks. Place in greased bowl; turn greased side up. Cover; let rise in warm place until double in size (about 1 hour).

Dough is ready if indentation remains when touched. Punch down dough; divide into thirds. Shape each third into loaf. Place loaves in 3 greased 8 x 4-inch loaf pans. Cover; let rise until double in size (about 1 hour).

In small bowl combine 1 egg and water; gently brush over top of loaves. Sprinkle each loaf with 1 tablespoon oats. Heat oven to 350 degrees. Bake for 25–35 minutes, or until loaf sounds hollow when tapped. Remove from pans immediately.

In small bowl stir together honey butter ingredients; serve with bread. Makes 3 loaves and ½ cup honey butter.

Grandma's Cheese Bread

2 cups shredded cheddar cheese
4 cups flour
2 tablespoons sugar
2 packages dry yeast
1 cup milk
2 teaspoons salt
Extra flour

Scald milk; add sugar, salt and cheese. Stir to melt cheese; cool to lukewarm and add yeast; mix well. Place 4 cups flour in large bowl, make a well in center; pour in mixture. Gradually stir flour into liquid; mix well. Knead on floured surface, adding flour as needed, until dough is very smooth and elastic.

Place dough in bowl; grease top; let rise in warm place. Punch down; let rise a second time until double in bulk. Place in 2 small greased loaf pans. Grease top; let rise until not quite double in bulk. Bake at 400 degrees for 10 minutes; lower heat to 350 degrees and bake for 45 minutes or until done. Cool before slicing. This is a very old recipe and very good. If desired 2 cakes compressed yeast may be used instead of dry yeast.

Frosty Orange Muffins

2 cups sifted self-rising flour*
⅓ cup sugar
1 tablespoon grated orange peel
1 egg
¾ cup orange juice
¼ cup vegetable oil
Orange Icing (recipe follows)

Preheat oven to 400 degrees. Grease muffin cups. Stir together flour, sugar and orange peel in mixing bowl. Beat egg in separate bowl; stir in orange juice and oil. Add liquid mixture to dry ingredients, stirring just until blended. Batter will be slightly lumpy.

Spoon batter into prepared muffin cups, filling each ⅔s full. Bake for 18–20 minutes, or until golden brown. Remove muffins from pan and cool for 5 minutes. Spread with Orange Icing. Makes about 12 medium muffins.

*If using all-purpose flour, sift 1 tablespoon baking powder and ¾ teaspoon salt with flour.

Orange Icing

1 (3-ounce) package cream cheese, softened
2 tablespoons sugar
1 teaspoon grated orange peel
2 teaspoons orange juice

Combine cream cheese, sugar and orange peel in small bowl; blend well. Add orange juice and stir until smooth.

Broccoli Bread

2 packages corn bread mix with jalapeños
1 stick margarine, melted
1 (10-ounce) package frozen chopped broccoli, thawed
1 cup frozen vegetable seasoning mix
1 can chopped green chilies
½ cup self-rising corn bread mix
1 cup cheese, grated
4 eggs

Mix together and spread into prepared pans. I bake mine in a cast-iron skillet. This is enough for 2 (8-inch) skillets. Bake at 400 degrees for 20 minutes, or until done. This is really a treat for corn bread lovers.

Foolproof Sourdough Starter

1 tablespoon (1 package) active dry yeast
2½ cups warm water (105–115 degrees), divided
2½ cups unbleached *or* all-purpose flour

Dissolve yeast in ½ cup warm water in a jar, crock or glass container. Mix in well the remaining warm water and all-purpose flour. Cover with cloth and place in a warm place to stand for 3–5 days. The starter should be loosely covered. The mixture will become bubbly.

Walnut Biscuits

¼ cup butter
2 tablespoons honey
1 egg, beaten
1¼ cups whole-wheat flour
1 teaspoon baking powder
¾ cup chopped walnuts
1 teaspoon almond extract

Preheat oven to 350 degrees. In a saucepan, heat butter and honey together until melted. Cool mixture and add beaten egg. Mix flour and baking powder; stir into honey mixture. Add walnuts and almond extract. Form into a soft dough. Shape into small balls using 1 tablespoon of mixture.

Place on a greased baking sheet and flatten with a knife. Bake for 15–20 minutes. Cool on wire rack. Makes 1 dozen.

Oatmeal Hawaiian Bread

4 eggs
1½ cups sugar
2½ cups flour
2 teaspoons salt
2 teaspoons soda
1½ cups quick oats
1 (20-ounce) can crushed pineapple, undrained
3 cups flaked coconut

Combine eggs and sugar; beat until light. Sift flour, salt and soda. Add to egg mixture; blend until smooth. Add remaining ingredients; mix well. Spoon into 2 greased and floured 9 x 5-inch loaf pans. Bake at 325 degrees for 1 hour. Remove from pans immediately.

Rice Bread

1½ cups orange juice
2 cups sugar
2 eggs
2 teaspoons grated orange peel
¼ cup margarine, melted
3½ cups flour
2 teaspoons baking powder
1 teaspoon baking soda
1 teaspoon salt
1 cup cooked, cooled rice
¾ cup finely chopped pecans
½ cup confectioners' sugar
3 tablespoons orange juice
½ teaspoon grated orange peel

Combine orange juice, sugar, eggs, orange peel and margarine. In separate bowl, mix flour, baking powder, baking soda and salt. Add orange juice mixture to dry ingredients and mix well. Fold in rice and pecans.

Pour batter into 2 greased and floured 9 x 5 x 3-inch loaf pans. Bake at 350 degrees for 1 hour, or until toothpick inserted in center comes out clean. Cool in pans 5 minutes, then turn out to cool. Combine confectioners' sugar, orange juice and peel. Drizzle this mixture over loaves when cool.

Strawberry Muffins

2¼ cups sifted all-purpose flour
⅓ cup sugar
2 eggs
3 teaspoons baking powder
½ teaspoon salt
½ cup oil
½ cup milk*
1 cup sliced strawberries
1 teaspoon vanilla

Stir together flour, sugar, baking powder and salt. Beat eggs. Blend in oil, vanilla and milk. Add liquid ingredients to dry ingredients. Stir quickly, just until moistened. Fold in strawberries. Spoon into well-greased 2½-inch muffin cups or paper-lined muffin cups. Bake at 400 degrees for 25 minutes, or until golden brown. Remove to wire rack. Serve warm.

**For Strawberry Yogurt Muffins:* Omit milk and use yogurt, also reduce baking powder to 1 teaspoon and add 1 teaspoon soda.

Lemon-Cheddar Bread

5 cups flour
2 teaspoons baking powder
½ teaspoons black pepper
1 tablespoon grated lemon peel
1 tablespoon lemon juice
¼ cup diced green onion
2 cups lemon yogurt
2 tablespoons prepared mustard
2 tablespoons sugar
1 teaspoon salt
1 teaspoon baking soda
2 cups shredded cheddar cheese
4 eggs
¼ cup diced onion tops
⅔ cup vegetable oil

Heat oven to 350 degrees. Grease 2 (9 x 5-inch) loaf pans. In large bowl, combine flour, sugar, baking powder, salt, pepper, baking soda, lemon peel and cheese. Mix well and set aside. In smaller bowl, combine remaining ingredients, mixing thoroughly. Pour egg batter into the dry mixture and stir just until combined. Batter will be stiff. Pour into pans, spreading evenly and smoothing the tops. Bake for 1 hour. Cool in pans on rack.

Whole-Wheat Bread

2 cups milk
⅓ cup honey
4 teaspoons salt
⅓ cup margarine
3 cakes yeast
2 cups warm water
10 cups whole-wheat flour

Scald milk. Add honey, salt and margarine. Cool. Proof yeast and warm water. Add to cooled milk. Beat in thoroughly 5 cups whole-wheat flour. Let rise until foamy and doubled in large bread pan.

Add remaining 5 cups flour. Let rise again until doubled. Knead lightly for 15–20 minutes. Dough will be somewhat sticky. Grease dough board and hands with margarine. Cover and allow to double in bulk. Shape into 3 loaves. Let stand in greased pans about 30 minutes. Grease top of loaves. Bake in a 375-degree oven for 1 hour, or until done. Makes 3 loaves.

Cottage Cheese Rolls

- 1/4 cup margarine
- 1/2 cup brown sugar
- 1/4 cup chopped pecans
- 1 3/4 cups flour
- 1/8 teaspoon salt
- 1 1/2 teaspoons baking powder
- 1/8 teaspoon baking soda
- 1/4 cup sugar
- 1 cup cottage cheese
- 1 egg
- 1/4 cup margarine, softened
- 1/4 cup sugar
- 1 teaspoon cinnamon

Melt margarine and brown sugar together and spread in an 8 x 8-inch pan. Sprinkle with pecans. Mix together flour, salt, baking powder, baking soda and sugar. Add cottage cheese and egg; mix. Knead it a little to get it to form a ball. Flour ball of dough and roll it out on a floured surface. Brush dough with 1/4 cup softened margarine; sprinkle with sugar and cinnamon. Roll as for cinnamon rolls. Cut into 12 pieces with a sharp knife and place in pan. Bake at 375 degrees for 20–25 minutes. Turn out of pan at once.

Easy Hot Cross Buns

- 1 (16-ounce) loaf white frozen bread dough
- 3/4 cup raisins
- 1 teaspoon ground cinnamon
- 1 egg white, slightly beaten
- 2/3 cup sifted confectioners' sugar
- 1/4 teaspoon vanilla

Let dough soften to room temperature, but do not let rise. Mix raisins with cinnamon. Knead into dough. Divide dough into 10 pieces; shape each into a round ball, flatten slightly. Place balls on greased baking sheet, 1 1/2 inches apart. Cover and let rise until almost doubled. Cut a shallow cross in each bun; brush tops with slightly beaten egg white, reserving remainder. Bake at 350 degrees 15–20 minutes until lightly browned. Let cool slightly before frosting. For frosting combine remaining egg white with confectioners' sugar and vanilla; mix well. Make crosses on tops with frosting using spoon or pastry tube.

Oat Bran Orange Banana Bread

- 3/4 cup oat bran
- 1/2 cup orange juice
- 1 cup mashed bananas (3 very ripe medium-size bananas)
- 3 tablespoons honey
- 1/3 cup vegetable oil
- 1 teaspoon vanilla
- 2 eggs, beaten until frothy
- 1 1/2 cups whole-wheat flour
- 3 teaspoons baking powder
- 1/4 teaspoon salt
- 1/2 teaspoon grated orange peel
- 1/2 cup coarsely chopped walnuts

Combine oat bran and orange juice; set aside for 30 minutes. Mix together mashed bananas, honey, oil, vanilla and eggs. Stir into orange juice mixture. Combine dry ingredients, orange peel and nuts. Mix into banana mixture. Preheat oven to 350 degrees. Pour batter into 9 x 5-inch greased loaf pan. Bake 55 minutes, or until toothpick inserted in center comes out clean. Cool in pan on wire rack 10 minutes; remove from pan and cool completely on rack.

Irish Soda Bread

- 2 cups flour
- 1/2 teaspoon baking soda
- 2 teaspoons baking powder
- 1 tablespoon sugar
- 1/2 teaspoon salt
- 3 tablespoons margarine
- 1/4 cup raisins
- 1/4 cup currants
- 2 teaspoons caraway seed
- 1 cup sour milk
- Sugar and cinnamon

Mix flour, soda, baking powder, sugar and salt. Cut in margarine. Add raisins, currants, caraway seed and milk; mix thoroughly with tablespoon. Knead for 2–3 minutes. Place in greased 8- or 9-inch greased cake pan. Shape into round mound and with a greased knife cut a cross in top center of bread dough. Lightly sprinkle with sugar and cinnamon. Bake in a 350-degree oven for 30–45 minutes.

Note: One cup milk with 1 1/2 teaspoons vinegar will create sour milk for recipe.

Louisiana Cornmeal Hush Puppies

- 1 cup stone-ground cornmeal
- 1/2 cup all-purpose flour
- 1 teaspoon salt
- 1 teaspoon baking powder
- 1 teaspoon garlic powder
- 1/2 teaspoon cayenne pepper
- 1/2 cup milk
- 1 egg, beaten
- 5 drops hot pepper sauce
- 3 tablespoons minced onion
- 1 tablespoon vegetable shortening
- Corn oil (enough for depth of 2 inches)

Heat corn oil until hot. Mix all ingredients; drop dough 1 1/2 inches wide, 2 inches long and 1/8 inch thick, into oil using a slotted spoon. Cook 3 minutes, or until golden brown. Delicious served with fish, meat or poultry. Makes 20.

Hush Puppies

- 1 cup cornmeal
- 1/4 cup flour
- 1 teaspoon baking powder
- 1 1/2 tablespoons sugar
- 3/4 cup chopped green onions
- 1/2–3/4 cups boiling water
- 1 egg
- Salt to taste
- Oil for deep-frying

Mix first five ingredients.Stir in 1/2 cup boiling water to make thick batter, adding more water 1 tablespoon at a time if needed. Add egg and stir. Drop into oil; fry until golden brown.

Fat Cat Popovers

- 1 cup milk
- 2 eggs
- 1/2 teaspoon salt
- 1 cup flour

Have all ingredients at room temperature. Pour milk into a bowl; break eggs on top. Add salt. Pour flour over milk and stir with a spoon until all flour is moistened. Grease 6–8 custard cups. Divide batter into cups, filling only half full. Place cups on a baking sheet, and put in a cold oven. Set oven at 400 degrees and bake for 30 minutes. Do not peek while the "fat cats" are baking.

Fruited Ricotta Bread

4 cups flour
2 teaspoons baking powder
1/4 teaspoon salt
2 cups ricotta cheese
3 large eggs, beaten
1 teaspoon vanilla
2/3 cup sugar
3 tablespoons candied fruit
2 tablespoons golden raisins
1 tablespoon chopped almonds
1 tablespoon grated lemon peel
1 tablespoon margarine, melted
1 tablespoon confectioners' sugar

Preheat oven to 375 degrees. Grease and flour cookie sheet. Sift flour, baking powder and salt into large bowl. Make a well in center and stir in ricotta cheese, eggs, vanilla, sugar, candied fruit, raisins, almonds and lemon peel. Knead lightly until dough holds together. Shape into a 12-inch-long loaf and place on prepared cookie sheet. Bake 50–60 minutes, until toothpick inserted in center comes out clean. Transfer to wire rack. Brush margarine over warm loaf; sift confectioners' sugar over top. Cool completely.

Fresh Apple Bread

2 cups flour
1 teaspoon soda
1 teaspoon baking powder
1/2 teaspoon salt
1/2 cup shortening
1 cup sugar
2 eggs
2 cups chopped apples (3 medium)
1/2 cup chopped nuts
1 teaspoon vanilla flavoring
1/4 cup sugar
1 1/2 teaspoons cinnamon

Sift first 4 ingredients together; cream sugar and shortening. Add eggs and beat well. Add apples, nuts and vanilla. Stir in flour mixture. Pour batter into well-greased bread pan and sprinkle with 1/4 cup sugar and 1 1/2 teaspoons cinnamon. Bake for 1 hour at 350 degrees.

Turn pan on side to cool after removing from oven. Do not slice until bread is cool. Makes 1 loaf.

Eggnog Bread

3 cups flour
1/2 cup sugar
4 teaspoons baking powder
1/2 teaspoon salt
1/2 teaspoon nutmeg
1 egg, beaten
1 3/4 cups eggnog
1/2 cup oil
1/2 cup chopped pecans
1/2 cup golden raisins
1/2 cup confectioners' sugar
2–3 teaspoons eggnog

In large bowl, stir together flour, sugar, baking powder, salt and nutmeg. Combine egg, eggnog, and oil; add to dry mixture. Stir in nuts and raisins. Pour into a 9 x 5-inch greased loaf pan.

Bake at 350 degrees for 60–70 minutes. Cover with foil after 50 minutes, if browning too much. Cool 10 minutes; remove from pan. Stir together confectioners' sugar and eggnog; drizzle over bread.

Irish Raisin & Caraway Biscuits

5 1/2 to 6 cups all-purpose flour
3 tablespoons double-acting baking powder
2 teaspoons salt
1 cup sugar
2 tablespoons unsalted butter, softened, plus additional butter as an accompaniment
2 large eggs, beaten lightly
2 cups milk
1 teaspoon caraway seed
3 cups raisins

Into a large bowl sift together flour, baking powder, salt and sugar. In another large bowl stir together 2 tablespoons butter, eggs, milk, caraway seed and raisins. Make a well in center of flour mixture and add milk mixture, stirring until mixture forms a sticky, but manageable, dough.

Knead dough on a floured surface for 30 seconds; roll to 1/4-inch-thickness; with a 2 1/2-inch cookie cutter cut out rounds. Bake rounds on greased baking sheets in middle of a preheated 375-degree oven for 12–15 minutes, or until golden. Serve biscuits warm with additional butter. Makes 2 dozen.

Orange Cranberry Bread

1/2 cup butter, softened
3/4 cup sugar
1 egg
1 teaspoon grated orange peel
2 1/2 cups all-purpose flour
2/3 cup orange juice
1/3 cup milk
1 tablespoon baking powder
1 teaspoon salt
3/4 cup coarsely chopped fresh *or* frozen cranberries
1/3 cup chopped pecans

Heat oven to 350 degrees. In large mixer bowl combine butter, sugar, egg and orange peel. Beat at medium speed, scraping bowl often, until well-mixed (1–2 minutes). Add remaining ingredients, except cranberries and pecans. Continue beating, scraping bowl often, until well-mixed (1–2 minutes). By hand, stir in cranberries and pecans.

Spoon into greased 9 x 5-inch loaf pan or 3 greased 5 3/4 x 3-inch miniature loaf pans. Bake for 50–60 minutes for 9 x 5-inch loaf or 30–40 minutes for miniature loaves, or until wooden pick inserted in center comes out clean. Cool 10 minutes; remove from pan. Makes 1 (9 x 5-inch) loaf or 3 (5 3/4 x 3-inch) miniature loaves.

Peanut Butter Bread

3/4 cup peanut butter, smooth *or* chunky style
1/4 cup margarine, softened
2 cups all-purpose flour
1/2 cup sugar
2 teaspoons baking powder
1 teaspoon salt
1 egg
1 1/4 cups milk
1 tablespoon grated orange peel

Beat peanut butter and margarine together until fluffy; add flour, sugar, baking powder and salt. Mix until crumbly. In a small bowl, combine egg, milk and orange peel. Stir into crumbly mixture just until moistened. Bake in a greased 9 x 5 x 3-inch loaf pan at 350 degrees for about 1 hour. Makes 1 loaf.

Zucchini Banana Bread

- 1½ cups flour
- 3 teaspoons baking powder
- ½ teaspoon salt
- ¾ teaspoon cinnamon
- 1 cup regular rolled oats
- 2 large ripe bananas
- ¾ cup sugar
- ⅔ cup vegetable oil
- 2 large eggs
- ¾ cup zucchini (slightly packed), unpared and grated
- ½ cup chopped walnuts

On waxed paper, stir together flour, baking powder, salt and cinnamon; stir in oats. Slice bananas in a bowl with electric beater on high speed. Beat until mashed. Add sugar and oil; blend at high speed; add eggs. Beat until blended. Add flour mixture at low speed. Beat only until dry ingredients are moistened. With a spatula fold in zucchini and walnuts. Pour into greased and floured 9 x 5-inch loaf pan. Bake at 350 degrees for 1 hour. Cool on rack.

Harvest Corn Bread

- 1 cup cornmeal
- 1 cup flour
- 2 tablespoons sugar
- 2 teaspoons baking powder
- ½ teaspoon salt
- 1 egg
- 1 cup milk
- ⅓ cup butter *or* margarine, melted
- ½ cup chopped green pepper
- ½ cup chopped tomato
- ¾ cup grated sharp cheddar cheese

Preheat oven to 400 degrees. Grease an 8 x 8 x 2-inch baking pan. In medium bowl mix cornmeal, flour, sugar, baking powder and salt. In small bowl lightly beat egg with fork; stir in milk and butter or margarine.

Add milk mixture to cornmeal mixture all at once. Stir just until cornmeal mixture is moistened. Do not overmix; a few lumps may remain. Fold in green pepper, tomato and cheese. Spoon mixture into baking pan; spread evenly. Bake 40 minutes, or until golden. Cut into squares. Serve warm. Serves 6.

Apple Bran Muffins

- 2 cups whole-wheat flour
- 1½ cups wheat bran
- ½ teaspoon salt
- 1 tablespoon grated orange rind
- 1 cup chopped apple
- ½ cup blackstrap molasses
- 1¼ teaspoons baking soda
- ½ cup raisins
- ½ cup chopped nuts
- Juice of 1 orange
- 2 cups buttermilk
- 2 eggs, beaten
- 2 tablespoons oil
- ½ teaspoon nutmeg

Preheat oven to 350 degrees. Toss flour, bran, salt, soda and nutmeg together. Stir in orange rind, apples, raisins and nuts.

Pour juice of 1 orange into a 2-cup measure and add buttermilk to make 2 cups. Add to eggs, molasses and oil; stir thoroughly. Stir liquid ingredients into dry ingredients with a few swift strokes. Pour into greased muffin tins, filling them ⅔ full. Bake for 25 minutes. Makes 24 muffins.

Honey 'n' Wheat Corn Bread

- 1½ cups cornmeal
- 1 cup whole-wheat flour
- 1 tablespoon baking powder
- ½ teaspoon salt
- 1½ cups milk
- 2 eggs
- ⅓ cup honey
- ¼ cup vegetable oil
- ⅔ cup shredded carrot
- ¼ cup green-onion slices

Stir together cornmeal, flour, baking powder and salt; mix in just until moistened milk, eggs, honey and oil. Stir in carrot and onion. Spread into a greased 9-inch square baking pan or a 9 x 5-inch loaf pan.

Bake at 400 degrees for 25 minutes for the square pan and 45 minutes for the loaf pan, or until golden and pick inserted in center comes out clean. Great with a hearty bean or vegetable soup. Makes 1 loaf.

Poppy Seed Rolls

- 2 cakes yeast
- 2 tablespoons sugar
- 1 cup lukewarm milk
- 4 cups sifted flour
- ½ cup margarine
- 1 teaspoon salt
- 2 egg yolks
- 1 can poppy seed filling

In a small bowl, place yeast, sugar and milk. Allow to dissolve; set aside. Use a pastry blender to cut in margarine with flour and salt until crumbly. Make a well in the center of the mixture and add egg yolks. Add yeast mixture and mix dough several minutes.

Place on a lightly floured board and cut into 4 pieces. Roll out each part as thin as possible and spread with filling. Roll up jelly roll style and place on a greased pan. Brush top with milk and let rise about 1 hour. Bake at 400 degrees for about 25 minutes.

Old-Fashioned Brown Bread

- 1 (1-pound) coffee can, washed and buttered (Steamer required)
- ½ cup cornmeal
- ½ cup whole-wheat flour
- ½ cup white flour
- ½ teaspoon salt
- 2 tablespoons brown sugar
- ¼ cup molasses
- ½ teaspoon baking soda
- 1 cup buttermilk
- ½ cup seedless dark raisins

Blend all dry ingredients. Stir in molasses and buttermilk; stir well to blend. Add raisins. Place in coffee can. Make a cap of aluminum foil that will stand up about 1½ inches away from top of can. Tie around the can and foil with string.

Place can in large steamer, upright, and steam over boiling water for 2 hours. Do not let the water reach the can; this will mean checking every little while to keep water level up.

When bread is done, shake out of can. Slice thickly and serve hot with butter. (Slicing bread too thin when hot will break it up).

Pop-Up Poppy Seed Cheddar Cheese Bread

- 3 –3½cups all-purpose flour, divided
- 1 (¼-ounce) package active dry yeast
- ½ cup milk
- ½ cup water
- ½ cup vegetable oil
- ¼ cup sugar
- 1 teaspoon salt
- 1 tablespoon poppy seed
- 2 eggs, beaten
- 1 cup (4 ounces) shredded cheddar cheese

Combine 1½ cups flour and yeast. Heat milk, water, oil, sugar and salt until warm (120–130 degrees), stirring to blend. Add to flour mixture along with eggs and cheese. Stir in poppy seed.

Beat with electric mixer until batter is smooth. Using a spoon, mix in remaining flour (batter will be stiff.)

Divide batter into 2 portions; spoon into 2 clean 1-pound coffee cans. Cover with plastic lids. Let rise in warm place until batter is ¼–½ inch below lids. Remove lids. Bake at 375 degrees for 30–35 minutes. Cool 15 minutes in cans. Remove from cans and finish cooling on wire rack. Makes 2 loaves.

At Christmastime omit the poppy seed and use 1 tablespoon each diced sweet red and green peppers to make it festive.

Pimiento Cheese Biscuits

- 2 cups buttermilk biscuit mix
- 1 cup (4 ounces) shredded sharp cheddar cheese
- 2 tablespoons chopped pimiento, drained
- ¼ teaspoon oregano
- ⅔ cup milk

Preheat oven to 425 degrees. Combine biscuit mix, cheese, pimiento and oregano. Add milk. Mix until a soft dough is formed. Drop by tablespoons onto lightly buttered baking sheet. Bake 10–12 minutes, or until lightly browned. Serve warm with butter. Makes 1 dozen.

Buttery Poppy Seed Crescents

- ½ cup butter
- 4 cups sifted flour
- 3 egg yolks
- 1 cake yeast
- 3 tablespoons sugar
- ⅓ cup warm milk
- 1 can poppy seed filling

Cut in butter with 2 cups of flour until mixture is crumbly; set aside. Combine milk, yeast and sugar in a small bowl. Set aside for about 10 minutes. Add yolks to yeast mixture. Add mixture to the remaining flour. Chill about 1 hour and divide into 8 portions. Roll out thin and cut into 12 wedges. Spread surface with poppy seed filling; sprinkle with crumbly flour mixture and roll up from the wide end to the small end. Place on an ungreased cookie sheet and bake for 20 minutes at 375 degrees.

Orange Bread

- 1 cup orange rind, cut into small pieces (takes 2 oranges)
- ½ teaspoon soda
- 4 cups water
- 1 cup sugar

Batter

- 1 cup sugar
- 3 tablespoons margarine
- 3 eggs, well-beaten
- 1 cup milk
- 3½ cups flour
- 3 teaspoons baking powder
- ¼ teaspoon salt
- 1 cup chopped nuts

Combine orange rind, soda and water, and bring to a boil; cook until rind is tender. Rinse in hot water until clear. Drain and add sugar; stir and cool.

To make batter, cream sugar and margarine until fluffy. Add eggs and stir. Alternately add milk with the flour, baking powder and salt, mixing well. Stir in orange rind and nuts. Fill 2 large bread pans, greased and floured (3 smaller pans may also be used), to half-full. Bake in a 350-degree oven for 40–60 minutes. Test for doneness. This recipe won first prize in the Quick Bread Contest in our local newspaper.

Golden Pumpkin Bread

- 1½ cups all-purpose flour
- 1 cup firmly packed brown sugar
- 1 cup cooked pumpkin
- ½ cup butter, softened
- 2 eggs
- 1 teaspoon baking powder
- 1 teaspoon baking soda
- 1 teaspoon salt
- 1½ teaspoons cinnamon
- ½ teaspoon cloves
- ½ teaspoon ginger

Heat oven to 350 degrees. In large mixer bowl, combine all ingredients. Beat at medium speed, scraping bowl often, until well-mixed (2–3 minutes). Pour into greased 9 x 5-inch loaf pan or 3 greased 5¾ x 3-inch miniature loaf pans.

Bake for 45–55 minutes for 9 x 5-inch loaf, or 30–35 minutes for miniature loaves, or until wooden pick inserted in center comes out clean. Cool 10 minutes; remove from pan. Cool completely; store refrigerated. Makes 1 (9 x 5-inch) loaf or 3 (5¾ x 3-inch) miniature loaves.

★★★

The zest of orange and rich cream cheese icing make these refreshing muffins good enough for dessert.

Homemade Flour Tortillas

- 4 cups all-purpose flour
- ⅛ teaspoon baking powder
- 2 teaspoons salt
- ⅔ cup shortening
- 1 cup plus 3 tablespoons hot water

Combine flour, baking powder and salt; stir well. Cut in shortening with pastry blender until mixture resembles coarse meal. Gradually add water, stirring until mixture forms a dough. Divide dough into 24 equal portions. Roll each with a rolling pin to a very thin circle about 6 inches in diameter, turning dough and rolling both sides.

Place on an ungreased skillet over medium heat. Cook tortillas 2 minutes on each side, or until lightly browned, being careful not to let tortillas wrinkle. Pat tortillas lightly with a spatula while browning the other side. Makes 2 dozen.

Dilly Casserole Bread

- 1 package dry yeast
- 1/4 cup warm water
- 1 cup creamed cottage cheese, heated to lukewarm
- 2 tablespoons sugar
- 1 tablespoon instant onion, (mixed)
- 1 tablespoon butter (soft)
- 2 teaspoons dill seed
- 1 teaspoon salt
- 1/4 teaspoon soda
- 1 egg, unbeaten
- 2 1/4 to 2 1/2 cups flour

Soften yeast in water; combine in mixing bowl cottage cheese, sugar, onion, butter, dill seed, salt, soda, egg and softened yeast. Add to flour to form stiff dough, beating well after each addition. Cover with waxed paper or plastic wrap and put Turkish towel over top of this. Let rise in warm place (85–90 degrees) until light and doubled in size, 50–60 minutes.

Bake in a round layer cake pan at 350 degrees for 45 minutes, until golden brown. Remove from oven, brush with soft butter over top and sprinkle lightly with salt. Makes 1 round loaf.

Cheese-Filled Monkey Bread

- 1 (16-ounce) loaf frozen bread dough, thawed
- 4 ounces cheddar cheese, cut into 32 cubes (about 1/2-inch size)
- 2 tablespoons butter *or* margarine, melted

Cut bread dough into 32 equal pieces. Place 1 cheese cube in center of each dough piece, shaping dough into a ball around the cheese. Pinch dough to seal.

Dip balls in melted butter. Layer balls, seam side up, in greased tube pan. Cover and let rise in a warm place (85 degrees) free from drafts for 30–40 minutes, or until doubled in bulk. Bake at 375 degrees for 30 minutes or until golden brown. Invert onto platter and serve warm. Makes 1 (10-inch) ring.

This is delicious and easy to make, although it looks like it took a lot of work.

Beignets (Doughnuts)

- 2 cups milk
- 1 package active dry yeast
- 1/4 cup warm water
- 1/3 cup sugar
- 1/2 cup vegetable oil
- 2 teaspoons salt
- 7 cups sifted flour
- 2 eggs, beaten
- Vegetable oil
- Confectioners' sugar

Scald milk and set aside to cool. Soften yeast in water and set aside. Combine sugar, vegetable oil and salt. Stir in yeast mixture and milk. Add flour slowly, beating well. Add eggs; mix. Knead dough and place in warm place until doubled in size. Punch down and roll out to about 1/2 inch thick, cutting dough into squares. Cover and let rise.

Heat vegetable oil and deep-fry for 2–3 minutes; remove carefully and drain. Sprinkle with confectioners' sugar and enjoy while hot!

Cloud Biscuits

- 2 cups flour
- 1 tablespoon sugar
- 4 teaspoons baking powder
- 1/2 teaspoon salt
- 1/2 cup shortening
- 1 egg, beaten
- 2/3 cup milk

Put dry ingredients together. Cut in shortening. Combine egg and milk; add all at once, mixing until dough follows fork. Knead 20 times. Roll out dough and cut out with biscuit cutter. Bake on an ungreased sheet for 10–14 minutes at 450 degrees. Makes 1 dozen.

Spoon Bread

- 1 package corn muffin mix
- 2 eggs, well-beaten
- 1 cup sour cream
- 1/2 cup liquid oil
- 1 cup cream-style corn, not drained

Grease 1 1/2-quart casserole. Combine all ingredients and pour into dish. Place casserole into pan of water. Bake in oven for 45–50 minutes at 350 degrees. Serve hot with butter.

Tasty Bread Sticks

- 1 1/4 cups biscuit mix
- 1 tablespoon sugar
- 2 tablespoons cold butter
- 1/4 cup cold water
- 1 egg, beaten
- Powdered garlic-and-herb flavoring

Preheat oven to 400 degrees. Mix baking mix and sugar; cut in butter with fork. Stir in water until dough cleans side of bowl. Gather into a ball and turn dough onto floured surface. Knead 5 times. Roll into 12 x 8-inch rectangle. Cut crosswise into 1/2-inch strips.

Place strips 1 inch apart on lightly greased cookie sheet. Brush with egg; sprinkle with flavoring. Bake until golden brown, 9–12 minutes. Cool slightly before removing from cookie sheet. Makes 2 dozen.

Blueberry Muffins

- 1/2 cup sugar
- 2 cups sifted flour
- 1/2 teaspoon salt
- 4 teaspoons baking powder
- 2 tablespoons margarine
- 1 cup milk
- 1 1/2 cups blueberries

Combine dry ingredients and sift. Cut in margarine until mixture is crumbly. Add milk and stir well. Fold in blueberries. Pour into greased muffin tins. Bake at 375 degrees for 30 minutes. Serve hot!

Pear Bran Muffins

- 1 (29-ounce) can pears
- 2 1/2 cups wheat bran flakes cereal
- 1/2 cup margarine
- 1/2 cup sugar
- 2 eggs
- 2 cups flour
- 2 teaspoons baking powder
- 1/2 cup coarsely chopped nuts
- Salt, as desired

Drain and finely chop pears; combine with cereal and let stand 2 minutes. Cream margarine and sugar; beat in eggs and pear mixture. Combine flour, baking powder, salt and nuts; stir into pear mixture until moistened. Spoon batter into 18 greased muffin tins and bake at 400 degrees for 25–30 minutes.

Margaret's Zucchini Banana Bread

3 cups flour
1 teaspoon salt
3 eggs, beaten
2 teaspoons cinnamon
2 teaspoons vanilla
1 cup salad oil
2 cups sugar
1 teaspoon baking soda
1 teaspoon baking powder
2 cups grated zucchini
1 cup mashed bananas
1 cup chopped nut meats

Combine flour, salt, soda, baking powder and cinnamon in large bowl. Add remaining ingredients; mix well. Bake in 2 greased and floured 9 x 4 x 3-inch baking pans, at 350 degrees for 1 hour.

Carrot Cheese Muffins

1 cup finely shredded carrots
1/2 cup butter, melted
2 eggs, beaten
1/2 teaspoon salt
1/2 cup grated, sharp cheddar cheese
1 cup milk
2 cups all-purpose flour
2 teaspoons baking powder
1 tablespoon granulated sugar
Paprika (optional)

In a bowl, combine carrots, melted butter, eggs and cheese. In another bowl, combine flour, baking powder, salt and sugar. Combine wet and dry ingredients alternately with milk, stirring only until dry ingredients are just dampened. Batter will be lumpy. Spoon into greased muffin pans, filling two-thirds full. Sprinkle with paprika, if used. Bake at 400 degrees for 20 minutes. Carefully remove from pans. Serve hot or warm.

Apple-Molasses Bread

1/2 cup butter *or* margarine
1 cup sugar
3 eggs
2 cups sifted all-purpose flour
1 teaspoon baking powder
1/2 teaspoon salt
1/2 teaspoon cinnamon
1/2 teaspoon nutmeg
1 cup canned applesauce
1/4 cup molasses
1 cup raisins
1/2 cup chopped pecans

Cream together butter and sugar. Add eggs, 1 at a time, beating well after each addition. Sift together flour, baking powder, salt, cinnamon and nutmeg. Combine applesauce and molasses. Add flour mixture, alternating with applesauce mixture, to egg mixture. Beat well after each addition. Fold in raisins and nuts. Pour into greased and floured 9 x 5 x 3-inch loaf pan. Bake at 350 degrees for 1 hour.

Hawaiian Bread

1 cup flour
2 teaspoons cinnamon
1 1/2 teaspoons baking soda
1/2 teaspoon salt
3 eggs
1 1/2 cups sugar
3/4 cup oil
1 cup raisins
1 cup chopped nuts
2 cups grated carrots
1 teaspoon vanilla

Sift flour, cinnamon, salt and baking soda. Add eggs, sugar and oil. Add raisins, nuts, grated carrots and vanilla. Mix well and place in greased loaf pan. Let stand for 25 minutes before baking. Bake at 350 degrees for 1 hour.

Poppy Seed Bread

1 package 2-layer white cake mix
1 (6-ounce) package vanilla pudding
3 eggs, beaten
1/2 cup vegetable oil
1 cup boiling water
3/4 cup poppy seed

Combine the dry cake and pudding mixes. Make a well in center; add eggs and vegetable oil. Beat well. Add boiling water and poppy seed. Beat until smooth. Pour batter into 2 greased loaf pans and bake for 40 minutes at 350 degrees.

Dumplings

2 cups flour
2 teaspoons baking powder (rounded)
1/4 teaspoon salt
1 egg, unbeaten
Milk (enough to make a soft dough)

Combine ingredients to make soft dough; roll out as for biscuits. Cut in small pieces. Cook on top of meat or sauerkraut for 15 minutes with lid on pan. Cook until tender and test with a fork for doneness.

This was my mother's recipe and she always made them when she served boiled spareribs and sauerkraut or her favorite chicken and dumplings.

Pizza Dough

5–6 cups flour
3 teaspoons sugar
3 teaspoons salt
2 packages yeast
2 cups hot water
4 tablespoons oil

Mix 1/3 the amount of flour, all the sugar, salt and yeast in mixing bowl. Add oil and hot water; work in more flour by hand until smooth. Place in greased bowl; let rise until double in bulk, about 45 minutes. Grease pans with shortening. Stretch dough with palms of your hands. Bake at 375 degrees for 20–25 minutes. Makes 3 (14-inch) pizzas.

Cheese Garlic Biscuits

2 cups biscuit mix
2/3 cup milk
1/2 cup shredded cheddar cheese (2 ounces)
1/4 cup margarine *or* butter, melted
1/4 teaspoon garlic powder

Preheat oven to 450 degrees. Combine biscuit mix, milk and cheese until soft dough forms; beat vigorously for 30 seconds. Drop dough by spoonfuls onto an ungreased cookie sheet.

Bake 8–10 minutes, or until golden brown. Mix margarine and garlic powder; brush over warm biscuits before removing from cookie sheet. Serve warm. Makes 10–12.

Whole-Wheat Banana Bread (No Eggs)

1½ cups whole-wheat flour (pastry flour, if available)
1 teaspoon salt
2 teaspoons baking powder
1 cup walnuts, chopped
1¼ cups mashed bananas
3 tablespoons oil
¼ cup honey
½ cup bran or wheat germ
½ to 1 cup White raisins
½ to 1 teaspoon vanilla extract
Grated rind of ½ lemon (optional)

Sift together flour, salt and baking powder. Add nuts and raisins; mix. Add remaining ingredients. Stir (no more than 40 strokes—batter is stiff.) Bake in a greased 4½ x 8½-inch loaf pan at 350 degrees for 45 minutes. Or make 3–4 miniature loaves; check at 40 minutes to see the baking progress.

Spicy Gingerbread

⅓ cup butter
⅓ cup sugar
1 egg, beaten
⅔ cup molasses
2 cups flour
¾ teaspoon baking soda
1½ teaspoons baking powder
¾ teaspoon cinnamon
¾ teaspoon ginger
¼ teaspoon cloves
¼ teaspoon salt
⅔ cup hot water

Cream butter by stirring. Add sugar, beaten egg and molasses. Sift together flour, baking soda, baking powder and spices; stir in. Add hot water. Bake in 9-inch square pan or a single-layer pan for 35 minutes at 350 degrees.

60-Minute Yeast Rolls

2 cakes yeast *or* 1 package quick-rise yeast
½ cup warm water
1 egg
1¼ cups lukewarm milk
2 tablespoons butter, melted
3 tablespoons sugar, divided
1 teaspoon salt
4⅓ cups flour

Dissolve yeast and ½ teaspoon sugar in water. Beat egg. Add to milk. Combine yeast and milk; add butter and dry ingredients. Allow to stand for 15 minutes; shape in half the size you want the finished roll to be. Let rise in pan to double in size. Bake 15 minutes at 375 degrees or until golden brown.

Rhubarb Bread

1 cup brown sugar
⅔ cup oil
1 cup sour milk
1 teaspoon vanilla
1½ cups diced rhubarb
½ cup chopped nuts
½ cup sugar
2 eggs
1 teaspoon salt
2½ cups flour
1 teaspoon soda
2 tablespoons margarine, melted
5 tablespoons sugar

Mix all ingredients except margarine and final sugar, adding rhubarb and nuts last. Pour into 5 foil baby loaf pans, 5¾ x 3¼ inches (greased). Before baking, top each loaf with 1 teaspoon melted margarine, then sprinkle 1 tablespoon sugar over each loaf. Bake at 350 degrees for about 30 minutes, or until lightly browned.

Walnut Peach Bread

1 cup dried peaches
¾ cup chopped walnuts
¼ cup butter
½ cup white sugar
1 egg
2½ cups sifted flour
3 teaspoons baking powder
1 teaspoon salt
1 cup half-and-half

Cut peaches into small pieces with knife or scissors. It is not necessary to soak them first. Cream butter, sugar and egg together. Sift flour, baking powder and salt together; add to creamed mixture, alternately with half-and-half. Stir in walnuts and peaches.

Turn into greased 9½ x 5½-inch loaf pan. Bake at 375 degrees for 50–55 minutes. Turn out onto rack to cool. Makes 1 loaf.

Pineapple Macadamia Nut Bread

4 eggs
1 cup sugar
½ cup oil
¾ cup pineapple juice
½ cup canned crushed pineapple with juice
1 tablespoon baking powder
3 cups flour
½ cup chopped macadamia nuts

Combine eggs, sugar, oil, juice and pineapple; mix well. Sift together baking powder and flour; mix into pineapple mixture. Fold in nuts. Pour into greased 9 x 5-inch loaf pan lined with waxed paper, and bake at 350 degrees about 50 minutes. Makes 1 loaf.

Blueberry Nut Bread

2 eggs
1 cup milk
3 tablespoons margarine
1 cup sugar
3 cups sifted flour
½ teaspoon salt
3 teaspoons baking powder
½ teaspoon cinnamon
1 cup blueberries
1 cup chopped walnuts

Combine eggs and margarine, beating well. Set aside. Sift together the dry ingredients and add to egg mixture alternately with milk. Carefully fold in nuts and blueberries. Bake in a loaf pan for 1 hour at 350 degrees.

Brunch FARE

Eggs With Pink Mayonnaise

- ½ package unflavored gelatin
- ¼ cup water
- ½ cup mayonnaise
- 2 tablespoons chili sauce
- ¼ teaspoon salt
- 4 drops liquid hot red pepper seasoning
- 8 hard-cooked eggs, shelled
- Celery leaves and stems
- Mayonnaise
- Hard-cooked egg yolk
- Watercress *or* other greens

Sprinkle gelatin over water in small saucepan. Dissolve over very low heat. Mix mayonnaise, chili sauce, salt and hot pepper seasoning in small bowl until smooth. Gradually stir in half the dissolved gelatin. Dip eggs, 1 at a time, in mixture to coat evenly. Arrange in a baking pan. Refrigerate just until set. Keep remaining gelatin at room temperature. Cut celery leaves into bladelike leaf shapes, ¼ x 1-inch in size. Cut stems into thin ¼-inch slivers about 1 inch long. Dip in gelatin remaining in pan. (Reheat if it has solidified.)

For decoration, arrange leaves and a stem on each egg. Make a small paper cone with waxed paper. Fill with spoonful of mayonnaise. Cut tip to ¼-inch opening. Pipe a daisy on each egg at tip of stem. Sprinkle center of daisy with mashed egg yolk.

Cover top of pan with plastic wrap so that it does not touch eggs. Chill until ready to serve, up to 2 hours. Transfer eggs with broad spatula to watercress-lined plate. Serves 8.

Frittata With Leftovers

A great way to use up odds and ends from the refrigerator: diced, cooked vegetables, bits of meat, ham, chicken, fish, cheese, etc.

- 8 eggs
- 2 tablespoons butter
- ¼ cup chopped onion
- 1 tablespoon milk
- Salt and pepper to taste
- 2 cups diced leftovers: meat, vegetables, cheese, chicken, ham, etc.

In large non-stick skillet, melt butter. Add onion. Add leftovers until heated; add milk and season. Beat eggs in a bowl; pour over skillet contents, lifting edges carefully with spatula to allow egg to run underneath. Cook until bottom is browned and eggs are set. Slide onto plate; cut into 4 wedges. Serves 4. *Note:* Halve ingredients to make 2 servings.

Cinnamon Drops

- 1 (7½-ounce) package pancake mix (2 cups)
- 2 tablespoons sugar
- ⅓ cup water
- 1 egg

Heat 1 inch oil in pan to 375 degrees. Combine mix, sugar, water and egg. Stir until moistened. Drop by spoonfuls into hot fat. Brown on both sides. Drain on paper towel.

Blend ¾ cup sugar and 2 teaspoons cinnamon. Roll drops in mixture.

Variations

Add ½ cup mashed banana to batter to flavor or coat drops with confectioners' sugar.

Brunch Green Bean & Egg Pie

- 1 (1-pound) can green beans
- 1 tablespoon butter *or* margarine
- 1 tablespoon vegetable oil
- ½ onion, minced
- 1 clove garlic, minced
- 6 eggs, lightly beaten
- 3 tablespoons water
- 1½ tablespoons American cheese, grated
- 1½ tablespoons Parmesan cheese, grated
- ¼ teaspoon salt
- ¼ teaspoon pepper
- ¼ teaspoon nutmeg

Drain beans in colander; rinse. In a skillet melt butter; add oil. Cook beans, onion and garlic. Mix eggs with water; add cheeses, salt, pepper and nutmeg. Pour egg mixture over green beans; cook until eggs are set. Cut into pie-shaped wedges; serve with hot buttered toast and broiled peach half. Serves 5.

Whole-Wheat Pancakes

- ¾ cup whole-wheat flour
- 2 teaspoons baking powder
- ½ teaspoon salt
- 1 tablespoon honey *or* sugar
- 1 cup milk
- 1 egg
- 1½ tablespoons oil

Combine dry ingredients. Combine liquids and stir into dry ingredients until just moistened. Spoon ¼ cupfuls on hot griddle. We also use this recipe for waffles. Our family loves the rich taste.

Blueberry Pancakes

1 cup flour
1½ teaspoons baking powder
1 tablespoon sugar
½ teaspoon salt, if desired
¼ teaspoon cinnamon
2 tablespoons margarine, melted
1 egg, separated
¾ cup milk
¾ cup blueberries, drained

Sift flour, baking powder, sugar, salt and cinnamon together. Add melted margarine to beaten egg yolk and stir in milk. Add to dry ingredients, mixing just enough to moisten. Fold in stiffly beaten egg white; add blueberries and mix lightly. Pour batter on hot greased griddle and bake on both sides until done. Serve with margarine and favorite syrup.

Cornmeal Pancakes

1 cup flour
1 cup cornmeal
2 teaspoons baking powder
½ teaspoon soda
2 cups buttermilk
2 eggs, well-beaten
½ cup water
1 teaspoon salt, if desired

Sift all dry ingredients together. Add 2 cups buttermilk and 2 well-beaten eggs. Thin batter with ½ cup water. Batter should be thin. Pour a tablespoon of batter onto hot, greased griddle; flip once. These should be the size of silver dollars. Keep stirring batter because cornmeal has a tendency to settle to bottom of bowl. Makes 8 servings.
You can flip over pancakes any time of the day or night.

Orange Apple Pancakes

2 cups buttermilk pancake and waffle mix
1½ cups water
2 tablespoons shredded orange peel
1 teaspoon ground cinnamon
1 cooking apple, cored and cut into thin wedges
1 tablespoon margarine
¾ cup syrup
⅓ cup coarsely chopped pecans

Combine pancake mix, water, orange peel and cinnamon in medium-size bowl; stir until fairly smooth. In skillet, cook apple wedges in margarine until tender, about 4 minutes. Stir in syrup and nuts; heat through and keep warm. For each pancake, pour ¼ cup of batter onto well-greased griddle. Turn when tops are covered with bubbles and edges look dry. Top with warm syrup mixture. Serves 4.

Banana Peanut Pancakes

These are a hit with "kids" of all ages.

2 cups buttermilk pancake and waffle mix
1½ cups water
1¼ teaspoons cinnamon
Dash nutmeg
1 cup diced fresh bananas
¾ cup syrup
½ cup sliced fresh bananas
⅓ cup coarsely chopped peanuts

Combine pancake mix, water, cinnamon and nutmeg in bowl; stir in diced bananas. Heat syrup, if desired; stir in sliced bananas and peanuts. Keep warm until serving. For each pancake, pour ¼ cup of batter onto hot, well-greased griddle. If electric, griddle should be set at 425 degrees. Top pancakes with warm syrup mixture. Serves 4.

Sunday Morning Chive Potato Pancakes

3 eggs
1 tablespoon flour
1 teaspoon salt
4 large new white potatoes, peeled and coarsely shredded
3 tablespoons snipped chives
Salad oil

Beat eggs with fork, gradually adding flour and salt. Add potatoes and chives; mix thoroughly. Heat just enough salad oil in frying pan to cover bottom. Bake over medium heat until crispy brown on edges; turn and brown on other side. Serves 6–8.

Blueberry Pancakes

1 cup milk
2 tablespoons light corn syrup
1 egg, lightly beaten
1 cup pancake mix
¾ cup blueberries
⅓ cup cottage cheese

In mixing bowl, combine milk, corn syrup and egg. Add pancake mix. Stir until dry ingredients are moistened. Batter will be lumpy. Stir in blueberries and cottage cheese. Carefully pour ¼ cup batter onto hot griddle. Cook until brown, turning once. Repeat cooking until all batter is used.

Beer Buttermilk Pancakes

3 eggs
1 cup buttermilk
⅓ cup beer
½ cup sour cream
2 tablespoons margarine, melted
1½ cups buttermilk pancake mix

Beat eggs; add buttermilk, beer, sour cream and melted margarine. Add pancake mix and beat until almost smooth. Spoon out into saucer-size circles on medium-hot ungreased griddle or heavy frying pan. Bake until golden brown on both sides. Makes 18.

Cottage Cheese Fruit Pancakes

3 eggs, well-beaten
1 cup cream-style cottage cheese
2 tablespoons salad oil
¼ cup sifted flour
¼ teaspoon salt, if desired
Raspberry jam
Confectioners' sugar

Combine eggs, cottage cheese and salad oil; mix well. Sift flour and salt together; add to egg mixture and beat only until well-blended. Bake 4-inch cakes on lightly greased griddle. Place about 1 tablespoon jam in center of each cake; bring edges of pancake together and roll. Sprinkle with confectioners' sugar and serve at once. You may vary the flavor of jam.

Puff Pancakes

- 1/2 cup flour
- 1/2 cup milk
- 2 eggs
- 1/4 teaspoon nutmeg
- 6 tablespoons butter
- Confectioners' sugar
- Lemon juice
- Strawberries (optional)

Melt butter in a 9-inch pie plate. Mix flour, milk, eggs and nutmeg. Pour batter into bottom of pie plate. Bake 15 minutes at 450 degrees. Sprinkle top with confectioners' sugar and lemon juice, or it may be served with fresh strawberries. Serve immediately after baking.

Crusty Swiss Potato Pancakes

- 4 potatoes
- 1 1/4 cups Swiss cheese, shredded
- 1/2 cup butter *or* margarine
- 1/2 teaspoon paprika
- 2 tablespoon fresh parsley, chopped
- 1/2 teaspoon salt
- 1/8 teaspoon pepper

Cook potatoes until just tender, about 10 minutes; cool. Peel and shred potatoes; add cheese, 1/2 the butter, paprika, parsley, salt and pepper. Add remaining butter in a 12-inch skillet; flatten potato mixture; fry over medium heat.

After mixture is golden and crusty on bottom, invert onto a plate in 1 piece; slide carefully back into skillet. Cook until golden and crusty on 2nd side. Cut into wedges to serve; garnish each serving with parsley. Serves 4.

Apple Pancakes

- 2 cups flour
- 2 tablespoons sugar
- 4 teaspoons baking powder
- 2 cups milk
- 2 eggs, separated
- 2 tablespoons margarine, melted
- 1 cup apple, grated and peeled

Combine flour, sugar and baking powder in mixing bowl. Combine milk, well-beaten egg yolks and margarine; mix well and add to flour mixture. Beat until smooth; add apple. Fold in beaten egg whites. Grease griddle for first pancakes only. Pour batter by 1/2 cupfuls onto griddle. Bake until puffy and bubbly; turn and brown other side. Serves 4–6.

Baked "Overnight" French Toast

- 1/4 cup butter, room temperature
- 12 (3/4-inch-thick) French bread slices
- 6 eggs
- 1 1/2 cups milk
- 1/4 cup sugar
- 2 tablespoons maple syrup
- 1 teaspoon vanilla
- 1/2 teaspoon salt
- Confectioners' sugar
- Maple-Walnut Syrup (recipe follows)

Spread butter over bottom of heavy large baking pan with 1-inch-high sides. Arrange bread slices in pan. In large bowl beat eggs, milk, sugar, syrup, vanilla and salt to blend. Pour mixture over bread. Turn bread slices to coat. Cover with plastic and refrigerate overnight.

Preheat oven to 400 degrees. Bake French bread 10 minutes. Turn bread over and continue baking until just golden, about 4 minutes longer. Transfer cooked toast to plates and sprinkle with confectioners' sugar. Serve at once, passing Maple-Walnut Syrup separately. Serves 6.

Maple-Walnut Syrup

- 2 cups maple syrup
- 1 cup chopped walnuts, toasted

Combine syrup and walnuts in heavy medium saucepan. Bring to simmer. Serve hot. Makes 3 cups.

Croissant French Toast

- 2/3 cup half-and-half
- 3 eggs
- 1/3 cup orange juice
- 1 teaspoon sugar
- 1 teaspoon vanilla
- 1 teaspoon grated orange peel
- 1/4 teaspoon ground cinnamon
- 1/8 teaspoon ground nutmeg
- 4 day-old croissants, halved lengthwise
- 2 tablespoons unsalted butter
- Confectioners' sugar
- Maple syrup

Whisk first 8 ingredients in medium bowl. Add croissants to egg batter and turn until thoroughly coated. Melt butter in heavy large skillet over medium-high heat. Add croissants and cook until golden brown on both sides, about 3 minutes per side. Sift confectioners' sugar over. Serve with maple syrup. Serves 4.

Ricotta-Stuffed French Toast

- 1 (1-pound) loaf Italian bread
- 1 (8-ounce) cup ricotta cheese
- 4 eggs
- 1/2 cup light cream
- 1 tablespoon vanilla extract
- 1/2 teaspoon nutmeg
- 1/2 teaspoon cinnamon
- 1 tablespoon butter *or* margarine
- Confectioners' sugar
- Maple syrup (optional)

Slice bread into 24 thin slices. Spread 12 slices with ricotta cheese; top with remaining bread slices. Beat eggs, cream, vanilla extract, nutmeg and cinnamon together. Dip each sandwich into egg mixture. In skillet, melt 1 tablespoon butter. Grill sandwiches slowly until golden brown; turn and grill other side. Dust with confectioners' sugar. Top with maple syrup, if desired. Makes 12.

French Toast With Currant Jelly Sauce (Challah Egg Bread)

- 1 cup milk
- 1/2 cup half-and-half
- 2 eggs
- 2 tablespoons *plus* 1 1/2 teaspoons sugar
- 2 teaspoons grated orange peel

½ teaspoon vanilla extract
½ teaspoon salt
¼ teaspoon ground cardamom
4 (1-inch-thick) slices egg bread *or* French bread
¼ cup butter
Currant Jelly Sauce (recipe follows)

Whisk first 8 ingredients in shallow dish to blend. Add bread and soak 15 minutes, turning once. Melt butter in heavy large skillet over medium-low heat. Add bread and cook until outside is golden brown, but inside is still custardlike, about 5 minutes per side. Transfer to plates. Spoon sauce over. Serves 2.

Currant Jelly Sauce

½ cup red currant jelly
¼ cup fresh orange juice
½ teaspoon (scant) ground cardamom
2 tablespoons butter *or* margarine

Melt jelly with orange juice and cardamom in heavy small saucepan over medium heat, stirring constantly. Boil until syrupy, about 3 minutes. Remove from heat and whisk in 2 tablespoons butter.

Peachy Cinnamon Toast

1 (1 pound 14-ounce) can (3½ cups) sliced peaches
1 tablespoon cornstarch
¼ teaspoon salt
1 tablespoon lemon juice
¼ cup butter *or* margarine
3 slices bread, slightly dry
¼ cup butter *or* margarine, melted
⅓ cup sugar
½ teaspoon cinnamon
¼ teaspoon nutmeg

Drain peaches, reserving 1 cup syrup. Combine cornstarch and salt; slowly blend in reserved syrup. Cook and stir until mixture comes to boiling. Reduce heat; cook and stir 2 minutes. Add lemon juice, ¼ cup butter and peaches. Heat just to bubbling. Turn into 10 x 6 x 1½-inch baking dish. Cut bread lengthwise into 1-inch strips; dip into ¼ cup melted butter, then into a mixture of sugar, cinnamon and nutmeg. Arrange over hot peaches. Bake at 375 degrees for 25 minutes, or until toasty. Serve with whipped cream if desired. Serves 6.

"Highly Unorthodox" French Toast

6 eggs
¼ cup triple sec *or* orange liqueur
2 tablespoons maple syrup
1 tablespoon heavy cream
1 teaspoon ground cinnamon
3–4 tablespoons unsalted butter
1 (1-pound) loaf brioche or challah (egg bread), cut into 12 thick slices
Confectioners' sugar
Orange slices

Beat eggs, triple sec, maple syrup, cream and cinnamon in large bowl until smooth. Melt 1 tablespoon of the butter in large skillet over medium heat. Dip 4 slices of brioche in egg mixture until well-saturated. Sauté in butter, turning once, until golden brown on both sides, about 5 minutes. Transfer to warm serving platter. Dust with confectioners' sugar. Keep warm.

Repeat with remaining brioche slices, adding more butter to skillet as needed. Dust with sugar. Garnish with orange slices. Serves 6.

French Toast With Brandied Lemon Butter

4 eggs
2 tablespoons and 1 teaspoon sugar
½ teaspoon salt
1 cup whole milk
¼ teaspoon vanilla extract
12 thick slices bread (cut and left overnight to dry out)
Butter
Confectioners' sugar
Brandied Lemon Butter (recipe follows)

In shallow dish, beat eggs, sugar, salt, milk and vanilla. Soak bread in the mixture. Heat butter over medium-high heat and cook each slice until slightly brown on each side.

Serve with Brandied Lemon Butter and lemon slices, if desired. Sprinkle with confectioners' sugar. Serves 6.

Brandied Lemon Butter

½ cup butter *or* margarine
1 cup sugar
Juice of 2 lemons
4 teaspoons grated lemon rind
3 ounces rum *or* brandy

Melt butter over low heat. Spoon off any foam that forms. Pour into a dish, leaving sediment in the pan. Wash pan. Pour in the clarified butter and sugar. Stir continuously until sugar dissolves. Add rind, juice and rum; stir until smooth. Pour over hot toast.

Stuffed French Toast

8 slices ¾-inch-thick heavy bread, cubed, crusts removed
2 (8-ounce) packages cream cheese, cubed
12 eggs, beaten
⅓ cup maple syrup, warmed
Dash cinnamon
Dash sugar

Place half the bread cubes in the bottom of a 9 x 13-inch baking pan. Top with cubed cheese. Put the rest of the bread cubes on top of this. Pour beaten eggs over all. Cover and refrigerate overnight. Bake at 375 degrees and serve with warmed maple syrup, cinnamon and sugar.

Quick Easter Carrot Bread

1 (16-ounce) package nut bread mix
1 cup coarsely grated carrots
½ teaspoon grated lemon rind
½ teaspoon cinnamon
¾ cup orange juice
1 egg

Combine all ingredients in large bowl. Stir 75 strokes, or until dry ingredients are moistened. Pour into a well-greased and floured 8 x 4-inch pan. Bake at 350 degrees for 45–55 minutes, or until bread tests done. Remove from pan and cool completely on rack before slicing.

Cream Cheese Pumpkin Coffee Cake

1 (8-ounce) package cream cheese
1/4 cup sugar
1/2 teaspoon vanilla
1 cup packed brown sugar
3/4 cup sugar
2/3 cup vegetable oil
2 eggs
3/4 cup buttermilk
3/4 cup cooked *or* canned pumpkin
2 cups flour
1/2 teaspoon baking powder
1/2 teaspoon baking soda
1/2 teaspoon salt
1 teaspoon cinnamon
1 teaspoon nutmeg
1/4 teaspoon ginger

Microwave cream cheese on HIGH for 30–45 seconds; blend in sugar and vanilla until creamy; set aside. Combine sugars and oil in large bowl; blend well. Beat in eggs 1 at a time; beat well after each addition. Blend in buttermilk and pumpkin; add flour, baking powder, soda, salt, cinnamon, nutmeg and ginger; beat just until smooth.

Use tube microwave springform pan; spray lightly with non-stick cooking spray. Pour cake batter into pan; spread evenly. Spoon cream cheese mixture by teaspoonfuls onto batter, staying away from edge of pan.

Microwave on MEDIUM (50 percent) power, uncovered, 15–16 minutes; rotate pan once. Microwave on HIGH 5–6 minutes; rotate pan twice, if necessary. Let stand 10 minutes. When springform pan is not available use a 12 x 8-inch baking dish. Top with cream cheese mixture; swirl lightly, microwave on MEDIUM (50 percent) power for 12 minutes; rotate dish once. Microwave on HIGH 6–8 minutes.

Maple Nut Coffee Cake

1/4 cup brown sugar, firmly packed
1/4 cup chopped nuts
1 1/2 cups all-purpose flour
1 teaspoon baking powder
1/4 teaspoon baking soda
1/4 teaspoon salt
2 cups raisin, rice and rye cereal
1 egg, slightly beaten
2/3 cup milk
1/2 cup margarine *or* butter, softened
2 tablespoons brown sugar, firmly packed
1/3 cup maple syrup

Mix together first 2 ingredients for topping; set aside. Stir together flour, baking powder, soda and salt; set aside. In large bowl, crush cereal slightly. Stir in egg and milk. Let stand 5–10 minutes until cereal is softened. Add margarine. Beat well. Stir in sugar, maple syrup and flour mixture. Spread evenly in 9-inch round or square greased pan. Sprinkle evenly with topping. Bake at 350 degrees for 35 minutes or until browned and tests done. Cool slightly before serving. This coffee cake is truly delicious. Serves 9.

Jubilee Coffee Cake

1/2 cup sugar
1/2 cup chopped nuts
1/2 teaspoon cinnamon
2 packages refrigerated biscuits
1/3 cup butter, melted
1 (12-ounce) jar apricot preserves

Combine sugar, nuts and cinnamon. Sprinkle 1/4 cup of mixture into greased 6 1/2-cup ring mold. Cut each biscuit in half. Roll in balls. Dip each ball in butter. Layer biscuit balls, cinnamon mixture and 1/2 cup preserves in ring mold. Bake in a 350-degree oven for 35 minutes. Invert on serving plate; top with remaining preserves. Serve with butter, if desired. Serves 6–8.

Mini Chips Blueberry Breakfast Cake

1 (14.5-ounce) package blueberry nut quick bread mix
1 cup dairy sour cream
1/4 cup water
1 egg
1/2 cup miniature semisweet chocolate chips
Topping (recipe follows)

Heat oven to 350 degrees. Grease bottom only of 9-inch square baking pan. In medium bowl, combine bread mix, sour cream, water, egg and miniature chocolate chips; stir until well-moistened and blended. Spread into prepared pan. Sprinkle topping over batter. Bake 40–45 minutes, or until golden brown. Cool; cut into squares. Serves 9.

Topping

In small bowl, combine 1/4 cup all-purpose flour, 1/4 cup sugar and 2 tablespoons softened butter or margarine until crumbly. Stir in 1/4 cup miniature chocolate chips.

Peachy Coffee Cake

4 cups flour
2 cups sugar
2 large eggs
4 teaspoons baking powder
1 stick margarine *or* butter
4 tablespoons milk *or* cream
2–3 pounds sliced fresh peaches

Mix all ingredients, except peaches, to a smooth dough (use hands). Place 3/4 of the dough into a greased 12 x 18-inch edged cookie sheet (jelly roll pan). Roll with rolling pin or press with hands to cover entire pan, including edges. Spoon peaches over dough and sprinkle with a little sugar. Roll remaining dough into strips and cover peaches.

Combine 1 1/2 cups flour, 1 stick margarine and 1 cup sugar, and work into crumbs. Sprinkle crumbs over peaches. I added a little almond flavoring to peaches. Bake 30 minutes at 350 degrees. This is a large coffee cake and freezes well.

Good Morning Marmalade Coffee Cake

1/4 cup shortening
1/2 cup sugar
1 egg, beaten
1 tablespoon grated orange rind
1 3/4 cups all-purpose flour
2 teaspoons baking powder
1/4 teaspoon salt
1/2 cup milk
3 tablespoons butter, melted
1 cup flaked coconut

3/4 cup orange marmalade
1 tablespoon sugar

Cream shortening; add 1/2 cup sugar; mix well. Add egg and orange rind. Sift together dry ingredients; add alternately with milk to creamed mixture; beat well. Spread dough in greased 9-inch square pan. Brush top with 1 tablespoon butter. Blend coconut and marmalade; add remaining butter. Spread evenly on top of dough. Sprinkle with 1 tablespoon sugar. Bake at 350 degrees for 45 minutes.

Eggs Parisian

(an oldie, but a goodie!)

- **3 cups well-mashed potatoes, instant *or* fresh cooked**
- **3 tablespoons butter**
- **1 small onion, minced**
- **Salt and pepper to taste**
- **2 tablespoons minced, fresh parsley, *or* 1/2 teaspoon dried parsley**
- **6 eggs**
- **1/2 cup grated American *or* cheddar cheese**
- **Paprika**

Mix potatoes with butter, onion, salt, pepper and parsley. With large spoon divide potatoes into 6 mounds on a greased cookie sheet; indent the center to form a hollow, making nest-shaped rounds. Place 1 teaspoon butter into each nest; then carefully break 1 egg into each mound. Sprinkle with paprika; top each with grated cheese. Place in a 325-degree oven; bake until eggs are set and potatoes lightly browned. Carefully remove to platter with spatula. Serves 6.

Eggs, of course, also mean desserts. I found a delightful Eggnog Ice Cream recipe in an old recipe book, and converted it to refrigerator freezing.

Hot Deviled Eggs

(A switch from the usual cold deviled eggs!)

- **1 1/2 cups canned tomatoes**
- **1/2 cup diced celery**
- **1/2 cup green pepper**
- **1/4 cup diced onion**
- **1 teaspoon Worcestershire sauce**
- **Dash hot sauce**
- **1/4 teaspoon oregano**
- **Salt and pepper to taste**

White Sauce

- **1 tablespoon margarine**
- **1 tablespoon flour**
- **2/3 cup milk**
- **6 hard-cooked eggs, sliced**

Mix tomatoes, celery, green pepper, onion, Worcestershire sauce, oregano, salt, pepper and hot sauce together in saucepan. Simmer for 20 minutes. Make white sauce by melting margarine in another saucepan; blend in flour and add milk slowly, stirring over low heat until thickened. Carefully and slowly stir tomato mixture into white sauce. Add sliced eggs. Serve over toast, or in patty shells.

Ham & Egg Pudding

- **1/4 cup butter, melted**
- **1 pound sliced ham**
- **White pepper**
- **6 eggs, well-beaten**
- **2 cups milk**
- **2 cups flour, sifted**
- **1 teaspoon salt**

Preheat oven to 425 degrees. Spread butter evenly in a 9 x 13-inch pan. Line bottom of pan with ham slices and sprinkle with pepper. Beat eggs until light. Beat in milk. Add flour and salt; beat until smooth. Pour mixture evenly over ham. Bake for 40–45 minutes, or until brown and crusty. Cut into squares and serve. May be topped with your favorite brown gravy, if desired. Serves 8.

Lemon Egg-Nut Loaf

- **3/4 cup margarine**
- **2 cups sugar**
- **4 eggs**
- **3 cups flour**
- **2 teaspoons baking powder**
- **1 cup milk**
- **1 tablespoon grated lemon rind**
- **1/2 cup chopped walnuts**

Glaze

- **1/4 cup sugar**
- **3 tablespoons lemon juice**

Cream sugar and margarine until fluffy. Add eggs, 1 at a time, beating after each addition. Mix flour and baking powder together. Add to creamed mixture alternating with milk. Beat well. Fold in nuts and grated lemon rind. Pour into 2 greased (medium-size) loaf pans or into 1 large loaf pan. Bake at 350 degrees for 45 minutes. Cool for several minutes; remove from pans. Mix glaze and pour over loaves. Cool before slicing.

Eggs Olé

- **1 small onion, chopped**
- **1 small green pepper, diced**
- **1/2 clove garlic, minced**
- **2 tablespoons oil or butter**
- **1/3 cup tomatoes, canned *or* fresh, chopped**
- **6 stuffed olives, sliced**
- **Salt and pepper to taste**
- **Dash hot sauce (optional)**
- **6 eggs, beaten slightly**
- **3 tablespoons water**

Sauté onion, green pepper and garlic in oil or butter in skillet. Add tomatoes, olives, salt, pepper and hot sauce. Stir and simmer for 3 or 4 minutes. Combine eggs and water and add to mixture. Cook on low heat until fluffy and thickened, stirring often. Serves 4–5.

Cheddar Spinach Quiche

- **1 (10-ounce) package frozen, chopped spinach, cooked and drained**
- **2 cups (8 ounces) shredded cheddar cheese**
- **2 tablespoons flour**
- **1 cup milk**
- **2 eggs, beaten**
- **3 slices bacon, crisply cooked and crumbled**
- **1/2 teaspoon salt**
- **Dash pepper**
- **1 (9-inch) unbaked pastry shell**

Preheat oven to 350 degrees. Drain spinach well. Toss cheese with flour; add spinach and remaining ingredients, mixing well. Pour into pastry shell; garnish with additional bacon, if desired. Bake at 350 degrees for 1 hour.

Cakes

TO BAKE

Strawberry Crunch Cake

- 2 (10-ounce) packages frozen, sliced strawberries, thawed
- 1 cup butter *or* margarine, softened
- 1 1/4 cups sugar
- 2 eggs
- 1 cup dairy sour cream
- 2 cups flour
- 1 teaspoon baking powder
- 1/2 teaspoon baking soda
- 1/2 teaspoon salt
- 1/2 cup chopped walnuts
- 1/2 cup packed brown sugar
- 2 tablespoons sugar
- 1 teaspoon cinnamon
- 4 teaspoons cornstarch
- 1 (9-ounce) container whipped topping

Preheat oven to 350 degrees. Drain strawberries, reserving juice; set aside. Cream together butter or margarine and 1 1/4 cups sugar until light and fluffy. Add eggs; beat well. Blend in sour cream. Stir together flour, baking powder, baking soda and salt. Add to creamed mixture, mixing well.

Spread half of batter into a greased 13 x 9-inch baking pan. Spoon drained strawberries over batter. Combine walnuts, brown sugar, 2 tablespoons sugar and cinnamon. Sprinkle half of nut mixture on top of strawberries. Spread remaining batter over all. Sprinkle with remaining nut mixture. Bake for 30–35 minutes, or until cake tests done.
In a small saucepan, combine cornstarch and reserved syrup. Heat and stir until thickened and bubbly; cool. To serve, top each piece with whipped topping and then drizzle thickened syrup over top. Serves 12.

Rhubarb Coffee Cake

- 2 1/2 cups flour
- Pinch salt
- 1/2 cup brown sugar
- 1/2 cup butter
- 3 teaspoons baking powder
- 2/3 cup milk
- 1 egg, slightly beaten
- 1 quart diced, uncooked rhubarb
- 1 (3-ounce) package black raspberry gelatin

Streusel Topping

- 1 cup sugar
- 1/2 cup flour
- 1/4 cup butter

Mix first 5 ingredients like pie dough. Add milk and egg; press into greased 9 x 12-inch pan. Cover with rhubarb; sprinkle gelatin on top of rhubarb. Mix topping ingredients; sprinkle topping over gelatin. Bake at 350 degrees for 45 minutes.

"Sunny" Easter Cake

- 1 package chocolate *or* spice cake mix
- 1 (1-pound 14-ounce) can apricot halves, drained
- Whipped cream

Bake cake according to package directions in a greased 13 x 9 x 2-inch pan. Drain apricot halves. To serve, cut cake in squares and place on serving plates. Place a heaping spoonful of whipped cream on each, then put a drained apricot half cut-side down on the center of cake square. Serves 8.

Blueberry Tea Cake

- 1/3 cup shortening
- 1 cup sugar
- 2 cups flour
- 3/4 cup milk
- 2 teaspoons baking powder
- 1 egg
- 1/4 teaspoon salt
- 1 cup blueberries

Stir shortening to soften. Add flour sifted with baking powder, salt and sugar. Add milk; beat vigorously for 2 minutes. Add egg; beat 1 minute. Stir in blueberries; pour into greased 8 x 8 x 2-inch pan. Bake at 350 degrees for 25–30 minutes, or until pick inserted in center comes out clean.

Poppy Seed Nut Cake

- 4 eggs
- 1 cup vegetable oil
- 1 cup milk
- 2 cups sugar
- 3 cups sifted flour
- 1/2 teaspoon baking powder
- 1/2 cup chopped nuts
- 1 (12-ounce) can poppy seed filling
- Confectioners' sugar

In a large mixing bowl, combine eggs, vegetable oil and milk. Carefully add sugar, flour and baking powder. Beat until well-blended. Add nuts and fold in Poppy Seed Filling last. Place in a lightly greased pan; bake at 350 degrees for at least 60 minutes, or until toothpick inserted in center comes out clean. Remove from oven and sprinkle with confectioners' sugar.

Holiday Fruit-Nut Cake

- 1 cup butter *or* margarine, softened
- 2 cups sugar
- 6 eggs, separated
- 4 cups all-purpose flour, divided
- 2 teaspoons baking powder
- 1/8 teaspoon ground nutmeg
- 1 cup whiskey
- 4 cups pecan halves
- 1 (8-ounce) package chopped dates
- 1/2 pound chopped candied cherries

Cream together butter and sugar. Add egg yolks, 1 at a time, beating well after each addition. Combine 3 3/4 cups flour, baking powder and nutmeg. Add alternately with whiskey to sugar mixture, mixing well. Combine remaining 1/4 cup flour, pecans, dates and cherries. Stir into flour mixture.

Beat egg whites until stiff. Fold into cake batter. Spoon into greased and floured 10-inch tube pan. Bake at 350 degrees for 1 hour and 40 minutes. Cover top of cake with foil if needed to prevent overbrowning. Cool on wire rack. Makes 1 (10-inch) cake.

Almond Cold-Oven Cake

- 1/2 cup sliced almonds
- 1 cup butter
- 1/2 cup margarine
- 3 cups sugar
- 6 eggs
- 3 cups all-purpose flour
- 1/2 teaspoon baking powder
- 1 cup milk
- 1/2 teaspoon vanilla
- 1 1/2 teaspoons almond extract

Grease and flour a 10-inch tube pan. Sprinkle sliced almonds on bottom of pan. Cream butter, margarine and sugar. Add eggs, 1 at a time, beating well after each addition. Sift together flour and baking powder. Alternately add flour and milk to mixture. Beat well. Add extracts. Blend well. Pour into prepared tube pan. Place in a cold oven and bake at 350 degrees for 1 hour and 30 minutes. Cool cake on a wire rack. Remove from pan after 10 minutes.

Chocola Cake

- 2 cups flour
- 2 cups sugar
- 2 sticks (1 cup) butter
- 1 cup cola beverage
- 1/2 cup buttermilk *or* sour milk
- 2 eggs, beaten
- 1 teaspoon baking soda
- 1 teaspoon vanilla
- 1 1/2 cups miniature marshmallows
- 3 tablespoons cocoa powder

Combine flour and sugar in a large bowl. In medium pan heat butter, cocoa and cola to boiling point, stirring constantly. Pour over flour mixture and add milk, eggs, baking soda and vanilla. Blend well; fold in marshmallows. Pour into 9 x 13-inch baking pan that has been greased and floured. Bake at 350 degrees for 30–35 minutes.

Icing

- 1/2 cup butter
- 3 tablespoons cocoa
- 6 tablespoons cola beverage
- 1 pound confectioners' sugar
- 1 cup chopped pecans

Combine butter, cocoa and cola in a saucepan; heat to boiling. Pour over confectioners' sugar in a mixing bowl and beat well. Add pecans and spread on hot cake.

Pineapple Carrot Cake

- 3 cups cake flour
- 1 teaspoon baking powder
- 1 (8-ounce) can crushed pineapple
- 1 1/2 cups oil
- 2 cups sugar
- 1/2 teaspoon salt
- 1 teaspoon cinnamon
- 3 eggs
- 2 cups finely shredded carrots
- Confectioners' sugar

Beat together the oil and sugar until well-blended. Add eggs, 1 at a time, beating well after each addition. Sift dry ingredients; add to previous mixture. Add pineapple and carrots; pour into a greased and floured 13 x 9 x 2-inch pan. Bake at 350 degrees for about 45 minutes. Cool in pan. Dust with confectioners' sugar. Cut in squares.

Cola Cake

- 1 cup flour
- 1 cup sugar
- 1/4 teaspoon baking soda
- 1/2 cup margarine
- 1/2 cup carbonated cola beverage
- 1/4 cup miniature marshmallows
- 2 tablespoons unsweetened cocoa
- 1/4 cup buttermilk
- 1 egg, beaten
- Chocolate-Cola Icing (recipe follows)

In large bowl mix flour, sugar and soda; set aside. In saucepan over low heat stir margarine, cola, marshmallows and cocoa until blended and marshmallows melt. With whisk or fork, stir into flour mixture. Stir in buttermilk and egg until blended. Turn into greased 8 x 8 x 2-inch pan. Bake in a 350-degree oven for 30 minutes, or until pick inserted in center comes out clean. Cool in pan on rack.

Chocolate-Cola Icing

- 1/4 cup margarine
- 2 tablespoons cocoa
- 2 tablespoons carbonated cola beverage
- 1 1/2 cups confectioners' sugar
- 1/4 cup chopped pecans or walnuts

In saucepan over low heat stir margarine, cocoa and cola until melted. Remove from heat. With whisk or fork beat in sugar until smooth. Stir in nuts. Spread on cake.

Hummingbird Cake

- 3 cups all-purpose flour
- 2 cups granulated sugar
- 2 cups mashed bananas
- 3 eggs
- 1 1/2 cups oil
- 1 (8-ounce) can crushed pineapple
- 1 1/2 cups chopped walnuts
- 1 1/2 teaspoons vanilla extract
- 1 teaspoon salt
- 1 teaspoon soda
- 1 teaspoon cinnamon

Mix all ingredients together by hand. Pour into a greased and floured fluted tube pan. Bake for 1 1/2 hours at 300 degrees. Cool in pan for 10 minutes; remove from pan and finish cooling on wire rack.

Chocolate Potato Cake

2 cups flour
½ cup cocoa
2 teaspoons baking powder
½ teaspoon salt
½ teaspoon cinnamon
1 cup shortening
2 cups sugar
4 eggs
1 cup mashed potatoes
1 teaspoon vanilla
⅓ cup milk
1 cup chopped walnuts
Ice cream *or* whipped topping (optional)

Sift together flour, cocoa, baking powder, salt and cinnamon; set aside. In large bowl of mixer cream shortening and sugar until light. Add eggs and beat until fluffy. Add potatoes and vanilla; mix well. Stir in flour mixture alternately with milk. Stir in nuts. Pour into greased 13 x 9 x 2-inch pan. Bake in preheated 350-degree oven 40–45 minutes, or until pick inserted in center comes out clean. Cool in pan on rack. Cut in squares. Serve with ice cream or whipped topping.

Fluffy Orange Coconut Cake

3⅓ cup sifted cake flour
2 cups sugar
2 tablespoons baking powder
1½ teaspoons salt
1 cup butter, softened
1⅓ cups milk
1 teaspoon vanilla
1 teaspoon orange extract
1 teaspoon grated orange rind
4 medium eggs
Filling (recipe follows)
Butter Cream Frosting (recipe follows)

Sift dry ingredients into bowl. Add butter and milk. Beat at low speed with electric mixer to blend. Beat 2 minutes at medium speed. Add flavorings and rind. Add eggs, 1 at a time, beating after each addition. Beat at moderate speed for 2 more minutes.

Pour into 2 greased and floured 9-inch layer cake pans. Bake at 350 degrees for 30–35 minutes. Cool well. Spread with filling between layers. Frost with Butter Cream Frosting.

Filling

1 cup sweetened condensed milk
3 egg yolks
1 cup sugar
1 stick butter (½ cup)
1½ cups coconut
1 cup chopped walnuts

Combine first 4 ingredients in saucepan. Bring to boil. Continue cooking until thickened. Remove from heat. Add coconut and nuts. Cool.

Butter Cream Frosting

½ cup butter, softened
1 (1-pound) box confectioners' sugar
⅓ cup milk
⅛ teaspoon salt
1 teaspoon vanilla
½ teaspoon orange extract
½ teaspoon coconut extract

Cream butter; add remaining ingredients. Blend well.

Tropical Chocolate Cake

2 (18.5-ounce) packages chocolate cake mix
1 pint heavy cream
2 bananas
½ pint fresh strawberries
1 small can peach slices
1 tablespoon ascorbic acid preservative

Prepare the mixes as directed on box; bake batter in round cake pans at 350 degrees for the time indicated on the mix box. With an electric mixer whip heavy cream until creamy and thick; refrigerate.

Cut bananas in small slices (to decorate); let them soak in a bowl of water and 1 tablespoon of preservative. Slice strawberries; drain peaches; set aside. After cakes have baked let them cool for 1 hour.

To decorate, spread whipped cream on top of first layer, then arrange some slices of banana, peaches and strawberries. Stack layers following the same procedure.

Cover entire cake with remaining whipped cream. Garnish alternating slices of banana, strawberries and peaches.

Cream Cheese Loaf Cake

1 (8-ounce) package cream cheese, softened
1¼ cups sugar
¾ cup butter *or* margarine, softened
4 eggs
1 teaspoon vanilla extract
1¾ cups all-purpose flour
1¼ teaspoons baking powder
¼ teaspoon salt
1 (4-ounce) bar German sweet chocolate
1 tablespoon butter

Combine cream cheese, sugar and ¾ cup butter in large bowl with electric mixer; beat until light and fluffy. Add eggs and vanilla, beating well. Combine dry ingredients and add to creamed mixture, beating on low speed until well-blended.

Melt chocolate and 1 tablespoon butter on low heat. Spoon half of batter into 9 x 5-inch loaf pan sprayed with vegetable cooking spray. Pour chocolate over batter, spreading if necessary. Top chocolate with remaining batter. Bake 70–80 minutes, or until toothpick inserted in center comes out clean. Cool on rack. Remove from pan and cool.

Zucchini Cake

3 eggs
2 cups sugar
1 cup vegetable oil
2 cups grated zucchini
1 cup chopped nuts
1 cup raisins
3 cups flour
1 tablespoon cinnamon
2 teaspoons soda
1 teaspoon salt
1 tablespoon baking powder
1 tablespoon vanilla

Beat eggs until frothy. Beat in vegetable oil, sugar and vanilla. Beat until thick and lemon-colored. Stir in zucchini.

Mix flour, cinnamon, soda, salt and baking powder. Add to zucchini mixture. Fold in nuts and raisins.

Place in a well-greased and floured tube pan. Bake in a 300-degree oven for about 1 hour and 10 minutes

Apple Butter Cake

2 cups all-purpose flour
1 teaspoon baking powder
1 teaspoon baking soda
1/2 cup margarine
1 teaspoon vanilla
1 cup sugar
2 eggs
3/4 cup apple butter
1/2 cup whole-bran cereal
1 cup sour cream

Topping

1/2 cup light brown sugar
3/4 cup chopped walnuts
1 teaspoon cinnamon
1/2 teaspoon nutmeg

Combine ingredients for topping; set aside. Sift together flour, baking powder, baking soda; set aside. Cream margarine with vanilla; gradually add sugar, beating until fluffy. Add eggs, 1 at a time, beating thoroughly. Blend in apple butter and cereal. Alternately add dry ingredients and sour cream in thirds to creamed mixture. Mix only until smooth.

Turn half of batter into a greased 13 x 9-inch pan. Sprinkle half of topping over batter in pan. Spoon remaining batter into pan; sprinkle remaining topping over batter. Bake at 350 degrees for 30 minutes, or until done. Cool in pan. Cut into squares; serve warm. Top with whipped cream for added goodness!

Frosted Banana Pudding Cake

1–2 small, ripe bananas, mashed
1 (2-layer) box yellow cake mix
1 large package banana cream *or* vanilla pudding and pie filling
1 cup water
1/4 cup oil
1/2 cup chopped pecans *or* walnuts
4 eggs
Banana Nut Frosting (recipe follows)

Combine cake mix, pudding, water and oil; add eggs, 1 at a time, mixing well after each addition. Fold in bananas and chopped nuts. Pour into 13 x 9-inch pan and bake in a 350-degree oven for 50–55 minutes. Cool and frost with Banana Nut Frosting.

Banana Nut Frosting

1/2 cup mashed banana
1 teaspoon lemon juice
1/3 cup butter *or* margarine, softened
1 (16-ounce) package plus 3 cups confectioners' sugar, sifted
3–4 tablespoons milk
1 cup flaked coconut, toasted
2/3 cup finely chopped pecans

Combine bananas and lemon juice; set mixture aside. Cream softened butter at medium speed of electric mixer; add confectioners' sugar and milk, mixing well. Add banana mixture, beating until fluffy. Stir in toasted coconut and chopped pecans. Makes 3 1/2 cups.

Note: This cake is best eaten within a few days of baking. It grows sweeter the longer it sits.

Nectarine Carrot Cake

1/2 cup wheat germ
1 cup flour
3/4 cup sugar
3/4 teaspoon baking soda
1/2 teaspoon baking powder
1/2 teaspoon salt
1 1/2 teaspoons cinnamon
1/2 teaspoon nutmeg
2 eggs, lightly beaten
1/2 cup vegetable oil
1 teaspoon vanilla extract
1 cup grated carrots
1 fresh nectarine, diced (1 cup)
1/2 cup chopped walnuts
Confectioners' sugar *or* cream cheese icing of choice (optional)

Preheat oven to 350 degrees. Mix together wheat germ, flour, sugar, baking soda, baking powder, salt, cinnamon and nutmeg. Add eggs, oil and vanilla. Stir in carrots, nectarine and walnuts.

Pour into well-greased and floured 7- or 7 1/2 cup fluted tube pan or 9-inch tube pan. Bake 50 minutes, or until done. Cool 10-15 minutes in pan; invert onto a rack and cool. Top with confectioners' sugar or cream cheese icing, if desired. Serves 8–10.

Classy Chocolate Applesauce Cake

2 cups all-purpose flour, sifted
1 1/4 cups sugar
2 teaspoons baking soda
Pinch salt
1/2 teaspoon nutmeg
1 teaspoon cinnamon
1/2 teaspoon allspice
4 tablespoons cocoa
1 1/2 cups applesauce
1/2 cup sweet milk
1/2 cup butter, melted
2 tablespoons rum extract
1 cup raisins, chopped
1 cup pecans, chopped
Confectioners' sugar, sifted

Sift together flour, sugar, baking soda, salt, spices and cocoa. Stir in applesauce, milk, butter and rum extract; mix thoroughly; add raisins and nuts. Spread in a buttered 9 x 13 x 2-inch cake pan that has been dusted with cocoa. Bake at 350 degrees for 45 minutes, or until tested done in the middle. Cool 10 minutes in the pan; turn out onto rack to cool completely. Dust with confectioners' sugar.

Cupcakes Elegant

Very unusual—requires no frosting.

4 (1-ounce) squares semisweet chocolate
2 sticks margarine
1 1/2 cups broken pecans
1 3/4 cups sugar
1 cup unsifted flour
4 large eggs
1 teaspoon vanilla

Melt chocolate and margarine over hot water or use microwave oven. Stir in nuts only until well-coated. Combine sugar, flour, eggs and vanilla; mix only until blended. *Do not beat.* Add chocolate-nut mixture; again stir in carefully, not beating. Place paper liners in muffin cups. Fill paper liners two-thirds full of batter; bake 35 minutes at 325 degrees.

Easy to make, plus you do not need an electric mixer for this recipe.

Dainty Devil's Food Squares

- 1½ cups all-purpose flour
- 1 cup sugar
- ⅓ cup milk chocolate, finely grated
- ¼ teaspoon salt
- 1 teaspoon baking soda
- ¼ teaspoon ground ginger
- 1 egg, slightly beaten
- 1 cup sour cream
- ⅓ cup butter *or* margarine, melted
- 1 teaspoon vanilla
- Confectioners' sugar

Combine dry ingredients; set aside. Mix together liquid ingredients; combine with dry ingredients. Pour into lightly buttered 8 x 8 x 2-inch square baking pan. Bake at 350 degrees for 25 minutes, or until tested done in middle. Cut into small squares; dust with confectioners' sugar.

Patriot's Flag Cake

- 1½ cups butter, softened
- 2 cups sugar
- 6 eggs, separated
- 2½ cups flour
- 2 teaspoons baking powder
- ¼ teaspoon salt
- 2 tablespoons vanilla extract
- 2 tablespoons lemon juice
- Fresh blueberries
- Fresh strawberries
- Vanilla Cream Cheese Frosting (recipe follows)

Cream butter and 1 cup sugar in mixer bowl until light and fluffy. Add egg yolks, 2 at a time, beating well after each addition. Blend in dry ingredients. Stir in vanilla and lemon juice. Beat egg whites in bowl until soft peaks form. Add remaining 1 cup sugar gradually, beating until stiff peaks form. Fold gently into batter.

Pour into greased, waxed-paper–lined 9 x 13-inch cake pan. Bake at 325 degrees for 1 hour, or until cake tests done. Cool in pan on wire rack for 10 minutes. Invert onto rack to cool completely. Place cake on serving tray. Frost top and side of cake with Vanilla Cream Cheese Frosting. Decorate cake with blueberries and strawberry slices to resemble the American flag. Serves 16.

Vanilla Cream Cheese Frosting

- 1 (8-ounce) package cream cheese, softened
- 1 tablespoon vanilla extract
- 1 tablespoon milk
- 1 (16-ounce) package confectioners' sugar

Beat cream cheese, vanilla and milk in bowl until smooth. Add confectioners' sugar gradually, beating until mixture is creamy.

Marshmallow Cake

- 1 cup butter, softened
- 2 cups sugar
- 3 cups sifted cake flour
- 2 tablespoons baking powder
- 1 cup half-and-half
- 8 egg whites, at room temperature
- Marshmallow Glaze (recipe follows)

Cream butter; gradually add sugar and beat well. Combine flour and baking powder; add to creamed mixture, alternating with half-and-half, beginning and ending with flour. Beat egg whites until stiff peaks form; fold into batter.

Pour into a greased fluted tube pan. Bake at 350 degrees for 1 hour, or until done. Cool in pan 10 minutes. Remove and cool completely. Drizzle with Marshmallow Glaze.

Marshmallow Glaze

- 1 cup sugar
- ⅓ cup water
- 5 large marshmallows, chopped
- 1 egg white
- Pinch cream of tartar
- 1 teaspoon vanilla

Combine sugar and water in heavy saucepan. Cook over medium heat, stirring frequently until mixture comes to a boil and sugar is dissolved. Continue cooking, stirring frequently until soft-ball stage (240 degrees). Add marshmallows; cook 1 minute or until blended, stirring frequently. Combine egg white and cream of tartar; beat until foamy.

While beating on medium speed, slowly pour hot syrup in a thin stream over egg white. Turn mixer to high speed, add vanilla, and continue beating until stiff peaks form and mixture is thickened.

Popular Rhubarb Cake

- ½ cup butter *or* shortening
- 1½ cups white *or* brown sugar
- 1 egg
- 1 cup sour milk *or* buttermilk
- 1 teaspoon baking soda
- ½ teaspoon salt
- 2 cups flour
- 1½ to 3 cups finely chopped rhubarb

Topping

- ¼ cup brown sugar
- 1½ teaspoons cinnamon
- ¼ cup walnuts

Cream together butter and sugar. Add egg. Stir in milk. Add flour, salt and soda. Stir in rhubarb. Scoop into greased 9 x 13-inch baking pan. Mix together topping ingredients. Sprinkle topping over batter. Bake at 350 degrees for 35–40 minutes.

Broiled Orange Apricot Cake

- 1 package orange cake mix
- 1 (12-ounce) jar apricot preserves
- 1 tablespoon lemon juice
- 1 (3½-ounce) can flaked coconut (1⅓ cups)
- 2 cups miniature marshmallows

Preheat oven to 350 degrees. Grease and flour a 13 x 9 x 2-inch pan. Prepare and bake cake following package directions. While cake is baking, combine preserves, lemon juice, coconut and marshmallows in small bowl. Spread over top of hot cake. Broil 3 or 4 inches from heat about 2 minutes, or until the marshmallows are lightly browned. Cool before serving. Serves 12–16.

Tip: To prevent marshmallows from sticking to the knife you use to cut the cake, wet the blade before cutting.

Casseroles

CREATIVE

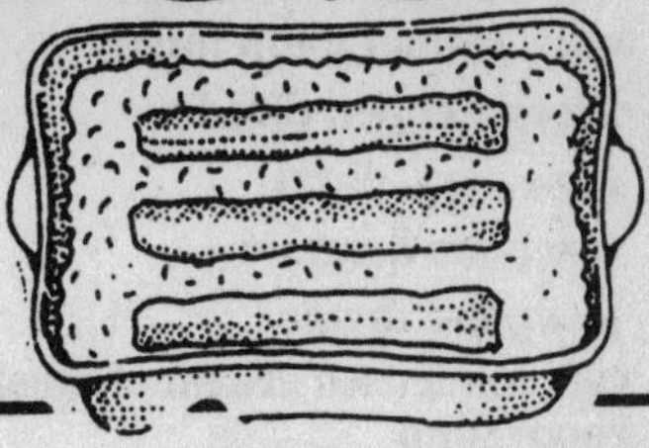

Shortcut Seafood & Chicken Casserole

1 (16-ounce) can whole tomatoes, undrained
1 (10-ounce) frozen green peas
1 (6 1/2-ounce) can minced clams undrained
1 (4 1/4-ounce) can broken shrimp, rinsed and drained
2 cups uncooked instant rice
2 tablespoons instant minced onion
1 teaspoon chicken bouillon granules
1 teaspoon paprika
1/4 teaspoon tumeric
1/4 teaspoon ground red pepper

Mix all ingredients in 3-quart casserole, breaking up tomatoes with fork. Cover tightly and microwave on high for 11–14 minutes, stirring after 5 minutes, until liquid is absorbed.

Crabmeat & Shrimp Casserole

1 medium onion, chopped
1 medium pepper, chopped
1 cup celery, chopped
1 (6 1/2-ounce) can crabmeat, flaked
1 (5 3/4-ounce) can shrimp
1/2 teaspoon salt
1/4 teaspoon pepper
1 teaspoon Worcestershire sauce
1 cup mayonnaise
1 cup bread crumbs, buttered

Combine all ingredients, except bread crumbs. Place in a casserole. Sprinkle with bread crumbs. Bake in 350-degree oven for 30 minutes. Serves 8.

Clam Pie Norfolk

1 (9-inch) unbaked single pie crust
1/4 cup onion, minced
1/2 cup button mushrooms
1/4 cup butter *or* margarine
2 cups boiling water
2 cups potatoes, diced
2 cups canned clams, minced, plus juice
2 cups milk
2 tablespoons flour
1/4 teaspoon herb seafood seasoning
Salt and pepper to taste

Sauté onion and mushrooms in butter; cover; cook 5 minutes. Add boiling water and potatoes; cover; cook 20 minutes. Add clams, clam juice and 1 3/4 cups milk; heat just to a simmer. Blend remaining milk with remaining ingredients; add to simmering liquid.

Turn mixture into 2-quart casserole. Make 3 small slashes in pie crust; place over top of casserole; crimp edges to casserole rim. Bake at 350 degrees for 25 minutes, or until crust is flaky and golden. Serves 6.

Brown Rice Chicken Bake

3 cups cooked brown rice
1 (10-ounce) package frozen green peas
2 cups cooked chicken breast, cubed
1/2 cup reduced-calorie mayonnaise
1/3 cup slivered almonds, toasted (optional)
2 teaspoons soy sauce
1/4 teaspoon ground black pepper
1/4 teaspoon garlic powder
1/4 teaspoon dried tarragon leaves
Vegetable cooking spray

Combine rice, peas, chicken, mayonnaise, almonds, soy sauce, pepper, garlic powder and tarragon in bowl. Transfer to 3-quart baking dish coated with cooking spray. Cover and bake at 350 degrees for 15–20 minutes. Serves 6.

Microwave Oven Instructions

Place mixture in 3-quart microwave-safe dish. Cover with waxed paper and cook on MEDIUM-HIGH (70 percent power) 5–7 minutes. Rotate dish after 2 1/2 minutes.

Eastern-American Casserole

1 cup cooked rice
2 cups diced, cooked chicken
1/2 cup celery
1/4 cup diced onion
1 cup coarsely chopped, roasted peanuts
1/4 teaspoon salt
1 (10 1/2-ounce) can cream of mushroom soup
1 cup hot water
1 tablespoon soy sauce
2 tablespoons cream-style peanut butter
1 cup chow mein noodles *or* 1 cup cracker crumbs

In a buttered casserole stir together rice, chicken, celery, onion, peanuts and salt. Mix soup with water, soy sauce and peanut butter. Pour over rice mixture, stirring to blend well. Sprinkle noodles or crumbs over top. Bake at 350 degrees for 25 minutes, or until top is nicely browned. Add more hot water if mixture is too thick. Serves 4–6.

Cubed Ham Green Noodle Bake

- 1½ pounds ham steak, cubed
- 1 tablespoon vegetable oil
- 1 clove garlic, mashed
- 2 cups Italian plum tomatoes
- 1 green pepper, diced
- 1 rib celery, diced
- ¼ teaspoon oregano
- ¼ teaspoon thyme
- 1 can condensed cream of mushroom soup
- ¼ soup can milk
- ½ pound green noodles, cooked and drained
- ¼ cup Swiss cheese, grated
- ¼ cup Italian bread crumbs

Trim all fat from ham; slice into squares; set aside. Sauté garlic in oil until light golden; add tomatoes, pepper, celery, oregano and thyme. Cover; simmer 10 minutes. Add soup, milk and cubed ham; simmer 10 minutes longer. In a large mixing bowl combine noodles and ham sauce. Spoon into a greased casserole or baking dish; top with combined cheese and bread crumbs. Bake at 350 degrees until the top is golden and crisp. Serves 4.

Cheese Grits

- 1⅓ cups water
- 1 clove garlic
- ⅓ cup quick grits
- 1 tablespoon cold butter *or* margarine
- 1 tablespoon Parmesan cheese
- ¼ teaspoon salt
- 1 cup coarsely grated sharp cheddar cheese
- 1 large cold egg

Preheat oven to 350 degrees. Lightly grease small baking dish, 3–4-cup capacity. Measure water into medium saucepan. While water comes to boiling mash garlic clove and add. Slowly stir grits into boiling water; return to boiling; reduce heat to medium-low; cook 4 minutes. Remove from heat. It will look watery. Whisk in butter, Parmesan cheese, salt and cheddar cheese. (I grate cheddar directly into pan.) Whisk in egg. Pour into prepared dish. Bake until just set in center, 25–30 minutes. Serves 2.

Beef Pie With Cornmeal Crust

- 1 pound lean ground beef
- ¼ pound ground pork
- 1 onion, sliced
- 1 small bell pepper, finely chopped
- 1 (8-ounce) can tomato sauce
- 1 (12-ounce) can whole-kernel corn
- 1 tablespoon chili powder
- ¼ teaspoon cumin powder
- ¼ teaspoon salt
- ¼ teaspoon pepper
- Cornmeal Crust (recipe follows)

In skillet cook beef and pork; add next 8 ingredients; pour into oblong baking dish. Cover with Cornmeal Crust; bake at 375 degrees for 35 minutes. Serves 6.

Cornmeal Crust

- 1¼ cups flour
- ½ cup cornmeal
- ¼ teaspoon salt
- ¼ teaspoon paprika
- ½ cup vegetable oil
- 3 tablespoons cold water

Mix all ingredients; press into ball. Roll between 2 sheets of waxed paper to fit top of baking dish; cut 2 or 3 slits in center of crust.

Hot Taco Rice

- 1 pound ground beef
- 1 onion, chopped
- 1½ cups medium salsa
- 1 (8-ounce) can tomato sauce
- 1 chicken bouillon cube
- 1½ cups instant long-grain rice

Garnishes

- Chopped tomatoes
- Sour cream
- Shredded cheddar cheese
- Tortilla chips
- Pitted ripe olives, sliced

Brown beef and onion in skillet. Add salsa, tomato sauce and bouillon cube. Bring to full boil; cover. Reduce meat and simmer 5 minutes. Meanwhile, prepare rice as directed on package. Serve beef mixture over rice; top with garnishes. Serves 4.

Deep-Dish Turkey Pie

- 1 cup sliced celery
- Generous dash of onion powder
- 2 tablespoons butter *or* margarine
- 1 (10¾-ounce) can condensed cream of chicken soup
- 1½ cups cubed, cooked chicken *or* turkey
- 1½ cups cooked carrots, cut in 1-inch pieces
- ¼ cup milk
- 2 teaspoons lemon juice
- ⅛ teaspoon ground nutmeg
- ½ cup biscuit mix
- 2 tablespoons cold water

In saucepan, cook celery with onion powder in butter until tender. Stir in remaining ingredients, except biscuit mix and water. Bring to boil; stir occasionally. Meanwhile, to make pastry, combine biscuit mix and water. Roll pastry to fit top of 1-quart casserole. Pour hot chicken mixture into casserole; top with pastry. Trim edges; make several slits in pastry. Bake at 450 degrees for 15 minutes, or until done.

Mexicali Quiche

- 1 (9-inch) prepared pie crust
- 6 slices bacon, fried crisp and crumbled
- 4 ounces chopped green chilies, drained
- 1 cup shredded Colby cheese
- ¼ cup chopped onion
- ¼ cup sliced black olives
- 2 tablespoons mild picanté sauce
- 4 eggs, slightly beaten
- 2 cups low-fat milk
- ½ teaspoon dried mustard
- ¼ teaspoon cumin
- Salt and pepper to taste

Preheat oven to 425 degrees. Follow package directions for pastry and place in 9-inch pie pan. Sprinkle in bacon, cheese, chilies, onion and olives. In large bowl, combine remaining ingredients and pour into pie crust. Do not cover. Bake for 15 minutes, then reduce heat to 300 degrees and bake another 30 minutes. Remove from oven and let quiche sit for 10 minutes before cutting. Serves 6.

Onion & Gorgonzola Pizza

- 1/4 cup virgin olive oil, divided
- 2 large yellow onions, quartered and sliced
- Salt to taste
- Freshly ground black pepper
- 1 pizza crust (recipe follows)
- Cornmeal (for dusting pizza)
- 3/4 cup Gorgonzola chunks (may substitute Roquefort or blue cheese)
- 1/4 cup grated mozzarella cheese
- 1/4 cup snipped fresh scallions
- Crushed dried red pepper, to taste
- 2 tablespoons fresh thyme leaves (may substitute snipped chives)

Place a pizza stone in the lower third of the oven and preheat to 550 degrees. In a large skillet over high heat, add 3 tablespoons olive oil. Add yellow onions, cooking until softened and caramelized, about 10 minutes. Add salt and pepper to taste. Dust bottom of crust with cornmeal.

Spread remaining tablespoon of olive oil across dough; cover with onion mixture, Gorgonzola and mozzarella cheeses and scallions. Top with red pepper to taste. Remove stone from oven. Place pizza on the stone and return to oven. Bake 10–15 minutes, until crust is golden. Remove from oven and sprinkle with thyme. Follow packing directions above. Makes 1 (9-inch) pizza.

Tomato, Caper & Basil Pizza

Bake the pizzas just before leaving for your tailgate party. The aroma will spark your appetite during the drive. After baking, place on a cardboard pizza round and cut into 12 small slices. Pack in a pizza box to prevent being crushed. To avoid becoming soggy, do not wrap in plastic. Serve on a platter when you arrive at your destination.

- 1 pizza crust (recipe follows)
- Cornmeal (for dusting pizza)
- 2 tablespoons virgin olive oil
- 1/4 cup grated fontina cheese
- 1/4 cup grated mozzarella cheese
- 1/4 cup capers, drained
- 1/4 cup diced tomatoes (peeled, seeded and drained)
- 1/4 cup grated aged Asiago cheese
- 2 tablespoons chopped fresh basil

Place a pizza stone in the lower third of the oven and preheat to 550 degrees. Dust bottom of crust with cornmeal. Spread olive oil across the dough; cover with fontina and mozzarella cheeses. Distribute capers and tomatoes over cheeses. Top with Asiago.

Place pizza on the stone. Bake 8–12 minutes, until the crust is golden. Remove from oven and sprinkle with basil. Makes 1 (9-inch) pizza.

Favorite Zucchini Casserole

- 6 cups zucchini, thinly sliced and unpeeled
- 2 egg yolks, slightly beaten
- 1 cup sour cream
- 2 tablespoons flour
- 2 egg whites, stiffly beaten
- 1 1/2 cups shredded cheddar cheese
- 6 slices bacon, fried crisp and drained
- 1 tablespoon butter, melted
- 1/4 cup bread crumbs

Cook zucchini in boiling water just until tender-crisp. Drain and salt. Combine egg yolks, sour cream and flour. Fold in stiffly beaten egg whites. Layer half each of zucchini, egg mixture, cheese, then bacon in a 9 x 13-inch pan. Repeat layers. Mix butter and bread crumbs; sprinkle over top. Bake at 350 degrees 20–25 minutes. Serves 8–10.

Cheesy Spinach Pie

- 1 (9-inch) frozen deep-dish pie shell
- 1 (10-ounce) package frozen spinach
- 1/4 cup finely chopped onion
- 1 cup (4 ounces) shredded Swiss cheese
- 3 eggs
- 2/3 cup evaporated milk
- 1/2 teaspoon salt
- 1/8 teaspoon nutmeg
- Cayenne pepper
- 1/4 cup Parmesan cheese

Place pie shell in oven-safe glass pie plate. When thawed press to plate; prick with fork; bake in conventional oven until browned. Place spinach and onion in 1-quart dish; cover with plastic wrap and vent. Microwave on high for 5 or 6 minutes; stir once and drain. Layer half of spinach mixture and Swiss cheese into bottom of pie shell; repeat layers.

Beat together remaining ingredients, except Parmesan cheese. Pour over spinach mixture; sprinkle with Parmesan cheese. Shield with foil ring (make a ring 3 inches wide to go around the pie). Microwave on medium (50 percent) for 10–11 minutes; rotate dish and remove foil ring after 5 minutes cooking time. Let stand 10 minutes before serving.

Chicken Breast Bake

- 2 small zucchini
- 4 split chicken breasts, skinned, boned and defatted (about 1 1/2 pounds)
- 1/2 cup white rice
- 1 can cream of chicken soup
- 1 cup chicken broth
- Basil
- Paprika

Peel zucchini and slice to about 1/4 inch thick. Layer on the bottom of a medium casserole. Sprinkle rice over zucchini. Lay chicken breasts on top. Mix soup with chicken broth and pour over chicken. Sprinkle with basil and paprika. Bake at 350 degrees for 1 1/4 hours, or until rice is tender.

Creole Red Beans

- 2 cups red kidney beans, soaked in water overnight
- 2 cups canned tomatoes
- 4 teaspoons molasses
- 1/2 teaspoon dry mustard
- 1/2 teaspoon salt
- 1/2 teaspoon pepper
- 1 cup shredded American cheese
- 1/2 pound bacon

After beans are softened, drain. Mix with tomatoes and molasses. Add dry seasonings and place in casserole. Top with cheese and bacon. Bake at 350 degrees for 20 minutes; place under broiler to make bacon crispy. Serve immediately.

Ground Beef Hash & Eggs

2 pounds ground beef
1 (6-ounce) package hash brown potato mix with onions
1 cup shredded cheddar cheese
1 teaspoon salt
6 eggs
2 tablespoons milk

Shape ground beef into a large patty in bottom of a large skillet. Brown 5 minutes, or until beads of moisture appear on top. Cut into quarters and turn. Brown 5 minutes longer. Remove from skillet with slotted spoon. Pour off and reserve 3 tablespoons fat.

Prepare potatoes, following label directions, adding cheddar cheese and salt, replacing butter or margarine with beef fat.

Mix beef, potatoes, cheese and salt. Turn into 10-cup shallow casserole. Make 6 indentations in beef mixture with spoon. Break 1 egg into each indentation. Bake in a 350-degree oven for 20 minutes, or until eggs are done as desired. Serves 6.

Corned Beef Hash Patties

2 pounds cooked corned beef, cut into small pieces, or shredded
1 cup sliced shitake mushrooms
5 scallions, white part only
1/3 cup chopped parsley
Salt and freshly ground pepper to taste
2 eggs, beaten (optional)

Toss together corned beef, mushrooms, scallions, parsley, salt and pepper in a mixing bowl. Pass through coarse blade of a meat grinder, or put in food processor with steel blade and process until well-chopped. (Do not overwork mixture.) Cover and refrigerate overnight.

Form mixture into small patties. If it seems dry and does not hold together easily (like hamburger), add beaten eggs. Sauté in non-stick skillet until crisp and brown on both sides. Serve while hot, topped with a poached egg. Serves 5–6.

Ham Hash

2 pounds potatoes
1 pound boiled *or* baked ham
2 tablespoons butter
1 1/4 cups milk
1/2 cup heavy cream
1/2 teaspoon Worcestershire sauce
3 dashes hot red pepper sauce
Freshly ground black pepper
Garlic salt to taste
Hot buttered toast
Spiced crab apples

Place potatoes in large saucepan. Cover with water and let simmer until half done (still firm but easily pierced). Drain; peel and chop. Chop ham.

Heat electric skillet to 300 degrees and put in butter (or put butter in regular skillet). When butter has melted, add ham and potatoes; stir until well-mixed. Blend in milk, cream and seasonings.

Cover and cook until mixture is thick but not dry, about 30 minutes. (Uncover and stir occasionally.) Serve on freshly-made hot, buttered toast and garnish each serving with spiced crab apples. Serves 4–6.

Red Flannel Hash

Leftover vegetables (including beets)
Fat and liquid left from boiled dinner
Salt and pepper to taste

Chop all leftover vegetables together. By using chopping bowl you can make it as fine as you like. Add fat and liquid left from cooking the boiled dinner. Mix well. Season with salt and pepper to taste. Store in refrigerator. When ready to cook, turn into baking dish and bake at 350 degrees for 1 hour … or use heavy cast-iron skillet and fry hash slowly, being careful not to burn.

Creamy Chicken Hash

2 tablespoons butter *or* margarine
1 small onion, diced
1 tablespoon all-purpose flour
1 teaspoon salt
3/4 cup half-and-half
2 cups cubed, cooked potatoes
2 cups cubed, cooked chicken *or* turkey
Chopped parsley (garnish)

In 10-inch skillet over medium heat, in hot butter or margarine, cook onion until tender, about 5 minutes; stirring occasionally. Stir in flour and salt. Gradually stir in half-and-half and cook, stirring, until thickened. Stir potatoes and chicken into mixture. Reduce heat to low. Cover skillet and simmer about 10 minutes, or until mixture is heated through; stirring occasionally. Garnish with parsley. Serves 4.

Mexican-Style Hash

2 cups chopped, cooked beef
1/3 cup chopped onion
2 tablespoons shortening
1 1/2 cups finely chopped raw potato
1 (12-ounce) can whole-kernel corn, drained
1 (10 3/4-ounce) can condensed tomato soup
1 1/2 teaspoon chili powder
Salt and pepper to taste

In 10-inch ovenproof skillet, cook beef and onion in shortening until onion is tender, about 5 minutes. Sprinkle with salt and pepper. Add potato, corn, soup and chili powder. Stir to combine. Bake, covered, at 350 degrees for 35–40 minutes. Serves 4.

Frankfurter-Vegetable Medley

1/2 pound (4–5) frankfurters cut in 1-inch pieces
1/2 cup long-grain rice
1 (8-ounce) can tomato sauce (1 cup)
1 cup water
1 (10-ounce) package frozen mixed vegetables, slightly thawed
1/4 cup chopped onion
1 teaspoon salt
Dash of bottled hot pepper sauce

Combine frankfurters with remaining ingredients in 2-quart casserole, breaking up frozen vegetables with a fork. Bake, covered, in a 375-degree oven for 1 hour, or until heated through. Stir once or twice during baking time. Serves 6.

Spanish Hash

- 3/4 cup gravy *or* thickened stock
- 1/2 cup tomato purée
- 1 teaspoon butter *or* margarine
- 2 tablespoons diced pimientos
- 1/4 cup chopped green pepper
- 1 tiny pod red pepper
- Boiled potatoes and onions, diced (enough to make 1 1/2 cups)
- Salt to taste
- 1 teaspoon Worcestershire sauce
- 1 1/4 cups cooked meat, diced
- 3 tablespoons bread crumbs
- 1 tablespoon butter *or* margarine

Heat gravy with tomato purée and butter. Add pimientos, green pepper, red pepper pod, boiled potatoes and onions, salt, Worcestershire sauce and meat. Heat thoroughly. Pour into shallow earthenware casserole. Sprinkle with bread crumbs. Dot with butter. Brown under broiler. Serves 2.

Chicken Gumbo

- 1 skinned, defatted chicken *or* 1 1/2 pounds skinned chicken breast
- 1/2 cup butter substitute
- 2 onions, chopped
- 2 cups small okra, sliced in rounds
- 1 clove garlic, finely diced
- 2 large bell peppers, chopped
- 1 small, whole chili pepper
- 1 large can chopped tomatoes
- White *or* brown rice

Place all ingredients, except okra and tomatoes, in a large pot. Cover with water and cook for 1 hour. Remove chicken; let cool slightly. Debone and chop meat into the broth. Add okra and tomatoes. Reheat and simmer for 30 minutes. Serve over your favorite rice.

Chicken Angelo

- 8 ounces fresh mushrooms, sliced, divided
- 4 large chicken breast halves, skinned and boned
- 2 eggs, beaten
- 1 cup bread crumbs
- 2 tablespoons butter
- 6 ounces sliced mozzarella cheese
- 3/4 cup chicken broth
- Hot cooked rice *or* noodles
- Fresh parsley, chopped

Place half the mushrooms in a 13 x 9-inch baking pan. Dip chicken into beaten eggs; roll in bread crumbs. In skillet, melt butter over medium heat. Brown both sides of chicken in skillet; place chicken on top of mushrooms. Arrange remaining mushrooms on chicken; top with cheese. Add chicken broth to pan. Bake at 350 degrees for 30–35 minutes. Serve chicken over hot cooked rice or noodles with chopped fresh parsley.

Baked Corned Beef & Cabbage

- 2 tablespoons butter
- 2 tablespoons flour
- 1 1/2 cups milk
- 1/3 cup mayonnaise
- 1 tablespoon vinegar
- Salt and pepper
- 1/2 teaspoon Worcestershire sauce
- 4 cups shredded cabbage
- 1/3 cup buttered bread crumbs
- 6 slices corned beef

Melt butter in saucepan; add flour and blend. Stir in milk gradually and cook over low heat until thickened. Remove from heat and add mayonnaise, vinegar, salt, pepper and Worcestershire sauce. Place cabbage in casserole; pour on sauce; cover. Bake in 350-degree oven for 40 minutes. Remove from oven; top with crumbs and slices of corned beef. Return to oven for 15 minutes, or until browned. Serves 6.

Layered Hamburger Squares

- 1 pound lean ground beef
- 1/4 teaspoon salt
- 1/8 teaspoon crushed sage
- 1 small onion, minced
- 1 cup soft bread crumbs
- 1 egg, beaten
- 1 cup tomato vegetable juice
- 1 cup prepared seasoned stuffing mix
- 1 tablespoon parsley, minced
- 1 (10 1/2-ounce) can cream of mushroom soup, undiluted

Combine first 7 ingredients; mix well. Press half the mixture into bottom of a well-buttered 8 x 8 x 2-inch dish; top with prepared stuffing mix and parsley. Cover with remaining meat mixture; spread soup across top; bake at 350 degrees for 1 1/2 hours. Cut into squares when ready to serve. Serves 8.

Impossible Ham Pie

- 2 cups fully cooked ham (boiled ham)
- 1 cup shredded natural cheese
- 4 ounces (1/3 cup) chopped green onions
- 4 eggs
- 1/2 teaspoon salt
- 1 cup buttermilk baking mix
- 1/4 teaspoon pepper

Heat oven to 400 degrees. Grease 10 x 1 1/2-inch round pie pan. Sprinkle ham, cheese and onions in pan. Beat remaining ingredients until smooth. Pour into pan. Bake in a 350-degree oven until golden brown and knife inserted in center comes out clean, 35–40 minutes. Cool 5 minutes before serving.

Macaroni & Cheese Soufflé

- 1 1/2 cups rotelle macaroni
- 2 tablespoons butter *or* margarine
- 3 tablespoons flour
- 1/4 teaspoon salt
- 1/2 teaspoon paprika
- 1/8 teaspoon cayenne
- 1 1/4 cups milk
- 1 1/2 cups sharp cheddar cheese, shredded
- 3 egg yolks
- 3 egg whites

Cook macaroni; drain; set aside. Melt butter in sauté pan; stir in flour, salt, paprika and cayenne. Add milk; cook until thickened; remove from heat; add cheese; stir until melted. Beat egg yolks; slowly add to cheese sauce; add cooked macaroni. Beat egg whites until stiff; fold into macaroni mixture. Pour into greased 2-quart casserole; bake at 350 degrees for 35–40 minutes. Serves 6.

Boston Baked Beans

1 pound Great Northern Beans
1 teaspoon salt
1 pound bacon, cooked and crumbled
1/2 cup onion, diced
1 cup brown sugar
1 cup tomato juice
1 cup ketchup
Dash sugar

Soak beans in lukewarm water overnight. Drain and boil in clean water until tender. Save 1 cup of water and mix all ingredients together. Bake in a casserole at 350 degrees for 2 hours.

All-At-Once Spaghetti

1 tablespoon margarine
1 large onion, chopped
1/2 pound ground beef
1 1/2 teaspoons salt
Pepper to taste
2 (8-ounce) cans tomato sauce
1 1/2 cups water
1/4 pound uncooked spaghetti
Grated cheese

Heat margarine in deep skillet. Add onion. Cook until soft; crumble in beef; stir; fry until meat loses red color. Sprinkle with salt and pepper. Pour tomato sauce and water over meat mixture; bring to a boil. Break spaghetti; sprinkle in a little at a time, stirring into sauce to keep it separated. Cover tightly; simmer 20–30 minutes, stirring occasionally. Serve with cheese. Serves 3–4.

Tamale Pie

3/4 cup cornmeal
1 1/2 teaspoons salt
3 cups boiling water
1 onion, chopped
1 tablespoon oil
1 pound ground beef
2 cups tomatoes
Dash cayenne pepper, *or*
1 green pepper, well-chopped
1 1/2 teaspoons salt

Make a mush by stirring cornmeal and salt into boiling water. Cook in double boiler 45 minutes. Brown onion in oil; add chopped meat and stir until red color disappears. Add tomatoes, pepper and salt. Grease baking dish, put in layer of mush, add seasoned meat and cover with mush. Bake 30 minutes in a 350-degree oven.

Chicken With Stuffing

2 cups frozen vegetables
2 tablespoons water
2 cups chicken-flavored stuffing mix
2/3 cup water
1 pound boneless, skinned chicken breast
Paprika
1 envelope chicken gravy mix

Combine vegetables and 2 tablespoons water in baking dish; cover with plastic wrap. Microwave on HIGH for 4 1/2–5 minutes; mix in stuffing mix and 2/3 cup water. Arrange chicken over stuffing; sprinkle with paprika; cover and vent plastic wrap. Microwave on HIGH for 7–8 minutes; rotate dish once. Let stand, covered, for about 5 minutes. Serve with prepared gravy.

Spanish Rice

2 cups uncooked rice
6 tablespoons shortening
2 small onions, finely chopped
2 cloves garlic, mashed
4 medium tomatoes, chopped, *or* 1 large can stewed tomatoes
4–6 cups chicken broth
1 small can chopped green chilies
2 tablespoons chopped parsley
1 cup pimiento-stuffed green olives, chopped

Brown rice lightly in shortening. Add onions, garlic and tomatoes. Cook for 3 minutes. Add 3 cups of the chicken broth and chilies. Pour into greased baking dish and cover. Bake at 350 degrees for about 1 hour. Add more broth as needed. Rice should have no liquid remaining when finished. Sprinkle parsley and chopped olives on surface of rice before serving.

Ham Balls

1 pound ground beef
1 pound ground ham
2 eggs
1 1/2 cups cracker crumbs
1 cup light brown sugar, firmly packed
1 teaspoon prepared mustard
1/2 cup water
1/2 cup vinegar

Preheat oven to 350 degrees. In a large bowl, mix beef, ham, eggs and cracker crumbs until well-blended. Shape into balls; place on a large rimmed baking sheet. In a separate bowl, stir together remaining ingredients until well-blended. Pour over ham balls. Bake 1 1/2 hours. Makes 60 balls.

Chicken-Rice Casserole

1 can cream of mushroom soup
2 cans cream of chicken soup
1 1/3 cup non-fat dry milk, prepared
1/2 package dry onion soup (stir contents well before dividing)
1 cup white *or* brown rice
2 pounds chicken breasts, skinned and defatted

Combine all ingredients, except chicken. Place in a 9 x 13-inch pan greased with butter substitute. Lay chicken pieces on top. Pepper chicken as desired and bake for 2 hours at 350 degrees.

Cheesy Ham Scramble

1/4 cup cubed ham
2 tablespoons shredded cheddar cheese
1/8 teaspoon seasoned salt
1 egg
1 tablespoon water
1/2 (6-inch size) pocket pita bread

Combine cheese, ham, salt, egg and water in microwave-safe mug or dish; beat with fork. Microwave on HIGH, uncovered, 1 1/2–2 minutes or until egg is just about set, stirring twice. Place pocket bread half on napkin; microwave 10–15 seconds. Spoon egg mixture into bread.

Cookies

& BARS

Caramel Pecan Bars

Crust

1 cup butter
1/2 cup brown sugar, packed
3 cups flour
1 egg

Filling

3 cups pecan halves
3/4 cup butter
1/2 cup honey
3/4 cup brown sugar, packed
1/4 cup whipping cream

To make crust, combine all ingredients until blended, using electric mixer or food processor. Press evenly into a 15 x 10 x 3/4-inch jelly roll pan. Bake at 350 degrees for 15 minutes.

To make filling, spread pecans evenly over crust. In large, heavy saucepan, melt butter and honey. Add brown sugar. Boil 5–7 minutes, stirring constantly, until it's a rich caramel color. Remove from heat. Stir in cream. Mix well and pour over pecans. Bake 15 minutes longer. Cool; cut into bars. Freezes well.

These are irresistible. The glossy appearance and texture look so fabulous! I never have enough bars because my family keeps sneaking them frozen, right out of the freezer! Makes 4 dozen.

Molasses Applesauce Bars

1/2 cup butter *or* margarine, softened
1 cup granulated sugar
1/4 cup dark molasses
2 eggs
2 1/3 cups sifted flour
1 teaspoon baking soda
1 teaspoon ground cinnamon
1/2 teaspoon salt
1/2 teaspoon ground nutmeg
1/2 teaspoon ground ginger
1 cup applesauce
1 cup raisins, chopped
1 tablespoon grated orange peel
Confectioners' sugar

Preheat oven to 350 degrees. In large bowl, cream butter and granulated sugar until light and fluffy. Add molasses and eggs; mix well. In medium bowl, sift together flour, baking soda, cinnamon, salt, nutmeg and ginger. Add flour mixture alternately with applesauce to creamed mixture, mixing well after each addition.

Stir in raisins and orange peel. Spread into greased and floured 13 x 9-inch baking pan. Bake 25–30 minutes, or until wooden toothpick inserted in center comes out clean. Cool completely in pan on wire rack. Sprinkle with confectioners' sugar. Cut into bars.

Easter Egg Cookies

1 cup butter *or* margarine, softened
1 3/4 cups confectioners' sugar
1 egg
2 teaspoons vanilla extract
Rind of 1 lemon, finely grated
2 tablespoons lemon juice
2 1/2 cups all-purpose flour
1 teaspoon baking soda
1/4 teaspoon salt
1 cup whipping cream
1 tablespoon confectioners' sugar
Food colorings

Cream butter and 1 3/4 cups confectioners' sugar until light and fluffy. Beat in egg, vanilla, rind and lemon juice. Add flour, soda and salt; mix until blended. Divide dough. Wrap each half in plastic wrap and pat into a round. Place in refrigerator several hours until firm. On a floured surface roll 1 round about 1/4 inch thick. Cut with egg-shaped cutter. (Bend a 2 1/2-inch round metal cutter into egg shape, then it may be bent back into round shape). Bake on an ungreased cookie sheet in a preheated 325-degree oven for 12–15 minutes, or until very lightly browned. Cool on wire racks. Repeat with remaining dough. To decorate, stir 1 tablespoon confectioners' sugar into cream and divide into small bowls. Add various colorings to each bowl to make intense pastel shades. Use small paintbrushes to paint cookies with colored cream. Makes 3 dozen.

No-Bake Bars

2 cups *or* 1 (12-ounce) package chocolate chips
1/2 cup peanut butter
1/2 cup butter *or* margarine
1 (10 1/2-ounce) package miniature white marshmallows
1/2 cup nuts
3/4 cup coconut

Melt chocolate, peanut butter and butter in saucepan. Watch closely so mixture does not burn. Cool; add next 2 ingredients. Press into greased pan. Sprinkle coconut on top. Put in refrigerator. Cut in squares when ready to serve.

Two Thumbs-Up

- 1/4 cup margarine
- 1/2 cup brown sugar, packed
- 2 tablespoons light corn syrup
- 1/4 cup peanut butter
- 3 cups rice cereal
- 12 caramels, unwrapped
- 1 tablespoon milk
- Chocolate coating disks, melted

Combine margarine, brown sugar and corn syrup in 2-quart bowl. Microwave on HIGH, uncovered, for 2–2 1/2 minutes until mixture boils vigorously and is blended; stir once. Blend in peanut butter.

Place 1 cup rice cereal in plastic bag; crush; add to peanut butter along with remaining rice cereal. Stir until evenly coated. Spread in an 8-inch baking dish. Combine caramels and milk in glass measure; microwave on HIGH, uncovered, for 1–1 1/2 minutes; stir once. Stir until smooth.

Pour evenly over rice mixture; spread to cover. Let stand 20 minutes, or until caramel is set. Top with warm chocolate coating; spread to cover. Cut into squares after chocolate is set. These treats freeze well.

Thin Chocolate Bars

For chocolate lovers—the small amount of coffee intensifies the chocolate flavor.

- 2/3 cup flour, spooned lightly into cup
- 1/2 teaspoon baking powder
- 1/4 teaspoon salt
- 1/2 cup butter *or* margarine
- 2 (1-ounce) squares unsweetened chocolate
- 1/4 teaspoon dry instant coffee (optional)
- 1 cup sugar
- 1/2 teaspoon vanilla
- 2 large eggs
- 1/2 cup chopped walnuts *or* pecans
- Chocolate Glaze (recipe follows)

Preheat oven to 350 degrees. Prepare 15 1/2 x 10 1/2 x 1-inch pan. (I line pan with foil and spray with pan release.)

Measure flour, baking powder and salt into a small bowl; mix with whisk or fork; set aside. Measure butter or margarine into medium (2-quart) saucepan. Set over low heat; add chocolate and coffee crystals, if using. Stir until chocolate melts; set off heat.

Whisk in sugar, vanilla and eggs, 1 at a time. Stir in dry ingredients and nuts. Pour in a thin stream over bottom of prepared pan; spread evenly with knife blade.

Bake just until set, 12–15 minutes—do not overbake. Set pan on rack while preparing glaze. Pour glaze over fudge bars while still warm; spread evenly with knife blade.

When glazed bars are cooled, cut into desired size; freeze. Makes 25 (2 x 3-inch) bars.

Chocolate Glaze

- 1 (1-ounce) square unsweetened chocolate
- 1 tablespoon butter *or* margarine
- 3 tablespoons water *or* coffee (I use water and 1/4 teaspoon instant coffee)
- 1 cup unsifted confectioners' sugar

In small saucepan combine chocolate, butter and water or coffee. Stir over lowest heat with rubber spatula until smooth. Add sugar. (I usually have to add a few drops of hot tap water to thin to honey consistency.)

Lemon Pecan Squares

- 1 1/2 cups flour
- 1/3 cup sugar
- 1 tablespoon lemon rind, divided
- 3/4 cup margarine, softened
- 1 (7-ounce) can flaked coconut
- 1 (14-ounce) can condensed milk
- 1 cup chopped pecans

Combine flour, sugar and 1 teaspoon lemon rind in bowl. Cut margarine into flour mixture until it resembles cornmeal. Press firmly into a 9 x 13-inch pan. Bake at 350 degrees for 15 minutes. Sprinkle coconut over crust; set aside.

Combine milk and remaining lemon rind. Drizzle evenly over coconut. Sprinkle pecans on top; press down slightly. Bake at 350 degrees for about 20 minute. Cool and cut into squares.

Lollipop Cookies

- 1 cup sifted flour
- 1/2 cup sugar
- 1 teaspoon baking powder
- 1/4 teaspoon salt
- 1/2 cup brown sugar
- 1/2 cup shortening
- 1 egg
- 1 teaspoon vanilla
- 1 teaspoon water
- 1 cup quick-cooking oatmeal, uncooked

Preheat oven to 350 degrees. Sift flour together with sugar, baking powder and salt. Add brown sugar, shortening, egg, vanilla and water. Beat until smooth, about 2 minutes.

Stir in oatmeal. Shape into 24 balls. Place on an ungreased cookie sheet. Flatten with bottom of glass dipped in flour. Insert wooden skewer into each. Bake in preheated oven for 10 minutes. Remove from cookie sheets; cool.

Using your favorite confectioners' sugar frosting, attach chocolate chips for eyes, red-hot cinnamon candies for mouth and coconut for hair, or decorate cookies with tube frosting.

Note: You can buy wooden skewers at craft shops. Use the type that you put in caramel apples or ice cream bars. Lollipop Cookies are a wonderful Easter-basket treat! Makes 24.

Peanut Butter Pieces

- 2 sticks butter
- 1 pound confectioners' sugar
- 1 cup graham cracker crumbs
- 1 cup peanut butter
- 1 (12-ounce) package chocolate chips

Place butter in large bowl and microwave on HIGH for 2–3 minutes. When butter is melted, add sugar, crumbs and peanut butter. Mix until smooth; press into 8 x 8-inch dish; microwave on HIGH for 2 minutes.

Put chocolate chips in large bowl and microwave at 50 percent for 3–4 minutes; stir several times while melting. When melted, spread over peanut butter layer; chill. Cut into squares and store in airtight container.

Traditional Rolled Sugar Cookies

- 3/4 cup (1 1/2 sticks) butter, softened*
- 3/4 cup sugar
- 1 egg
- 1 tablespoon grated lemon peel
- 1 teaspoon vanilla extract
- 2 1/4 cups all-purpose flour
- 1/8 teaspoon salt
- Water

Cream butter in large mixer bowl. Add sugar and beat until light and fluffy. Beat in egg, lemon peel and vanilla until well-blended. Gradually mix in flour and salt until well-blended. Beat in water, a few drops at a time, only until dough starts to come away from sides of bowl. Form dough into a large flat disk. Wrap dough in plastic wrap and refrigerated 2–3 hours.

Preheat oven to 350 degrees. Roll dough on lightly floured surface to 1/8-inch thickness. Cut with cookie cutters dipped in flour. Place on buttered cookie sheets. (Paint with Edible Tempera Color now—see below—or decorate after baking. If planning to use cookies as ornaments, make small hole in top of each with the end of a wooden pick.)

Bake 10–12 minutes, or until cookies begin to brown around edges. Carefully remove from cookie sheets. Cool completely on wire racks. Decorate with Royal Icing(see recipe below) and other cookie decorations if cookies have not been "painted" before baking.
Store in airtight metal containers in a cool place up to 1 month. Freeze up to 3 months. Makes 4 dozen 3-inch cookies.

*For ease in creaming butter taken directly from refrigerator, cut butter into 8–10 pieces and proceed as directed.

Giggle Bars

- 9 graham cracker squares
- 2 tablespoons dry vanilla *or* butterscotch pudding mix (cooked type)
- 1 teaspoon unflavored gelatin
- 1/4 cup milk
- 1/2 cup margarine
- 2 1/2 cups dry roasted peanuts
- 1 cup confectioners' sugar
- 25 (7 ounces) caramels, unwrapped
- 1 tablespoon milk
- Chocolate coating disks, melted

In an 8-inch square glass baking dish, place crackers to cover bottom. Set aside. Combine pudding mix, gelatin and 1/4 cup milk in a 1-quart bowl; mix well. Let stand 5 minutes; add margarine. Microwave on HIGH, uncovered for 1 1/2–2 minutes. stirring once.

Meanwhile, process 1/4 cup peanuts in food processor until in fine pieces. Add to pudding mixture; blend in sugar. Spoon onto cracker base; spread evenly. Refrigerate until set, about 30 minutes.

Combine caramels and 1 tablespoon milk in bowl; microwave on HIGH, uncovered, for 2–2 1/2 minutes; stir once. Stir until smooth; stir in remaining peanuts; spoon onto base and spread evenly. Refrigerate until set. Top with chocolate coating that has been melted. Let it set up and cool.

Surprise Packages

- 1 cup (2 sticks) butter
- 1 cup granulated sugar
- 1/2 cup firmly packed brown sugar
- 2 eggs
- 1 teaspoon vanilla extract
- 3 cups all-purpose flour
- 1 teaspoon baking soda
- 1/4 teaspoon salt
- 48 thin-layered chocolate mint wafers
- Red and green decorator icing

Cream butter and sugars in large mixer bowl until light and fluffy. Beat in eggs and vanilla. Combine dry ingredients. Gradually add to creamed mixture; mix well. Divide dough in half; wrap each in plastic wrap and refrigerate 1–2 hours for ease in handling.

Preheat oven to 375 degrees. Work with half of dough at a time, leaving remaining half refrigerated. Using 1 scant tablespoon dough, cover each mint, forming rectangular-shaped cookie. Place about 2 inches apart on lightly buttered cookie sheets. Bake 10–12 minutes. Cool completely on wire racks; decorate with decorator icing to look like a wrapped package. Makes 4 dozen.

Spiced Oatmeal Cookies

- No-stick spray
- 1/2 cup unsalted margarine
- 1/2 cup granulated sugar
- 1/2 cup brown sugar
- 1 egg
- 1 tablespoon vanilla
- 1 cup flour
- 1 1/2 teaspoons cinnamon
- 1 teaspoon baking soda
- 1/2 teaspoon nutmeg
- 2 cups old-fashioned rolled oats
- 1 cup seedless raisins *or* currants

Spray cookie sheet with oil. Use a large bowl and electric mixer at high speed; beat sugars and margarine until creamy. Add egg and vanilla. Beat until light and fluffy. In medium-size bowl combine flour, cinnamon, soda and nutmeg. Stir until mixture is well-blended with margarine mixture. Stir in oats and raisins. Drop by rounded teaspoons, 2 inches apart, on prepared cookie sheets. Bake in a 350-degree oven for 10–12 minutes, or until lightly browned. Makes 4 dozen.

Caramel Oatmeal Bars

- 3/4 cup butter *or* margarine, melted
- 1 cup all-purpose flour
- 1 cup oatmeal
- 1 cup brown sugar, packed
- 1 teaspoon baking soda
- 1 tablespoon cinnamon
- 32 caramels
- 3 tablespoons butter *or* margarine
- 4 tablespoons light cream
- 1 cup chocolate chips
- 1/2 cup walnuts, chopped

Combine first 6 ingredients. Put 3/4 of the butter mixture in a 9 x 13-inch pan; press evenly over bottom; bake at 350 degrees for 10 minutes. Combine caramels, butter and cream in a saucepan; heat until the caramels are melted.

Pour caramel mixture over crust; sprinkle with chocolate chips and nuts. Top with remaining butter/oatmeal mixture. Bake 15 minutes; cool; cut into bars. Makes 24 bars.

Raisin Bars

This is a recipe making the rounds of our tri-state area (Ohio, Indiana, Kentucky). Fern recommends them as a "go-with" for coffee.

- 1 cup raisins
- 1 cup water
- 1/2 cup salad oil
- 1 cup sugar
- 1 large egg
- 1 3/4 cups flour, spooned lightly into cup
- 1/4 teaspoon salt
- 1 teaspoon soda
- 1/2 teaspoon cinnamon
- 1/2 teaspoon nutmeg
- 1/2 teaspoon allspice
- 1/4 teaspoon cloves
- 1 cup coarsely chopped walnuts

Glaze

- 1 cup confectioners' sugar
- 2 tablespoons boiling water

Prepare 15 1/2 x 10 1/2 x 1-inch pan. Lightly grease or spray with pan release (I line with foil so I can lift out baked sheet of bars for easy cutting).

In a medium saucepan (2-quart) combine raisins and water; bring to boiling. Set off heat and stir in salad oil. Set aside to cool—this may be done hours ahead, if convenient.

When ready to proceed, preheat oven to 375 degrees. Whisk together flour, salt, soda, cinnamon, nutmeg, allspice and cloves; set aside. Stir sugar into raisins. Add egg; whisk vigorously so that egg is thoroughly incorporated. Whisk in dry ingredients. Stir in nuts. Spread evenly in prepared pan.

Bake on middle oven rack about 20 minutes, or until lightly golden. Set on rack to cool.

Immediately stir together confectioners' sugar and enough boiling water to make a glaze of thin spreading consistency. Spread as evenly as possible over sheet of hot bars. When cold, cut into desired-size bars; freeze. Makes 25 (2 x 3-inch) bars.

English Toffee Bars

- 1 cup (2 sticks) butter
- 1 cup sugar
- 1 egg yolk
- 1 3/4 cups all-purpose flour
- 1 teaspoon cinnamon
- 1 egg white, slightly beaten
- 1 cup chopped pecans
- 3 tablespoons milk
- 2 (1-ounce) squares semisweet chocolate

Preheat oven to 275 degrees. Cream butter in large mixer bowl. Gradually add sugar and beat until light and fluffy. Beat in egg yolk. Combine flour and cinnamon. Gradually add to creamed mixture. Press evenly into buttered 13 x 9-inch pan. Brush top with egg white. Sprinkle with pecans; press lightly into dough. Bake 1 hour.

Meanwhile, heat milk and chocolate together over low heat until chocolate is melted. Remove pan from oven; cool slightly. Cut into 1 1/2-inch squares or diamonds; drizzle with melted chocolate. Cool completely in pan on wire rack. Makes 5–6 dozen.

Topped with colored sugar or tinted frosting or just served plain, these delicate spritz cookies are simple to make and taste delicious.

The Best Butter Cookies

- 2 cups (4 sticks) butter
- 1 1/2 cups sugar
- 2 eggs
- 1 teaspoon vanilla extract
- 5 cups all-purpose flour
- 2 teaspoons baking powder
- 1/4 teaspoon salt

Cream butter in large mixer bowl. Gradually add sugar and beat until light and fluffy. Blend in eggs and vanilla. Combine flour, baking powder and salt. Gradually add to creamed mixture; mix well. Divide dough into 4 equal portions. Mix and shape dough for each variety as follows:

Cutouts

Preheat oven to 375 degrees. Roll 1/4 portion of dough on lightly floured surface to 1/8-inch thickness. Cut into desired shapes with floured cookie cutters. Place on unbuttered cookie sheets. Bake 6–8 minutes. Cool completely on wire racks; decorate as desired. Makes 2 dozen.

Peppermint Balls

Preheat oven to 375 degrees. Beat 1/4 cup crushed peppermint candy and 1/4 teaspoon peppermint extract into 1/4 portion of dough. Shape into 1-inch balls. Place on unbuttered cookie sheet. Sprinkle with red colored sugar. Bake 8–10 minutes. Cool completely on wire racks. Makes 2 dozen.

Spicy Fruit Balls

Preheat oven to 375 degrees. Beat 1/2 cup each currants and chopped mixed candied fruit and 1/2 teaspoon cinnamon into 1/4 portion of dough. Shape into 1-inch balls. Place on unbuttered cookie sheets. Bake 8–10 minutes. While still warm roll in confectioners' sugar. Cool completely on wire racks.

Chocolate Slices

Beat 1 ounce (1 square) melted unsweetened chocolate into 1/4 portion of dough. Shape into log approximately 1 1/2 inches in diameter. Roll in chopped nuts. Wrap in plastic wrap and refrigerate several hours or overnight. Preheat oven to 375 degrees. Cut dough into 1/8-inch thick slices. Place on unbuttered cookie sheets. Bake 6–8 minutes. Cool completely on wire racks.

★★★

Snappy flavor, festive shapes and do-your-own decorations make these a traditional favorite.

Blueberry Bars

- 1/4 cup shortening
- 1/2 cup sugar
- 1 egg
- 1 cup sifted flour
- 1/2 teaspoon salt
- 2 teaspoons baking powder
- 1/3 cup milk
- 1 pint blueberries
- 1/4 cup sugar
- 1/3 cup flour
- 1/4 teaspoon cinnamon
- 1/4 cup margarine

Cream shortening and sugar together. Beat egg and add. Sift together flour, salt and baking powder; add dry ingredi ents alternately with milk to egg mixture. Spread into a greased 8 x 8-inch cake pan. Top with blueberries and set aside. Combine other ingredients and sprinkle over blueberries. Bake at 375 degrees for 40 minutes and cool. Cut into bars and serve.

Candy Cane & Wreath Cookies

- $1\frac{1}{4}$ cups ($2\frac{1}{2}$ sticks) butter
- 1 cup confectioners' sugar
- 1 egg
- 1 teaspoon vanilla extract
- $\frac{1}{2}$ teaspoon almond extract
- $3\frac{1}{2}$ cups all-purpose flour
- $\frac{1}{4}$ teaspoon salt
- Red and green food color
- 1 egg white
- Red and green decorating sugar
- Cinnamon candies

Cream butter in large mixer bowl. Gradually add sugar and beat until light and fluffy. Beat in egg and extracts. Combine flour and salt. Gradually add to creamed mixture; mix well.

Set aside half of dough. Divide other half in 2 parts. Tint 1 part light green and the other light red with food color. Wrap all dough in plastic wrap. Refrigerate 30 minutes to 1 hour. Work with small amounts of dough. Keep remaining dough chilled for ease in handling.

Preheat oven to 350 degrees. For candy canes, roll, with hands, 1 teaspoonful of white dough and 1 teaspoonful of red dough into strips about 4 inches long. Place strips side by side and twist together gently. Carefully place on unbuttered cookie sheets and curve the top down to form a cane. Brush with egg white and sprinkle with red sugar. Bake 10–12 minutes.

For wreaths, roll 1 teaspoonful of white dough and 1 of green into strips about 4 inches long. Twist strips together; form into a circle on cookie sheet. Brush with egg white and sprinkle with green sugar. Use cinnamon candies for garnish and bake as for candy canes. Makes 4–5 dozen.

Fruit Cocktail Cookies

- $\frac{1}{2}$ cup butter, room temperature
- $\frac{1}{2}$ cup sugar
- $\frac{1}{2}$ cup light brown sugar, firmly packed
- 1 jumbo egg, beaten to blend
- $\frac{1}{2}$ teaspoon vanilla
- $\frac{1}{4}$ teaspoon almond extract
- $1\frac{1}{2}$ cups all-purpose flour
- $\frac{1}{2}$ teaspoon baking powder
- $\frac{1}{2}$ teaspoon baking soda
- $\frac{1}{2}$ teaspoon cinnamon
- $\frac{1}{2}$ teaspoon ground cloves
- $\frac{1}{8}$ teaspoon salt
- 1 cup canned fruit cocktail, very well-drained
- $\frac{1}{2}$ cup raisins

Preheat oven to 375 degrees. Grease and lightly flour baking sheets. Cream butter with sugar in large bowl. Blend in brown sugar. Add egg, vanilla and almond extract; beat until smooth. Combine dry ingredients in medium bowl and mix into butter mixture. Stir in fruit cocktail and raisins. Drop by heaping teaspoons onto prepared sheets. Bake 11–12 minutes, or until lightly golden. Cool on sheets 2–3 minutes. Transfer to wire racks to cool. Store cookies in airtight container. Makes 5 dozen.

Raspberry Meringue Bars

- 1 cup (2 sticks) butter
- $\frac{1}{2}$ cup firmly packed brown sugar
- 1 egg
- 2 cups all-purpose flour
- 1 (12-ounce) jar raspberry preserves
- $\frac{1}{2}$ cup seedless raisins
- $\frac{1}{2}$ teaspoon almond extract
- 2 egg whites
- $\frac{3}{4}$ cup sugar
- $\frac{1}{2}$ cup flaked coconut
- $\frac{1}{2}$ cup sliced almonds

Preheat oven to 325 degrees. Cream butter and brown sugar in large mixer bowl until light and fluffy. Blend in egg. Add flour; mix well. Spread dough in buttered 13 x 9-inch baking pan. Bake 25 minutes.

Meanwhile, combine preserves, raisins and extract. Spread over baked cookie base. Beat egg whites until foamy. Gradually beat in sugar. Continue beating until stiff peaks form. Gently fold in coconut and almonds. Spread over raspberry mixture.

Return to oven and bake until meringue is lightly browned, about 20 minutes. Cool completely in pan on wire rack. Cut into bars. Makes 4 dozen.

Cream Cheese Drops

- $\frac{1}{4}$ cup butter *or* margarine, softened
- 1 (3-ounce) package cream cheese, softened
- 1 cup sugar
- 2 cups all-purpose flour
- $\frac{1}{2}$ cup finely chopped walnuts
- 3 tablespoons milk
- 1 teaspoon vanilla
- $\frac{3}{4}$ cup semisweet chocolate pieces (approximately)

In large bowl with mixer at high speed, beat butter, cream cheese and sugar until fluffy. Reduce speed to low. Add flour, walnuts, milk and vanilla extract. Beat ingredients until well-mixed. Preheat oven to 375 degrees. Grease large cookie sheets. Drop dough by heaping teaspoonfuls, about 2 inches apart, onto cookie sheets. Lightly press a chocolate piece into center of each cookie. Bake cookies about 10 minutes, or until lightly browned. With pancake turner, remove cookies to wire racks to cool. Store in tightly covered container and use within 1 week. Makes 5 dozen.

Chocolate Pixies

- $\frac{1}{4}$ cup ($\frac{1}{2}$ stick) butter
- 2 (1-ounce) squares unsweetened chocolate
- 2 eggs
- 1 cup sugar
- $1\frac{1}{2}$ cups all-purpose flour
- 1 teaspoon baking powder
- $\frac{1}{4}$ teaspoon salt
- $\frac{1}{4}$ cup chopped walnuts
- Confectioners' sugar

Melt butter and chocolate in a heavy saucepan over low heat. Beat eggs and sugar in large mixer bowl. Gradually mix in chocolate mixture. Combine flour, baking powder and salt; gradually add to chocolate mixture. Stir in walnuts. Chill dough at least 1 hour.

Preheat oven to 300 degrees. Shape dough into 1-inch balls. Roll in confectioners' sugar. Place on buttered cookie sheets. Bake 15–18 minutes. Cool completely on wire racks. Makes 3 dozen.

Coffee Pecan Crescents

1 cup (2 sticks) butter
1/3 cup sugar
1 1/2 teaspoons instant coffee*
1 1/2 teaspoons water*
1/2 teaspoon vanilla extract
2 cups all-purpose flour
2 cups finely chopped pecans
1/4 teaspoon salt
Confectioners' sugar
Granulated sugar

Cream butter in large mixer bowl. Gradually add sugar and beat until light and fluffy. Dissolve coffee in water. Add to creamed mixture with vanilla. Combine flour, nuts and salt. Gradually stir into creamed mixture. Press dough into a ball. Wrap in plastic wrap and refrigerate at least 1 hour for ease in handling.

Preheat oven to 325 degrees. Shape teaspoonfuls of dough into crescents. Place 1 inch apart on unbuttered cookie sheets. Bake about 20 minutes, or until set, but not brown. While still warm, roll cookies first in confectioners' sugar, then in granulated sugar and again in confectioners' sugar. Cool completely on wire racks. Makes 5 dozen.

*Coffee and water may be deleted and dough shaped into 1-inch balls and flattened slightly; bake as above.

Golden Nuggets

1 cup butter
1 1/2 cups sugar, divided
2 eggs
3 1/2 cups flour
1/4 teaspoon salt
1/2 teaspoon baking soda
2 teaspoons cinnamon, divided
60 walnut halves

Cream butter and 1 1/4 cups sugar together. Mix in eggs. Sift together flour, salt, baking soda and 1 teaspoon cinnamon. Add to creamed mixture. Mix well; shape dough into small balls.

Combine 1/4 cup sugar and 1 teaspoon cinnamon. Roll balls in sugar-cinnamon mixture. Place on greased baking sheet; press walnut half on each. Bake in a 375-degree oven for 10–12 minutes. Makes 5 dozen.

Concord Oatmeal Cookies

1 stick margarine, softened
1 cup brown sugar, firmly packed
1/2 cup granulated sugar
1 egg, slightly beaten
1 teaspoon vanilla
1 cup rolled oats
1/2 cup chopped walnuts
1/2 cup wheat germ
1 cup unsifted flour
1/2 teaspoon baking soda
1/4 teaspoon baking powder
1/2 teaspoon salt
1/2 cup Concord grape jam

In mixer bowl, cream margarine at high speed. Beat in sugars gradually until light and fluffy. Stir in egg, vanilla, rolled oats, walnuts and wheat germ. Sift flour with baking soda, baking powder and salt. Stir into batter until well-blended. Drop by teaspoonfuls onto lightly greased cookie sheets.

Make indentation in center of each cookie using back of small spoon. Drop about 1/2 teaspoon concord grape jam into center of each cookie. Bake at 350 degrees until delicately browned, about 8–10 minutes. Remove from cookie sheet while still warm; cool on racks. Makes 5 dozen cookies.

Caramel Nut Crunch

1/2 cup brown sugar, packed
1/2 cup dark corn syrup
1/4 cup butter *or* margarine
1/2 teaspoon salt
6 cups toasted oat cereal
1 cup pecan halves or roasted peanuts
1/2 cup slivered almonds

Combine brown sugar, corn syrup, butter and salt in a microwave-safe bowl. Microwave on HIGH, uncovered, 3–4 minutes; stir once. Stir well, then microwave on HIGH 1 1/2 minutes; combine cereal and nuts in a large, buttered bowl. Pour hot mixture over cereal; mix until evenly coated. Microwave on HIGH, uncovered, 6–8 minutes or until cereal is toasted; stir every 2 minutes.

Spoon mixture onto waxed paper. Cool 5–7 minutes; break into pieces; cool completely. Store in covered container.

Gingerbread People

1 cup sugar
1 tablespoon ginger
2 teaspoons cinnamon
1 teaspoon cloves
1/2 cup water
1/2 cup corn syrup
1 cup (2 sticks) butter
4 cups all-purpose flour
1 1/2 teaspoons baking soda
1/4 teaspoon salt
Colored icing

Combine sugar, spices, water and corn syrup in small saucepan. Bring to boiling, stirring constantly. Remove from heat and pour over butter in large mixer bowl. Stir until butter melts; cool to lukewarm. Combine flour, baking soda and salt. Add to butter mixture; mix well. Cover and refrigerate dough overnight.

Preheat oven to 375 degrees. Roll dough on lightly floured surface to 1/8-inch-thickness. Cut with floured gingerbread people cutters. Bake on unbuttered cookie sheets 12–15 minutes, or until golden. Cool completely on wire racks; decorate as desired with icing. Makes 3 dozen.

Lemon Fluff Bars

1/3 cup butter
1/4 cup confectioners' sugar
1 cup flour
1/4 cup butter *or* margarine
1 cup sugar
1/4 cup flour
2 eggs, separated
1 tablespoon grated lemon peel
1/4 cup fresh lemon juice
1 cup milk

Mix 1/3 cup butter with confectioners' sugar; mix in flour and press mixture into bottom of an ungreased 9-inch square pan. Bake at 350 degrees for 12 minutes. Cream together 1/4 cup butter, 1 cup sugar and 1/4 cup flour. Beat in egg yolks, lemon peel and juice. Blend in milk. Beat egg whites until they stand in peaks. Fold into filling mixture and pour into baked crust. Bake at 350 degrees for about 40 minutes, or until deep golden brown. Cool in pan and cut into bars. These are delicious!

White Chocolate Chip Cashew Cookies

- 2½ cups all-purpose flour
- 1 teaspoon baking soda
- ¼ teaspoon salt
- ¼ teaspoon nutmeg
- 1 cup unsalted butter, room temperature
- 1 cup sugar
- ¼ cup unsulfured molasses
- 2 eggs
- 1 teaspoon vanilla
- 1½ cups roasted, unsalted cashews, chopped (about 7½ ounces)
- ½ cup white chocolate chips

Sift first 4 ingredients into medium bowl. Using electric mixer, cream butter, sugar and molasses in large bowl until fluffy. Beat in eggs and vanilla. Mix in dry ingredients. Add cashews and chocolate chips. Refrigerate 1 hour, or overnight.

Preheat oven to 350 degrees. Grease cookie sheets. Drop dough by rounded teaspoonfuls onto sheets, spacing 2 inches apart. Bake until golden brown, about 12 minutes. Cool on cookie sheets 2 minutes. Transfer to rack and cool completely. Store in airtight container. Makes 3 dozen.

Peanut Butter Marshmallow Cookies

- ½ cup shortening
- ½ cup sugar
- ½ cup brown sugar, firmly packed
- ½ cup peanut butter
- 1 cup miniature marshmallows
- 1¼ cups flour
- ¾ teaspoon baking soda
- ¼ teaspoon salt
- ¼ teaspoon baking powder
- 1 egg, beaten

Cream shortening, sugars, peanut butter and beaten egg. Combine dry ingredients; add to creamed mixture. Fold in marshmallows. Form into balls about 1 inch in diameter. Bake on a greased cookie sheet at 350 degrees for 8–10 minutes.

Cream Cheese Spritz

- 1 cup (2 sticks) butter
- 1 (3-ounce) package cream cheese, softened
- 1 cup sugar
- 1 egg yolk
- 1 teaspoon vanilla extract
- 2 cups all-purpose flour
- ½ teaspoon salt
- ¼ teaspoon baking powder

Preheat oven to 350 degrees. Cream butter and cream cheese in large mixer bowl. Gradually add sugar and beat until blended. Beat in egg yolk and vanilla. Combine flour, salt and baking powder. Gradually add to creamed mixture. Fill cookie press. Use attachments to form cookie designs on unbuttered cookie sheets. Bake 12–15 minutes. Cool completely on wire racks. Makes 7 dozen.

Note: Before baking, dough may be tinted or sprinkled with colored sugar or a cinnamon-sugar mixture; or decorate cookies with a tinted frosting after baking.

Favorite Maple Cookies

- ½ cup margarine, melted
- ¼ cup shortening
- ¾ cup brown sugar
- 1 egg
- 1 teaspoon maple flavoring
- 1½ cups all-purpose flour
- ½ teaspoon cream of tartar
- ½ teaspoon baking soda

Mix together melted margarine, shortening, brown sugar, egg and maple flavoring. Mix together flour, cream of tartar and baking soda. Gradually add dry ingredients to first mixture; mix well. Drop by teaspoonfuls on lightly greased cookie sheets. Press each cookie with bottom of a wet glass. Bake at 350 degrees for 8–10 minutes.

For a special treat, spread cookie with your favorite icing or frosting and top with a second cookie. Makes 4 dozen.

Frosted Krispies

- 1 cup sugar
- 1 cup light corn syrup
- 1 cup peanut butter
- 6 cups crispy rice cereal
- 1 (6-ounce) package chocolate chips
- 1 (6-ounce) package butterscotch chips

In saucepan combine sugar and syrup, bring just to a boil. Stir in peanut butter. Mix in rice cereal. Press mixture into a buttered 13 x 9-inch pan. Melt chocolate and butterscotch chips together over hot (not boiling) water. Spread over cereal mixture evenly. Chill in refrigerator for about 15 minutes. Cut into bars. Makes 4 dozen 2 x 1-inch bars.

Applesauce Dream Bars

- ½ cup butter *or* margarine
- ¾ cup brown sugar, firmly packed
- ½ cup nonfat dry milk powder
- 1¼ cups all-purpose flour
- 1 teaspoon cinnamon
- 1 teaspoon salt
- ½ teaspoon soda
- 2 cups oats (quick or old-fashioned), uncooked
- 1½ cups applesauce

Beat together butter and sugar until light and fluffy. Add combined flour and nonfat dry milk powder with cinnamon, salt and soda; mix well. Stir in oats. Press half of crumb mixture onto bottom of greased 13 x 9-inch pan. Spread with applesauce; sprinkle with remaining crumb mixture. Bake in preheated 400-degree oven for 30 minutes, or until golden brown. Cool; cut into bars.

Mincemeat Drop Cookies

- 1½ cups prepared mincemeat
- ¾ cup evaporated milk
- 3 cups prepared baking mix
- ½ cup brown sugar, packed
- ½ teaspoon salt

Heat oven to 375 degrees. Heat mincemeat and milk to boiling in 3-quart saucepan, stirring frequently. Reduce heat. Simmer until slightly thickened, about 10 minutes. Stir in remaining ingredients. Drop dough by rounded teaspoonfuls, 2 inches apart, onto ungreased cookie sheet. Bake about 10 minutes, or until light brown. Makes 4 dozen.

Peanutty Snickerdoodles

2 tablespoons sugar
2 teaspoons ground cinnamon
1 (15-ounce) package golden sugar cookie mix
1 egg
1 tablespoon water
1 cup peanut butter chips

Preheat oven to 375 degrees. In small bowl, stir together sugar and cinnamon; set aside. In medium bowl, combine cookie mix (and enclosed flavor packet), egg and water. Mix with spoon or fork until thoroughly blended. Stir in peanut butter chips.

Shape dough into 1-inch balls. (If dough is too soft, cover and refrigerate for about 1 hour). Roll balls in reserved cinnamon-sugar mixture; place on an ungreased cookie sheet. Bake 8–10 minutes, or until very lightly browned. Cool slightly; remove from cookie sheet to wire rack. Cool completely. Makes 2 dozen.

Easter Nests

1/2 cup coconut
Green food coloring
1/2 cup corn syrup
3 tablespoons sugar
1 tablespoon margarine
2 cups cornflakes
Assorted small jelly beans

Separate coconut and add a few drops of green food coloring. Combine syrup, sugar and margarine; bring to a boil and stir for 5 minutes. Remove from heat; add cornflakes and coconut; blend together. Drop by teaspoons and using hands, shape into miniature nests. Fill with colorful jelly beans.

Checkerboards

2/3 cup shortening
1 1/2 teaspoons vanilla
1 cup sugar
2 eggs
2 1/2 cups flour
1/2 teaspoon salt
3/4 teaspoon baking powder
Red food coloring
1 (1-ounce) square chocolate, melted

Cream together sugar, shortening and vanilla. Add eggs. Combine dry ingredients and add to creamed mixture. Divide dough in half. To 1 half mix in red food coloring and to other half mix in melted chocolate. Form each mixture into a loaf and chill.

Cut each loaf in half. Layer red and chocolate until you have 4 layers. Chill. Slice 1/4 inch thick and layer alternately, making a checkerboard. Chill again. Then slice 1/4 inch thick and bake at 350 degrees for 8–10 minutes, or until lightly browned on bottom.

Molasses Date-Nut Bars

1/4 cup shortening
1/2 cup sugar
1 egg
1/2 cup molasses
2 cups sifted flour
1/4 teaspoon salt
1/4 teaspoon baking soda
1 1/2 teaspoons baking powder
1/2 cup milk
1 cup chopped walnuts
1 cup chopped dates

Cream together shortening and sugar. Add egg; beat well. Add molasses. Sift together flour, salt, baking soda and baking powder; add alternately with milk to creamed mixture. Add chopped nuts and dates.

Line 2 greased 8 x 8 x 2-inch pans with greased waxed paper; pour in batter. Bake in 350-degree oven for 25–27 minutes. Cool 5 minutes. Remove from pan, cut in 4 x 1-inch bars. Makes 2 1/2 dozen.

Honey Orange Cookies

1 cup shortening
1 cup brown sugar
1/2 cup honey
2 eggs, well-beaten
1 cup sour milk
3 1/2 cups unsifted flour
2 teaspoons baking powder
1 teaspoon soda
1 teaspoon vanilla
1/2 cup nuts *or* raisins
Rind of 1 orange, grated
Orange Icing (recipe follows)

Combine all ingredients using an electric mixer. Drop by teaspoonfuls onto cookie sheet. Bake in 375-degree oven for 8–10 minutes.

Orange Icing

1 1/2 tablespoons orange juice
1 egg yolk
1 small orange rind, grated
1 cup confectioners' sugar

Combine ingredients thoroughly until of spreading consistency. Ice cookies while still warm.

Magic Cookie Bars

1/2 cup butter *or* margarine
1 1/2 cups graham cracker crumbs
1 (14-ounce) can sweetened condensed milk (not evaporated milk)
1 (6-ounce) package semisweet chocolate chips (1 cup)
1 (3 1/2-ounce) can flaked coconut
1 cup chopped walnuts *or* pecans

Preheat oven to 350 degrees. In a 13 x 9-inch baking pan, melt margarine in oven. Sprinkle crumbs over margarine; pour condensed milk over crumbs. Top with remaining ingredients. Press down firmly. Bake 25–30 minutes, or until lightly browned. Cool. Chill if desired. Cut into bars. Store loosely covered at room temperature. Makes 24–36.

Fudge Drop Cookies

5 1/4 cups unsifted confectioners' sugar
4 heaping tablespoons cocoa powder
2 cups coarsely chopped walnuts
1/8 teaspoon salt
1/2 cup egg whites (about 5 egg whites)

Combine sugar, cocoa, nuts and salt in mixer bowl. Mix at low speed until thoroughly blended. Add unbeaten egg whites. Mix just to moisten. Do not overmix. Line baking sheets with parchment paper. Drop by heaping tablespoons, 2–3 inches apart, on parchment paper. Bake at 300 degrees for 20 minutes. Makes 2 dozen.

Low-Cholesterol Brownies

- 1/2 cup vegetable oil
- 3 egg whites
- 3/4 cup sugar
- 1 teaspoon vanilla
- 1/2 cup all-purpose flour
- 6 tablespoons cocoa
- 1/2 teaspoon baking powder
- 1/4 teaspoon salt
- 1/2 cup chopped walnuts
- 1/2 cup raisins

Preheat oven to 350 degrees. Combine oil, egg whites, sugar and vanilla. Mix until smooth. Blend in flour, cocoa, baking powder and salt. Stir in raisins and nuts. Pour batter into greased 8-inch square pan. Bake about 15 minutes. Cool completely before cutting into squares.

Old-Fashioned Sugar Squares

- 1 cup margarine
- 1 1/4 cups sugar, divided
- 2 eggs
- 2 cups flour
- 1/2 teaspoon baking soda
- 1/2 teaspoon salt
- 1 teaspoon ground ginger
- 2 tablespoons milk
- 1 tablespoon lemon juice

Cream margarine and 1 cup sugar; add eggs; blend. Add dry ingredients. Mix lemon juice into milk and blend into cookie mixture. Spread into buttered 15 x 10-inch pan. Sprinkle with 1/4 cup sugar. Bake at 350 degrees for about 15 minutes until golden brown. Cool. Cut into squares.

Persimmon Cookies

- 1/2 cup shortening
- 1 cup sugar
- 1 cup persimmon pulp
- 1 cup chopped walnuts
- 1 cup raisins
- 2 cups sifted flour
- 1 teaspoon baking soda
- 1 teaspoon baking powder
- 1/4 teaspoon salt
- 1/2 teaspoon cinnamon
- 1/2 teaspoon cloves

Preheat oven to 350 degrees. Cream sugar with shortening until fluffy. Mix in persimmon pulp, nuts and raisins. Sift flour, baking soda, baking powder, salt and spices together. Add to creamed mixture; blend well. Bake as bar or drop cookies on parchment-lined cookie sheets at 350 degrees for 12–15 minutes.

Chocolate Kisses

- 1/4 teaspoon salt
- 1/8 teaspoon cream of tartar
- 3 egg whites
- 1 cup sifted confectioners' sugar
- 1/3 cup fine saltine cracker crumbs
- 1 (6-ounce) package chocolate chips, melted and cooled slightly

Sprinkle salt and cream of tartar on egg whites; beat with a rotary beater to a coarse foam; add sugar gradually and beat until stiff enough to hold a peak. Fold in cracker crumbs; fold in chocolate. Drop by spoonfuls on baking sheets covered with waxed paper. Bake in a 350-degree oven for 8–10 minutes. Cool 5 minutes; remove cookies from paper. Store in covered container. Makes 3 dozen.

Peanut Butter Drops

- 1 cup shortening *or* 3/4 cup butter, softened
- 1 cup sugar
- 1/2 cup light brown sugar, packed
- 1 teaspoon vanilla
- 2 eggs
- 2 cups unsifted all-purpose flour
- 1 teaspoon baking soda
- 1 cup peanut butter chips
- 1 cup semisweet *or* milk chocolate chips

Cream shortening, sugars and vanilla. Add eggs. Beat well. Combine flour and baking soda. Blend into creamed mixture. Stir in peanut butter chips and chocolate chips. Drop by teaspoonfuls onto ungreased cookie sheet. Bake at 350 degrees for 10–12 minutes, or until lightly browned. Cool slightly. Remove from cookie sheet. Makes 5 dozen.

Easy Gingerbread Cookies

- 1 (6-serving-size) package butter scotch pudding and pie filling (not instant)
- 3/4 cup butter *or* margarine
- 3/4 cup brown sugar, packed
- 1 egg
- 2 1/4 cups flour
- 1 teaspoon baking soda
- 3 teaspoons ginger
- 1 1/2 teaspoons cinnamon

Cream pudding mix with butter and sugar. Add egg and blend well. Combine flour, soda and spices; blend into pudding mixture. Chill dough until firm, about 5–10 minutes. Roll on floured board about 1/4 inch thick and cut with cookie cutter. Place on greased baking sheet. Bake at 350 degrees for 10–12 minutes. Cool on wire rack. Decorate as desired. Makes 16–18 cookies.

Jumbles

- 1/4 pound butter
- 3/4 cup sugar
- 1 egg, beaten
- 3/4 cup flour
- 1 cup flaked coconut
- 1/2 teaspoon mace (optional)

Cream butter and sugar well. Stir in egg, then flour and coconut. Add mace, if desired. Batter will be stiff. Grease 2 cookie sheets. Drop by the teaspoonful, 16–18 per pan. Bake at 425 degrees for 10–12 minutes. Cool on racks. Makes 2 dozen.

Melting Moments

- 1 cup all-purpose flour
- 2 tablespoons cornstarch
- 1/2 cup confectioners' sugar
- 1 cup butter *or* margarine, softened
- 1 1/3 cups coconut

Mix flour, cornstarch and sugar in bowl. Blend in butter until a soft dough is formed. If dough is too soft to handle, cover and chill. Shape into 3/4-inch balls. Roll in coconut. Place 1 1/2 inches apart on an ungreased baking sheet. Bake at 300 degrees for 20–25 minutes, or until lightly browned. Makes 3 dozen.

Peanut Butter Rocky Road

- 1 (6-ounce) package semisweet chocolate chips
- 1 (6-ounce) package butterscotch chips
- ½ cup peanut butter
- 3 cups miniature marshmallows
- ½ cup salted peanuts

Place chocolate chips, butterscotch chips and peanut butter in 2-quart bowl. Microwave, uncovered, on HIGH (100 pecent) until softened, 2–2½ minutes. Stir until melted and smooth. Mix in marshmallows and peanuts until evenly coated. Spread into buttered square 8 x 8.x 2-inch baking pan. Refrigerate until firm, at least 1 hour. Cut into squares.

Chocolate Nuggets

- 1 package devil's food, Swiss or dark chocolate cake mix
- ½ cup cooking oil
- 2 eggs
- 1 (6-ounce) package semisweet chocolate pieces
- Pecan halves

Preheat oven to 350 degrees. Blend cake mix, oil and eggs. Stir in chocolate pieces. Drop from a teaspoon onto an ungreased cookie sheet. Top each cookie with a pecan half. Bake for 10–12 minutes, until cookie tests done with a toothpick. Cool on cookie sheet about 1 minute; remove to racks to finish cooling. Makes 4–5 dozen.

Nut Bars

- 2 cups flour
- ¼ teaspoon salt
- ½ cup sugar
- 1 egg
- 2 teaspoons baking powder
- 1 tablespoon butter
- 1 cup chopped nuts
- 1 cup milk

Mix dry ingredients and add nuts. Cut in shortening. Add milk to egg and beat thoroughly. Combine mixtures. Place on floured board. Pat to ½-inch thickness. Cut into strips ½ inch x 3 inches. Fry in deep fat (375 degrees). Drain on unglazed paper. Rub in sugar and cinnamon.

Peanut Brittle Bars

- 1 cup sifted flour
- ¼ teaspoon baking soda
- ½ teaspoon cinnamon
- ½ cup butter *or* margarine, softened
- ½ cup brown sugar
- 1 egg
- 1 teaspoon vanilla extract
- 1 cup chopped salted peanuts

Mix and sift flour, soda and cinnamon. Combine remaining ingredients except peanuts; mix. Add dry ingredients; mix. Stir in half of the peanuts. Spread in greased 13 x 9 x 2-inch pan; press remaining peanuts lightly into dough. Bake in preheated 325-degree oven for about 20 minutes. Cool and cut into 24 bars.

Peanut Butter Bars

- 1 (18.5-ounce) package yellow cake mix
- ½ cup chopped pecans
- ⅔ cup evaporated milk
- ¼ cup margarine, melted
- ½ cup peanut butter chips
- ½ cup chocolate syrup

Combine dry cake mix, pecans, milk and margarine in a medium bowl; mix well. Pour half the mixture into a greased 9 x 13-inch baking pan. Bake 10 minutes at 350 degrees. Sprinkle over chips and drizzle with chocolate syrup. Top with small spoonfuls of remaining cake mixture. Bake for another 20 minutes. Cool and cut into bars.

Chewy Brownies

- 2 eggs
- 1 cup sugar
- ⅔ cup margarine, melted
- ¾ cup flour
- ⅓ cup unsweetened cocoa
- 1 teaspoon baking powder
- 1½ cups coarsely chopped pears
- ½ cup walnuts
- 1 teaspoon vanilla

Beat eggs, blend in sugar, margarine and vanilla. Combine flour, cocoa and baking powder; stir into egg mixture until batter is smooth. Fold in pears and nuts. Turn into a greased 8-inch square baking pan and bake at 350 degrees for 30–35 minutes.

No-Bake Peanut Butter Squares

- 12 ounces peanut butter
- ½ stick butter (¼ cup)
- 1½ cups graham cracker crumbs
- 1 box confectioners' sugar
- ⅓ cup boiling water
- 1 (12-ounce) package chocolate chips
- ½ stick butter (¼ cup)

Combine first 5 ingredients. Press into 9 x 13-inch pan. Heat chocolate chips with ½ stick butter over low heat until melted. Spread over peanut butter mixture. Let cool; cut into squares.

Crunchy Fudge Sandwiches

- 1 (6-ounce) package butterscotch chips
- ½ cup peanut butter
- 4 cups crisp rice cereal
- 1 (6-ounce) package chocolate chips
- ½ cup sifted confectioners' sugar
- 2 tablespoons butter
- 1 tablespoon water

Melt butterscotch chips and peanut butter in skillet; turn off heat. Add cereal and mix well. Press half of mixture into greased 8 x 8 x 2-inch pan and chill. Combine remaining ingredients in saucepan. Stir and heat until melted and smooth. Spread over chilled cereal mixture and spread remaining cereal mixture evenly over top.

Try This

Store crisp cookies in a cookie can that has a loose cover. If you tightly seal them they may lose their crispness.

Use a salt shaker filled with powdered or colored sugar for sprinkling candy or cookies. Make holes larger if needed.

—4001 Food Facts and Chef's Secrets
By Dr. Myles H. Bader

Desserts
DELICIOUS

Eggnog Ice Cream

- 6 eggs
- 1/2 cup sugar
- 1/4 teaspoon salt
- 4 tablespoons sherry, rum, brandy *or* 1 teaspoon vanilla
- 1 cup heavy cream, whipped until stiff
- Ground nutmeg

Carefully separate egg yolks from whites into 2 mixing bowls. Beat whites until stiff; add sugar and salt to yolks gradually and beat them until very thick. Mix yolk mixture with whites; stir in sherry, rum, brandy, or the vanilla. Fold in whipped cream. Pour into empty ice cube trays or a square 8 x 8-inch baking pan. Freeze for 4–5 hours, or until firm, with no stirring. Sprinkle with nutmeg before serving. Serves 4–6.

Chocolate & Pear Pâté

- 1 cup honey
- 1 cup lemon juice
- 5 large Comice pears
- 1 tablespoon mild paprika
- 15 ounces extra-bittersweet chocolate
- 1 cup heavy cream
- 4 tablespoons (1/2 stick) unsalted butter
- 2 large egg yolks
- 1 cup confectioners' sugar, sifted
- 2 cups Pear Creme Anglaise Sauce (recipe on page 51)
- Mint sprigs for garnish

Preheat oven to 375 degrees. In a small bowl, combine honey and 1/2 cup lemon juice. Peel and core pears, rubbing all surfaces with remaining lemon juice to retard browning.

Select a medium-size ovenproof pot large enough to accommodate all 5 pears. Bake on the lower rack of oven, basting frequently with honey mixture, until just tender, about 45 minutes. Remove from oven to rack to cool. Reserve 1 pear for sauce.

When the remaining 4 pears have cooled enough to handle, slice lengthwise about 3/8–1/2-inch thick. Using a spatula, carefully lay pears on a parchment sheet and sprinkle with paprika.

Combine chocolate, heavy cream and butter in top half of a double boiler over simmering water, cooking until chocolate is melted and warm, about 10 minutes. Transfer to a large warm bowl and add egg yolks, whisking until well-combined. Gradually add sugar and whisk until chocolate is very shiny.

Line a 3-cup terrine mold with parchment. Spoon chocolate mixture into mold to a depth of about 3/4 inch. Lay pear slices across chocolate and spoon on a little chocolate mixture to cover. Continue layering pears and chocolate until pears are used. Pour remaining chocolate mixture into the mold and refrigerate overnight.

Invert terrine, and pull on the edges of the parchment to unmold. If the terrine sticks to the mold, loosen it by dipping terrine in hot water for a few seconds, then inverting again. Refrigerate until ready to serve.

Cut chocolate into slices with a wire cheese cutter. Position slices in the center of a serving platter and cover with plastic to transport. To serve, unwrap, spoon sauce around chocolate, and garnish with mint. Serves 8.

Regal Fruit Combo

- 2 (20-ounce) cans pineapple chunks
- 3 large bananas, sliced
- 3 large apples, cut up
- 2 teaspoons cinnamon
- 1 teaspoon nutmeg
- 1 large can fruit cocktail, drained
- 1 pint whipping cream
- 1/4 cup sugar, *or* to taste
- 1 teaspoon lemon juice

Drain pineapple chunks well. Peel and core apples and cut into bite-size pieces. Slice bananas and sprinkle with lemon juice. With ice-cold beaters and cold metal bowl, whip cream until soft peaks form. Add sugar when cream is just about whipped. Add fruits and spices. Stir well. Serve chilled.

Fruit Crumble

- 2 cups diced red apples
- Juice of 1/2 lemon
- 1 (1-pound 4-ounce) can crushed pineapple with juice
- 1 (1-pound) can cranberry sauce
- 1 cup quick-cooking rolled oats
- 3/4 cup dark brown sugar
- 1/2 cup flour
- 1 teaspoon cinnamon
- 1/2 cup butter

In large baking dish, mix together the fruit with cranberry sauce and lemon juice. Combine half the sugar and the cinnamon; sprinkle over fruit. Cut butter into flour, remaining sugar and rolled oats until a crumble mixture is formed. Sprinkle crumble mixture evenly over top of fruit and bake in 350-degree oven for 35–40 minutes. Serve warm with whipped cream or topping.

Delicious Apple Deep-Dish Dumplings

There's an exception to every rule and this recipe is the delicious exception to the general advice not to cook Red Delicious. It combines the flavor of an apple dumpling with an exceptionally easy way to make it.

2 Red Delicious apples (about 6 ounces each) cored and cut into 1½-inch chunks
2 tablespoons raisins
2 teaspoons brown sugar, packed
2 teaspoons butter *or* margarine
Pastry for 1-crust (9-inch) pie
Whipped cream (optional)

Divide apple chunks and raisins between 2 (2 cups each) shallow baking dishes. Sprinkle with sugar; dot with butter. Cut pastry slightly smaller than top of dish; place on apple mixture. Bake at 450 degrees 10–12 minutes, or until pastry is golden. Serve warm and pass whipped cream to top dessert, if desired. Serves 2.

Apple Tart

This tart starts out upside down, then is turned over to right the apples on top of puff pastry crust.

2 tablespoons unsalted butter
1 cup sugar
¼ cup fresh lemon juice
½ cup water
½ cup blanched, sliced almonds
8 greening apples (or other tart variety), peeled, cored and cut into ¼-inch slices
¼ cup sugar
½ pound Puff Pastry (recipe follows, or use frozen)
Mint sprigs to garnish

Preheat oven to 400 degrees. Rub a 10-inch non-stick ovenproof saucepan with butter; reserve. In a medium-size saucepan, combine 1 cup sugar, lemon juice and water. Bring to a simmer over high heat and cook until light caramel, about 320 degrees on a candy thermometer. Add almonds and stir to coat. Pour into buttered saucepan.

Layer apples over the almond-caramel sauce. Sprinkle each layer of apples with sugar. Continue building layers of apples with remaining sugar.

Flour and roll out pastry to ⅛-inch thick. Lay over apples in pan. Trim pastry to ½ inch from edge of pan. Bake on the lower rack of oven until pastry is golden, about 30 minutes. Remove from oven.

Carefully invert onto a deep serving platter to prevent any juices from spilling in the car. Allow to cool at room temperature. Cut into slices and wrap with plastic to transport. To serve, unwrap and garnish with mint. Makes 1 (10-inch) tart.

Blueberry Kuchen

1½ cups sifted flour
½ teaspoon salt
2½ teaspoons baking powder
¾ cup sugar
1 egg
¼ cup milk
¼ cup margarine, melted
1 teaspoon vanilla
2 cups blueberries
1 teaspoon cinnamon

Combine dry ingredients and sift well. Beat in egg. Add milk, margarine and vanilla. Pour mixture into greased 8x8-inch pan. Sprinkle with blueberries and cinnamon. Bake at 350 degrees for 50 minutes and serve warm with whipped topping.

Praline Grahams

⅓ of a 16-ounce box graham crackers
¾ cup butter *or* margarine
½ cup sugar
1 cup chopped pecans

Separate each graham cracker into 4 sections. Arrange in a large flat pan with edges touching. Melt butter or margarine in saucepan; stir in sugar and pecans. Bring to a boil; cook 3 minutes, stirring frequently. Spread mixture evenly over graham crackers. Bake at 300 degrees for 12 minutes. Remove from pan, and allow to cool on waxed paper. Makes 3½ dozen.

Frosted Avocado Mold

1 (6-ounce) package lemon gelatin
2 cups boiling water
2 tablespoons lemon juice
1 cup cold water
1 tablespoon minced onion
2 (6–7-ounce) cans tuna, drained
1 avocado, chunked
½ cup chopped celery
2 hard-cooked eggs, diced
1 tablespoon sweet pickle relish
Frosting (recipe follows)

Dissolve gelatin in boiling water. Stir in lemon juice, water and minced onion. Chill until partially set. Add tuna, avocado, celery, eggs and pickle relish. Spoon into 1½-quart mold and chill until firm. Unmold on chilled platter with mixed greens and spread frosting on top of gelatin mold. Serves 8.

Frosting for Avocado Mold

1 avocado, mashed
¼ cup mayonnaise, yogurt or sour cream
Salt, as desired
Pinch of dill *or* garlic powder

April Showers Dessert

3 tablespoons cornstarch
2 cups cold water
Juice and grated rind of 2 lemons
1 cup sugar
3 egg whites, stiffly beaten
2–3 drops green food coloring
Chocolate wafers

Stir cornstarch into water; boil until thickened. Add remaining ingredients, except wafers. Line a loaf pan with chocolate wafers; pour ⅓ of mixture over cookies; repeat, making 3 layers. Chill thoroughly.

Sauce

1½ cups scalded milk
¼ cup sugar
3 egg yolks, beaten
4 drops mint flavoring

Combine sauce ingredients and heat until thickened; cool. Slice chilled dessert and serve with sauce. Serves 6.

Molded Blueberry

First layer

- **1 (3-ounce) package strawberry gelatin**
- **1 cup hot water**
- **1 cup cold water**

2nd layer

- **½ cup cold water**
- **1¼ ounces unflavored gelatin**
- **1 cup whipping cream, unwhipped**
- **1 cup sugar**
- **1 (8-ounce) package cream cheese**
- **1 teaspoon vanilla**
- **½ cup chopped nuts**

3rd layer

- **1 (3-ounce) package strawberry gelatin**
- **1½ cups hot water**
- **2 cups blueberries**

First layer—dissolve strawberry gelatin in hot water; add cold water and pour into 9 x 13-inch dish. Chill until firm.

2nd layer—Mix cold water and gelatin. Heat until gelatin is dissolved. Add whipping cream and sugar. Use blender and blend cream cheese until soft; add whipping cream mixture and vanilla. Blend until thick and frothy. Stir in chopped nuts and pour over first layer.

3rd layer—Mix strawberry gelatin and hot water, add blueberries. Pour over 2nd layer and chill until firm. Serves 12–15.

Glazed Fruit

- **2 (11-ounce) cans mandarin orange segments, drained**
- **6 medium-size bananas, sliced**
- **1 (No. 2) can crushed pineapple, drained (reserve juice)**
- **1 (6-ounce) package miniature marshmallows**
- **Drained pineapple juice**
- **2 eggs, beaten**
- **1 cup sugar**
- **1 tablespoon flour**
- **1 small package gelatin (apricot, peach *or* orange)**

Combine pineapple juice, eggs, sugar and flour. Cook over low heat until thick (about 5 minutes). Add gelatin. Stir until dissolved. Cool before adding orange sections, bananas, pineapple and marshmallows. Chill in refrigerator for several hours before serving. Serves 3–4.

Quick Rippled Ice Cream

Several hours ahead of serving, spoon 1 pint of slightly softened ice cream into an 8 x 8-inch baking pan. Swirl or fold in 1 of the following flavors through the ice cream. Freeze until firm. Serves 4.

Berry: With fork, swirl 1 cup fresh or thawed frozen strawberries or raspberries through vanilla ice cream.

Ginger: Fold 1 cup coarsely broken gingersnaps into vanilla ice cream.

Fruitcake: Fold 1 cup crumbled fruitcake into vanilla ice cream.

Maple: Fold maple or maple-blended syrup through butter-pecan ice cream.

Mincemeat: Swirl ½ cup prepared mincemeat through vanilla ice cream.

Special soft ice cream:

In bowl with mixer at low speed, beat vanilla ice cream just until soft, but not melted. Stir in 1 of the following:

Crumbled macaroons; diced fig-filled cookies; crushed peanut brittle or toffee; diced dried figs or prunes; grated unsweetened chocolate; plain or toasted flaked coconut, well-drained, canned crushed pineapple; diced maraschino cherries; ½-inch cubes of angel food cake. Spoon into sherbet dishes and eat while soft.

Lemon Ice Cream Rings

- **½ pint vanilla ice cream**
- **1 fresh pineapple**
- **2 tablespoons frozen lemonade concentrate**
- **¼ teaspoon ground ginger**

Place ice cream in refrigerator to soften slightly, about 15 minutes. Meanwhile, with sharp knife, cut off crown and stem of pineapple. Carefully cut off peel and remove eyes. Cut fruit crosswise into ½-inch slices. With round biscuit cutter or sharp knife, remove core from each slice.

In small bowl, mix softened ice cream, lemonade concentrate and ground ginger. Serve ice cream mixture with pineapple rings. Serves 4.

Ice Cream "Flowerpots"

- **1 pint vanilla (or other flavor) ice cream**
- **10 (2½-inch-long) pink sugar wafers**
- **11 (2½-inch-long) vanilla sugar wafers, cut crosswise in half**
- **1 (4.25-ounce) tube pink decorating icing, fitted with star tip**
- **1 (¾-ounce) tube green writing gel**
- **¼ cup chopped pistachios *or* peanuts**
- **Assorted lollipops**

Remove ice cream from container in 1 piece. Place on serving plate. Working quickly, press pink wafers upright around base of ice cream. Sandwich 2 cut wafers together with some icing. Press sandwiches into ice cream just above pink cookies. With tiny rosettes of green icing, decorate between sandwiches. With a tiny rosette of pink icing, decorate outside of sandwiches. Sprinkle nuts over top of ice cream.

With green icing, decorate lollipops. Insert pops "flowers" into "flowerpot." Place in freezer until serving time. To serve, cut lengthwise in wedges. Serves 4.

Quick Fruit Cream

- **2 large cans fruit cocktail, drained**
- **1 pint vanilla ice cream, softened**
- **½ cup chopped pecans, optional**

Empty cans of fruit cocktail into bowl. Add softened vanilla ice cream and stir until all fruit is coated. Add pecans. Stir until pecans are mixed in. Chill salad before serving. Serves 4–6.

Amaretto Crunch Ice Cream

- **1 pint vanilla ice cream**
- **½ cup chopped amaretto cookies *or* almond macaroons**
- **¼ cup amaretto liqueur**

Soften ice cream slightly in refrigerator. Transfer to medium bowl. Mix in cookies and amaretto. Immediately refreeze. Spoon ice cream into bowls and serve immediately. Serves 2–4.

Jamaican Ice Cream

1 quart vanilla ice cream
6 tablespoons dark rum
2 tablespoons instant coffee powder

Just before serving, scoop ice cream into stemmed goblets. Pour rum over. Sprinkle with coffee powder. Serve immediately. Serves 6.

Note: If coffee is granular, freeze-dried type, pulverize in blender before using.

Pumpkin-Pecan Ice Cream

1 quart vanilla ice cream, softened
1 (16-ounce) can solid-pack pumpkin
3 tablespoons maple syrup *or* maple-flavored syrup
1 cup chopped toasted pecans
Additional maple syrup (garnish)
Whipped cream (garnish)
Chopped pecans (garnish)

Oil an 8-cup mold. In a large bowl, beat or stir ice cream, pumpkin and maple syrup just until blended. Fold in nuts. Pour into prepared mold. Freeze until firm. To unmold, dip briefly in hot water and invert on serving platter. Drizzle with syrup. Garnish with whipped cream and nuts. Cut into 1-inch slices. Serves 12.

Pumpernickel Ice Cream

4 thin slices pumpernickel bread
2 tablespoons grated semisweet chocolate
1 teaspoon grated lemon peel
½ gallon vanilla ice cream, slightly softened
1 tablespoon sugar
1 tablespoon margarine

Finely chop bread in processor or blender. Set aside 2 tablespoons crumbs. Mix remaining crumbs, chocolate and lemon peel in small bowl. Stir into ice cream. Return to freezer. Combine reserved bread crumbs, sugar and margarine in small skillet and stir over medium-low heat until mixture begins to caramelize. Cool slightly. Spoon ice cream into bowls. Sprinkle with crumb mixture and serve. Serves 8.

Frozen Fruit Treat

1 (3-ounce) package cream cheese
3 tablespoons whipping cream
2 tablespoons lemon juice
1 cup mandarin orange segments, drained
1 cup pineapple tidbits, drained
½ cup chopped pecans
½ cup halved maraschino cherries
⅓ cup mayonnaise
1 cup whipping cream
2 tablespoons sugar
½ cup bing cherries, seeded and halved
Dash salt

Mix cream cheese thoroughly with 3 tablespoons cream. Add mayonnaise, lemon juice and dash of salt.

Combine pineapple, cherries, orange segments, sugar and chopped nuts. Add to cheese mixture.

Whip cream and add to cheese-fruit mixture. Fold carefully. Pour into a freezer-proof serving dish and freeze in a sealed container. Set salad out a few minutes before serving. You may dip this out with a sturdy serving spoon, or cut it into cubes or slices to serve.

Caribbean Ice Cream Roll

1 (20-ounce) can crushed pineapple in syrup, drained (reserve ¼ cup syrup)
¼ cup dark rum *or* ½ teaspoon rum extract
1 pint tub vanilla ice cream
½ cup flaked coconut, toasted (toasting optional)

In shallow serving bowl, mix reserved pineapple syrup with rum. Stir in pineapple. With scissors, cut ice cream container from top to bottom. Remove ice cream in 1 piece and roll in coconut, pressing gently so coconut sticks. Freeze until serving time, or cut in 6 slices and serve immediately with pineapple sauce. Serves 6.

Cream-Filled Chocolate-Covered Egg

1 (4-serving size) package instant chocolate, vanilla *or* butter scotch pudding and pie filling
1½ cups cold milk
1 cup heavy cream, whipped
½ cup walnuts, chopped
10 vanilla wafers, chopped
1 cup marshmallow creme
4 (1-ounce) squares semisweet chocolate, melted
2 tablespoons margarine, melted
1 tablespoon colored sprinkles
½ cup flaked coconut, tinted green with food coloring (garnish)

Prepare pudding mix according to package directions, using cold milk. Fold in 1 cup whipped cream, walnuts and vanilla wafers. Line a 4-cup mold or bowl with plastic wrap. Spoon half the pudding mixture into mold. Spread marshmallow creme over pudding to within ½ inch of edge. Top with remaining pudding mixture. Cover. Freeze 6 hours or overnight.

Unmold egg onto serving plate. Combine chocolate and margarine. Frost egg. Garnish with sprinkles and remaining whipped cream. Serve at once, or freeze until serving time. Serves 8.

Banana Foster

4 very ripe bananas or 1¾ cups total (use bananas that have black spots on skins to en sure they are well-ripened)
2 tablespoons unsalted butter
¼ cup sugar
2 tablespoons lemon juice
¼ cup water
¼ cup dark rum
1 pint vanilla ice cream (best quality)

Peel bananas and slice them crosswise. Heat butter and sugar in skillet; cook over medium heat, stirring occasionally for about 1 minute, until sugar starts to caramelize. Add bananas and sauté, stirring for about 1 minute. Then stir in lemon juice, water and rum. Cover and cook over medium heat for about 1 minute, until a sauce has formed. Spoon mixture onto dessert plates and top with ice cream. Serve immediately. Serves 4.

Ice Cream Mold for Easter

- 2 (1-pound) packages frozen strawberries, thawed
- 2 (3-ounce) packages strawberry gelatin
- 2 pints vanilla ice cream (or more)
- 1 cup whipping cream, whipped
- Milk
- Coconut

Thaw strawberries; drain and reserve syrup. Add enough milk to make 1 3/4 cups of liquid and bring to a boil. Add gelatin and stir until dissolved. Cut each pint of ice cream into 8 pieces and add to gelatin mixture. You may want to add more ice cream; stir until ice cream is melted and blended.

Chill until partially set. Fold in strawberries; pour into oiled melon-shaped mold and chill until firm. Unmold at serving time and decorate the Easter egg with whipped cream topped with coconut. Cut in slices to serve. Makes 8–10 servings.

Peanut Ice Cream

- 3 1/2 cups half-and-half
- 1 cup dry roasted, salted peanuts coarsely chopped
- 1/2 cup creamy peanut butter
- 1 cup sugar
- 1 teaspoon vanilla
- 1/2 cup whipping cream
- 3 egg yolks
- Pinch salt

Scald half-and-half in heavy medium saucepan over medium heat. Whisk yolks, sugar, vanilla and salt in medium-size bowl. Gradually whisk in hot cream. Return to saucepan; stir over medium-low heat until it thickens and leaves path on back of spoon when finger is drawn across, about 10 minutes. *Do not boil.* Remove pan from heat.

Whisk in cream and peanut butter. Strain in medium bowl filled with ice. Stir until cool. Cover and refrigerate until well-chilled. Transfer to ice cream maker and process according to instructions, adding nuts when almost set. Freeze in freezer container overnight. If frozen solid, let soften in refrigerator before serving.

Strawberry-Rhubarb Mold

- 2 cups rhubarb sauce *or*
- 1 (16-ounce) package frozen, sweetened rhubarb
- 1 (6-ounce) package strawberry gelatin
- 1 (9-ounce) can crushed pineapple, drained
- Crushed Pineapple Dressing (recipe follows)

Make rhubarb sauce; heat to boiling. Remove from heat and immediately add gelatin; stir until dissolved. Cool until partially set. Add drained pineapple; reserve 2 tablespoons for dressing. Pour into 1-quart salad mold. Chill until firm. Serve on lettuce leaves.

Crushed Pineapple Dressing

- 1/4 cup whipping cream, whipped
- 1/4 cup mayonnaise
- 2 tablespoons pineapple juice

Combine ingredients. Dollop or drizzle on salad. Serves 4–6.

Eggnog for the New Year

- 2 (3 3/4-ounce) cans crushed pineapple
- 1 tablespoon unflavored gelatin
- 3 tablespoons lime juice
- 1 1/2 cups prepared eggnog
- 3/4 cup chopped celery
- 1 (3-ounce) package raspberry gelatin
- 1 1/2 cups boiling water
- 1 package frozen orange-cranberry relish

If serving as a dessert, omit celery. Drain pineapple; pour juice into saucepan and heat to boiling. Soften unflavored gelatin in lime juice and dissolve in boiling pineapple juice. Cool.

Add eggnog and chill until partially set; add pineapple. Place in a 9.x 13 x 2-inch pan or a 5-quart mold. Dissolve raspberry gelatin in boiling water; add orange-cranberry relish, stirring until completely dissolved. Chill until mixture begins to thicken. Add chopped celery. Pour raspberry gelatin mixture over eggnog layer and chill until firm.

EZ Blueberry Delight

- 1 (1-pound 5-ounce) can blue berry pie filling
- 1/2 cup sugar
- 1/3 cup margarine
- 3/4 cup sifted flour
- 1/4 teaspoon salt
- 1/2 teaspoon cinnamon
- 1 (8-ounce) package cream cheese, whipped

Arrange pie filling in an 8 x 8-inch baking dish. Cut margarine into remaining ingredients, until mixture resembles coarse crumbs. Sprinkle over pie filling. Bake at 350 degrees for 40 minutes and serve with cream cheese spooned on top.

Peach Melba

- 1 (16-ounce) can peach halves, packed in fruit juice
- 1 cup raspberry preserves
- 1 teaspoon vanilla
- 4 scoops vanilla ice cream

Drain peach halves; save 2 tablespoons juice. Place 4 peach halves, cutside up, on individual plates. To make sauce, combine reserved juice, raspberry preserves and vanilla in a 4-cup glass measure with handle. Microwave on HIGH for 2 1/2–3 minutes; stir once. Top each peach half with scoop of ice cream and 2 tablespoons raspberry sauce; serve.

Elegant Ambrosia

- 1 (20-ounce) can pineapple chunks
- 1 (11-ounce) can mandarin orange segments
- 1 banana, peeled and sliced
- 1 1/2 cups seedless grapes
- 1 cup miniature marshmallows
- 1/2 cup flaked coconut
- 1/4 cup chopped almonds
- 1 (8-ounce) carton vanilla yogurt

Drain pineapple and oranges. Combine pineapple, oranges, banana, grapes, marshmallows, coconut and almonds. Fold in yogurt. Chill and serve. Serves 4–6.

Irish Whiskey Trifle

1 baker's sponge cake
Strawberry *or* raspberry jam
1 (14-ounce) can fruit cocktail, drained
1/2 cup Irish whiskey
1 cup cooked vanilla pudding, homemade *or* from mix
2 cups whipped cream
Cocktail cherries

Split sponge cake into 1-inch layers. Spread slices with jam. Put together again. Cut sponge cake into small cubes. Place in a glass bowl. Add fruit. Sprinkle with Irish whiskey. Pour pudding over cake. Chill. Before serving, decorate with whipped cream and cherries. Serves 6.

Thanksgiving Apricot Ring

1 (No. 2 1/2) can apricot halves
2 (6-ounce) packages lemon gelatin
Juice of 2 lemons
Juice of 1 orange
2 (3-ounce) packages cream cheese
1 cup chopped nuts (optional)

Drain apricots, reserving juice; put through a sieve. Add enough water to juice to make 2 cups. Pour liquid into saucepan and bring to a boil. Stir in gelatin until dissolved completely. Combine lemon and orange juice; add sufficient water to equal 1 cup. Stir liquids and apricots into gelatin and chill until slightly thickened.

Dice and soften cream cheese; add with nuts to dish. Chill in large mold and use as a centerpiece with colorful fresh fruits buried in greens. Serves 10–12.

Double Strawberry Bavarian Cream

1 (3-ounce) package strawberry-flavored gelatin
1 cup boiling water
1 (10-ounce) package frozen sliced strawberries in syrup
1 cup whipping cream, whipped
Whole strawberries

Dissolve gelatin in boiling water in large mixing bowl. Add frozen strawberries to hot gelatin mixture; as berries thaw, break up with a fork. Mixture should be partially set by the time strawberries have thawed; if not, place bowl in freezer 5–10 minutes.

Fold whipped cream into gelatin mixture. Pour into 4-cup mold. Refrigerate several hours or overnight. To serve, unmold onto serving plate. Garnish with whole strawberries. Serves 4–6.

Variation: Double Raspberry Bavarian Cream: Substitute red raspberry gelatin and frozen red raspberries in syrup for strawberries.

Golden Ginger Ale Fruit

1 tablespoon gelatin
2 tablespoons cold water
1/2 cup boiling water
1 tablespoon sugar
Dash salt
1 cup ginger ale
2 tablespoons fresh lemon juice
1/2 cup heavy cream, whipped
1/4 cup seedless white grapes, sliced
1/2 cup pineapple chunks
1/4 cup celery, diced
1 tablespoon candied ginger, chopped
1/3 cup pecans, chopped

Soften gelatin in cold water; add boiling water; stir until gelatin has dissolved. Add sugar, salt, ginger ale and lemon juice; chill. When slightly thickened, fold in remaining ingredients. Turn into individual dessert glasses; chill. Serves 6.

Cider-Baked Apples

6 firm tart apples, quartered and cored
1 cup apple cider
1/2 cup crunchy breakfast cereal
1/2 teaspoon cinnamon

Place apples in a casserole. Pour cider over apples; sprinkle lightly with cinnamon. Cover casserole and bake at 350 degrees until apples are soft. Sprinkle cereal over apples immediately before serving, so it stays crunchy.

Easter Basket Desserts

1/2 package (1 packet) meringue mix
1 pint strawberry ice cream
1 pint chocolate ice cream
1 pint pistachio ice cream
Frozen strawberries

Mix meringue according to package directions. Using pastry bag, make 5 individual shells. It takes about 1/2 cup meringue for each. Bake according to package directions. Use a small ice cream scoop. Fill each cooled shell with a scoop of each flavor of ice cream. Spoon partially thawed strawberries for topping. Serves 5.

April Apple Fool

6 apples, cored and sliced
2 cups apple juice
1 1/4 cups sugar
1 fresh lemon, cut into slices
1 cup cream
1 teaspoon vanilla

Slice lemon; place in a saucepan with apple juice and 1 cup sugar. Bring to a boil; cook 5 minutes; add apple slices; cook 10 minutes. Drain and discard lemon slices. Purée apples in a food processor; refrigerate. Beat cream until thick; add 1/4 cup sugar and vanilla; blend with apple purée. Pour into chilled parfait glasses. Serves 6.

Pineapple-Strawberry Parfaits

1 package coconut macaroon mix
2 cups commercial sour cream
2 tablespoons brown sugar
2 cups cubed, sweetened fresh *or* canned pineapple
1 cup strawberries, sliced, drained, sweetened

Prepare macaroons as directed on package. Cool. Finely crumble 10 macaroons into a bowl; blend in sour cream and sugar. Cover and chill 2–3 hours. When ready to serve, layer chilled fruits and sour cream mixture in parfait glasses. Serves 6–8.

Red Delicious Fruit Salad

1 Red Delicious apple, cored and sliced
1 orange, peeled, sliced and quartered
2 small kiwifruit, pared and sliced
1/2 cup pineapple chunks
Sweet Lemon Vinaigrette (recipe follows)
Lettuce leaves

Combine fruit; toss with Sweet Lemon Vinaigrette. Arrange in lettuce-lined bowl.

Sweet Lemon Vinaigrette

Combine 2 tablespoons lemon juice, 1 tablespoon *each* vegetable oil and sugar, dash *each* salt and cayenne pepper; mix well. Makes 1/4 cup. Serves 4–6.

Orange Delight

1 (10-ounce) package miniature marshmallows
2 cups orange juice
1/2 cup crushed pineapple, drained
1/2 cup coconut (optional)
Whipped cream

Microwave marshmallows in a large bowl on HIGH 2–3 minutes; they will puff up. Add orange juice and beat with a wire whisk. Juice and marshmallows should be smooth; stir in pineapple. Pour into small dessert dishes; chill. Top with whipped cream and sprinkle coconut over top.

Red Hot Gelatin

1/2 cup red hots (candy)
2 cups boiling water
1 (6-ounce) package raspberry gelatin
3 cups cinnamon-flavored applesauce
1 teaspoon lemon juice

Dissolve candies in hot water; stir in gelatin until completely dissolved. Add applesauce and lemon juice; mix together. Pour into gelatin mold (individual, round or loaf). Serves 6.

Pear Creme Anglaise Sauce

1/4 cup sugar
6 large egg yolks
1 teaspoon paprika
1 teaspoon vanilla extract
1 1/2 cups half-and-half, scalded
7 ounces white chocolate, broken into 1/2-ounce bits
1 roasted pear

In a medium-size saucepan, combine sugar, egg yolks, paprika and vanilla. Stir in half-and-half. Without boiling, cook over medium-low heat about 6 minutes, stirring continuously, until thickened to coat the back of a spoon.

Transfer to a bowl; add chocolate and stir to dissolve. In a blender, combine sauce with the pear and purée until smooth. Strain through a fine sieve. Refrigerate until ready to serve. Makes 2 1/4 cups.

Purple Cow

1 1/2 cups cold milk
3 tablespoons frozen grape juice concentrate
2/3 cup ice cream

Place cold milk, frozen grape juice concentrate and ice cream in blender; cover. Blend until smooth and frothy. Pour into 2 (12-ounce) glasses. Top with scoops of vanilla ice cream. Serve immediately.

Pineapple Slush

1 (5 1/4-ounce) can pineapple tidbits, undrained
1 medium banana, chilled
1/4 cup milk
2 cups pineapple sherbet

Combine all ingredients in blender; process until smooth.

Raspberry Frost

1/2 cup finely sieved raspberries
1 pint vanilla ice cream
1 1/2 cups cold milk
Sugar

In a bowl mix raspberries and half the ice cream. Beat until well-blended. Add milk. Beat until frothy. Sweeten to taste. Pour into 4 (8-ounce) glasses and top with remaining ice cream.

Mother's Day Cake With Coconut Topping

1 (8-ounce) container dairy sour cream
2 eggs
3/4 cup sugar
1 1/2 cups sifted all-purpose flour
2 teaspoons baking powder
1/2 to 1 teaspoon almond *or* vanilla extract
Coconut Topping (recipe follows)

Let sour cream and eggs warm to room temperature for easy mixing. Remove 2 tablespoons sour cream to small bowl. Reserve for Coconut Topping. Grease and flour an 8 x 8 x 2-inch baking pan. Preheat oven to 350 degrees.

Combine remaining sour cream, eggs, sugar, flour, baking powder and almond extract in a large bowl. Beat at medium speed with electric mixer for 1 minute, scraping down side of bowl with plastic spatula. Pour into prepared pan.

Bake in a 350-degree oven for 25 minutes, or until center springs back when lightly pressed with fingertips. Remove cake from oven. Spread Coconut Topping evenly over top. Return to oven. Bake 10 minutes longer. Cool in pan on wire rack. For a "Mother's Day touch" lay 2 or 3 pink roses on top.

Coconut Topping

Reserved sour cream
2 tablespoons butter, softened
1/2 cup brown sugar, firmly packed
1/2 cup flaked coconut

Combine all ingredients until well-mixed.

Glorified Rice

2 cups cooked rice
3/4 cups granulated sugar
1/4 teaspoon salt
1 teaspoon vanilla
2 cups crushed pineapple
1/2 cup diced marshmallows
1 cup coconut
1/2 cup whipped cream

Combine rice, sugar, salt and vanilla; mix well. Add pineapple. Chill in refrigerator for 1 hour, then add marshmallows, coconut and whipped cream.

Foreign & EXOTIC

Zucchini Moussaka

- ¼ cup dry bread crumbs
- 2 medium-size zucchini, sliced
- Olive oil
- 1½ pounds ground turkey *or* hamburger
- 1 medium onion, chopped
- ½ cup red cooking wine
- ¼ cup parsley, chopped
- 4 tablespoons tomato paste
- 2 cloves garlic, minced
- Salt and pepper to taste

Sauce

- 3 tablespoons butter *or* margarine
- 3 tablespoons flour
- 1½ cups milk, heated to boiling
- 2 egg yolks, beaten
- 1 cup cottage cheese
- ½ cup dry bread crumbs
- ½ cup Parmesan cheese
- 1 cup shredded mozzarella cheese

Spray a 3-quart baking dish with non-stick spray. Cover bottom with ¼ cup bread crumbs. Clean and slice zucchini in ½-inch rounds. Coat slices with olive oil and lay in single layer on broiler pan. Broil until lightly browned. (You may need to do 2 or 3 batches.) Lay on paper towels to absorb oil.

In a large skillet, brown ground turkey in a little olive oil. Add onions and garlic. Add cooking wine and simmer for a few minutes. Stir in parsley, tomato paste, salt and pepper to taste. Continue simmering while you prepare remaining sauce.

In a medium pan, melt butter. Stir in flour. Cook and stir for 3–4 minutes. Stir in hot milk and continue cooking until thick. Gradually stir about ⅓ of the hot white sauce into beaten egg yolks, then stir back into skillet. Do not allow to boil. Continue cooking for 3–5 minutes, stirring constantly. Remove from heat. Stir in cottage cheese; set aside.

Preheat oven to 350 degrees. In greased baking dish, layer half the zucchini and half the meat sauce. Sprinkle with ¼ cup bread crumbs and ¼ cup Parmesan cheese. Repeat layers until both are used. Pour cream sauce evenly over top. Cover with aluminum foil and bake for 45 minutes. Remove foil and top with mozzarella cheese; bake an additional 15 minutes. Let stand for 10–15 minutes before cutting.

Pork or Chicken Satay

- 1 pound boneless chicken *or* pork tenderloin
- ¼ cup coconut milk
- 2 tablespoons lime juice
- 1 tablespoon soy sauce
- 1 tablespoon brown sugar
- ½ teaspoon ground ginger
- ½ teaspoon garlic powder
- 1 teaspoon ground coriander
- 12 wooden bamboo skewers soaked in water for 1 hour
- Peanut Sauce (recipe follows)

Cut meat into bite-size chunks or strips. Mix remaining ingredients together in a glass bowl. Add meat. Marinate for 2 hours or overnight in refrigerator. Place meat on skewers. Cook in oven at 425 degrees for 12–15 minutes, turning once. Serve with sauce.

Peanut Sauce

Gently heat ½ cup creamy peanut butter in small saucepan. Add 1 tablespoon coconut milk, 3 tablespoons soy sauce, 2 tablespoons lime juice and ½ teaspoon cayenne pepper. Mix well. Heat until blended.

Gazpacho

- 1 onion, chopped
- ¼ teaspoon curry powder
- ¼ cup celery, chopped
- 1 cup stewed tomatoes
- 1 teaspoon basil
- 2 cups carrots, peeled and sliced
- ¼ teaspoon grated lemon peel
- ¼ cup green pepper, chopped
- 1 cup chicken broth
- Salt and pepper to taste

Combine all ingredients in saucepan and bring to a boil. Reduce heat; cover and simmer 1 hour or until vegetables are tender. Serve hot or cold. Serves 4.

Ragalach

- 1 cup sweet butter, softened
- 1 (8-ounce) package cream cheese, softened
- ¼ teaspoon salt
- 2 cups sifted all-purpose flour
- 1 cup chopped walnuts
- ½ cup granulated sugar
- 1 tablespoon cinnamon

Mix butter, cheese and salt until creamy. Mix in flour; shape into 14 balls. Refrigerate overnight.

Heat oven to 350 degrees. On lightly floured surface roll each ball to a 6-inch circle. Cut each into quarters. Mix nuts, sugar and cinnamon. Drop rounded teaspoonfuls on each quarter. Pinch together edges of dough, then form into crescents. Place on an ungreased cookie sheet. Bake 12 minutes until light brown. Best served fresh. Makes 5 dozen.

Lithuanian Kugelia (Potato Pudding)

- 8 large potatoes
- 2 large onions, finely chopped
- 1 stick butter *or* margarine
- 4 eggs, well-beaten
- 1 large can evaporated milk
- 3 teaspoons salt
- 1/4 teaspoon pepper

Melt butter in frying pan and sauté chopped onion until limp; set aside. Meanwhile grate the potatoes; do not purée in blender or food processor. Work quickly to avoid excess discoloration. Take out as much excess liquid from potatoes as you can. Retain potato starch in bottom of bowl.

Using a large bowl, add onion and butter to potato mixture. Add beaten eggs, evaporated milk, salt and pepper; mix well. Pour into a well-greased glass baking dish.

Bake in preheated oven at 450 degrees for 10 minutes. Lower oven temperature to 350 degrees and bake until edges are crispy brown, about 1 1/2 hours.

Depth of grated potato mixture should be no less than 2 inches in baking dish. Serve with applesauce or sour cream. May be used as a main course. Delicious!

Italian Shoulder Lamb Chops

- 4 lamb arm *or* blade shoulder chop
- Garlic salt
- Pepper
- Salt
- 4 teaspoons tomato sauce
- 1 large onion, cut into 1/4-inch slices
- 1 medium green pepper, cut into 1/4-inch rings
- 2 tomatoes, cut into 1/2-inch slices

Arrange chops in baking dish; sprinkle generously with garlic salt, pepper and salt. Spread 1 teaspoon tomato sauce on each lamb chop. Place onion slices, pepper rings and tomato slices on top of each chop. Bake in preheated 325-degree oven for 1 hour, or until lamb is tender.

Orange-Honey Crescents (Melomacarona)

- 1 1/2 cups salad oil
- 9 tablespoons frozen orange juice concentrate, divided
- 1/3 cup sugar
- 1 1/2 teaspoons grated orange peel
- 3 1/2 cups sifted flour
- 1 teaspoon cinnamon
- 3/4 cup baking powder
- 3/4 teaspoon soda
- 1/4 teaspoon salt
- 1/4 teaspoon cloves
- 1/4 teaspoon nutmeg
- 1 1/4 cups chopped pecans, divided
- 3/4 cup honey

Combine salad oil, 6 tablespoons orange juice concentrate, sugar and orange peel. Sift dry ingredients; add to orange juice mixture. Stir in 3/4 cup chopped pecans. Dough can be chilled. Shape into crescents. Bake at 350 degrees for 15–18 minutes. Cool. Combine honey and remaining orange juice concentrate; drizzle over cookies. Sprinkle with remaining pecans. Makes 3 1/2 dozen.

Baklava

- 1 1/4 cups *plus* 2 tablespoons granulated sugar
- 6 tablespoons honey
- 1 cup water
- Juice of 1/2 lemon
- 1 cup finely chopped almonds
- 1 1/2 teaspoons cinnamon
- 1 pound phyllo pastry sheets
- 1/2 pound butter

Boil sugar, honey, water and lemon juice for 20 minutes; allow to cool. Place nuts and cinnamon in a bowl; mix well. Butter a 14 x 10-inch baking pan and line with 8 sheets of phyllo pastry, buttering between each sheet with pastry brush. Spread some of nut mixture over top pastry sheet.

Alternate layers of pastry sheets and nut mixture until all nuts and sugar mixture are used. Top this with 8 sheets of pastry, remembering to butter each. Score pastry into diamond-shape pieces. Bake at 325 degrees for 30 minutes. Pour cool syrup over hot pastry and serve hot or cold. Makes 20 servings.

French Pancakes (Galettes)

- 3 eggs
- 1/2 cup flour
- 1/2 cup cream
- 1/4 teaspoon salt

Mix all ingredients and beat thoroughly with rotary eggbeater. Pour small quantity of batter into hot, well-buttered skillet and spread over bottom in thin sheet. When brown, turn to other side and finish cooking. Spread with tart jelly and roll up. To serve, place in center of platter and arrange tiny pork sausages on each side. Garnish with slices of lemon and sprigs of parsley. Serves 4–6.

Mexicali Chili Puff

- 2 (4-ounce) cans whole green chilies
- 1 1/2 cups Monterey Jack cheese, shredded
- 1 1/4 cups sharp cheddar cheese, shredded
- 3 eggs
- 1 cup masa harina *or* 1 cup flour
- 2 1/4 cups milk
- 1/4 teaspoon salt
- 1/4 teaspoon chili powder
- 1/4 teaspoon ground cumin
- Guacamole Mash (recipe follows)

Drain chilies; remove seeds; cut into 1-inch strips; place in bottom of buttered 2-quart casserole. Place 2 cheeses on chilies; spread evenly. Mix eggs, masa harina (or flour), milk, salt, chili powder and cumin; pour over cheeses. Bake at 350 degrees for 35–40 minutes until puffed and golden; serve with Guacamole Mash. Serves 4.

Guacamole Mash

- 1 ripe avocado
- 1 tomato, seeded and diced
- 2 tablespoons finely chopped onion
- 1 tablespoon fresh coriander, chopped
- 1/4 teaspoon minced garlic
- 2 tablespoons fresh lime juice
- 1/8 teaspoon cayenne pepper

Mash avocado pulp; add remaining ingredients; mix well. Serves 4.

Creamy Bacon-Mushroom Mostaccioli

- 8 slices bacon, cut up
- 2 (4.5-ounce) jars whole mushrooms, drained
- 8 ounces mostaccioli
- 3/4 cup half-and-half
- 1/3 cup butter *or* margarine
- 2 teaspoons parsley flakes
- 1/2 teaspoon salt, if desired
- 1 clove garlic, minced
- 1/3 cup grated Parmesan cheese
- 1/4 cup sliced green onions
- 8 drops hot pepper sauce

In medium skillet, cook bacon until crisp; remove. Add mushrooms to bacon drippings and cook until golden; drain. Cook mostaccioli according to package directions; drain; Set aside. In same saucepan, combine half-and-half, butter, parsley, salt, garlic and hot pepper sauce. Heat just until butter melts, stirring frequently.

Combine bacon, mushrooms, hot mostaccioli, half-and-half mixture and Parmesan cheese. Toss to coat. Place on warm serving platter; garnish with green onions. Serve immediately. We really like this!

Norwegian Lefse

- 2 cups mashed potatoes
- 1 cup dried apricots, diced
- 1/4 cup granulated sugar
- 1/4 teaspoon cinnamon
- Sliced almonds
- 1/2 cup flour
- 1/2 cup water
- 1/4 cup brown sugar
- 1/4 teaspoon nutmeg
- Whipped cream

Add flour to potatoes to make a stiff dough. Separate into 6 portions and roll out like pie crusts on a floured surface. Bake on floured griddle at 350 degrees until lightly browned; turn to bake other side. Place on plate in warm oven. Meanwhile, in large saucepan, combine apricots, water, sugars and spices. Bring to boil and simmer 5 minutes. Place 1 or 2 tablespoons of mixture along edge of each lefse and roll up. Top with whipped cream and almonds. Serve hot.

Goulash With Noodles

- 1 pound beef, cut into cubes
- 2 medium onions, minced
- 1/2 teaspoon dry mustard
- 1 1/4 teaspoons paprika
- 2 tablespoons brown sugar
- 1 1/4 teaspoons salt
- 3 tablespoons Worcestershire sauce
- 3/4 teaspoon cider vinegar
- 6 tablespoons ketchup
- 1 1/2 cups water
- 3 tablespoons flour
- 1 (6-ounce) package noodles

Brown meat on all sides in heavy fry pan or Dutch oven; add onions. Combine mustard, paprika, brown sugar and salt. Combine Worcestershire sauce, vinegar and ketchup; add to mustard mixture. Add to meat with 1 cup water. Stir and cover.

Cook over low heat for 2 1/2 hours, or until meat is tender. Blend flour with remaining water; add to meat mixture. Stir until thickened. Boil noodles in salted water until tender; drain. Serve meat mixture over noodles. Serves 8.

Polenta Parmesan

- 4 cups water
- 1 teaspoon salt
- 1 1/4 cups yellow cornmeal
- Butter
- 1/2 to 1 cup freshly grated Parmesan cheese

Bring water to a boil; add salt. Lower heat and stir in cornmeal, a little at a time, stirring constantly to prevent lumping and sticking (a whisk is good for this). Cook 15 minutes, or until polenta is very thick. Pour into a greased 8 x 4 1/2-inch bread pan and refrigerate until cool. Run a knife around edge of pan and remove loaf. Cut polenta into 1/2-inch-thick slices; place overlapping in a large, flat casserole. Place dots of butter between slices; sprinkle slices with freshly grated Parmesan cheese. The polenta can be assembled ahead of time to this point and refrigerated. Bake in a 350-degree oven until cheese is melted and edges are brown, about 25 minutes.

Oxtail Stew Madeira

- 5 pounds oxtails
- Flour (for dredging)
- 2 tablespoons oil
- 1 cup scallions, chopped
- 1 cup carrots, chopped
- 3 cloves garlic, minced
- 2 cups water
- 2 bay leaves
- 1 cup Madeira wine
- 1/4 cup flour

Trim oxtails of all excess fat and dredge in flour. Heat oil in large Dutch oven and brown oxtails on all sides. Place on paper towels to drain. Add scallions, carrots and garlic to remaining drippings, sauté a few minutes. Add water, bay leaves and oxtails; bring to a boil. Reduce heat and add 1/2 cup Madeira. Cover and simmer slowly for 2 3/4 hours. Add remaining Madeira and simmer an additional 15 minutes.

Drain meat, reserving cooking liquid. Place meat on serving platter surrounded by buttered noodles and keep warm.

Skim fat from cooking liquid and return liquid to pot. Blend 1/4 cup flour with enough cold water to make a smooth paste. Add to liquid and stir constantly until mixture boils and thickens. Pass sauce separately at table. Serves 6.

Gazpacho

- 2 (16-ounce) cans peeled tomatoes, undrained and chopped*
- 1/2 cucumber, peeled and chopped
- 1/4 cup chopped green bell pepper
- 1/4 cup vegetable oil
- 2 tablespoons wine vinegar
- 1 tablespoon grated onion
- 2 cups tomato juice
- 1 tablespoon Worcestershire sauce
- Salt and pepper to taste
- 4 drops Tabasco sauce

Combine all ingredients. Cover and refrigerate until thoroughly chilled. Serves 8.

*Six large fresh tomatoes, chopped, may be substituted for canned tomatoes.

Rugalah

8 ounces cottage cheese
3/4 cup plus 2 tablespoons butter
2 cups flour
Confectioners' sugar

Filling

3/4 cup finely chopped walnuts
3/4 cup light brown sugar, firmly packed
3/4 teaspoon cinnamon

In a medium bowl, combine cottage cheese with 1/2 cup butter. Cream until soft; add flour and mix well. Wrap dough in plastic wrap and chill overnight.

Preheat oven to 400 degrees. Lightly grease a cookie sheet. Make a filling by combining walnuts, brown sugar and cinnamon.

Roll out dough a third at a time, on a floured surface until it is 1/8-inch thick. Using a ruler and sharp knife, mark dough into strips 1 x 4 inches for small pastries, or 1 x 8 inches for large ones. Melt remaining butter; brush dough with butter.

Sprinkle dough with nut mixture; roll up pastries and place seam side down on cookie sheet. Brush tops with any remaining butter. Bake 18–20 minutes. Sprinkle confectioners' sugar on top to serve. Makes 4 dozen large or 8 dozen small.

Haluskhy (Slavic Dumpling)

2 cups flour
2 eggs
1 teaspoon salt
Dash pepper
1/4 cup milk
1 teaspoon baking powder
Kettle of hot water

Combine ingredients, except water, in bowl; mix until sides of bowl are clean. Add bit more flour, if needed. Cut off tiny bits of dough with tip of a teaspoon which has been dipped into the boiling, salted (1 teaspoon salt per quart) water in kettle. Drop bits of dough into boiling water. When bits of dough float to the top, cook 5 minutes more. Drain and use them with any of the following: fried cabbage, onions or process American cheese.

Hungarian Pork Paprika

2 tablespoons flour
1 tablespoon paprika
1/2 teaspoon salt
1/4 teaspoon pepper
1 pound boneless lean pork, cut in 1-inch cubes
4 teaspoons oil
2 (14 1/2-ounce) cans stewed tomatoes
1/2 cup sour cream, room temperature

Combine flour, paprika, salt and pepper. Toss with meat. In skillet, brown meat in hot oil. Stir in tomatoes. Cook, uncovered, over medium heat 20 minutes, or until meat is tender, stirring frequently. Remove pan from heat. Remove 1/2 cup of sauce from skillet and blend with sour cream. Return mixture to skillet; blend well. Do not boil. Serve over hot cooked noodles, potatoes or rice. Serves 4.

Equally as good with top sirloin or bottom round steak.

Sekanina (Easter Meat Loaf)

1 1/2 pounds ground pork
1 1/2 pounds ground veal
1/4 pound margarine
Salt to taste
Garlic to taste
2 cups fresh bread crumbs
1 bunch green onions, minced
1 dozen eggs, slightly beaten
Pepper to taste
1/2 cup chives chopped

Boil pork and veal together for 30 minutes. Drain. Add bread crumbs and minced green onions (tops and bottoms); mix well. Add eggs, margarine (at room temperature); season to taste with salt, pepper and garlic. Add 1/2 cup chopped chives. Mix thoroughly. Place in shallow pan; sprinkle with garlic salt, and bake at 350 degrees for 1 1/4 hours.

Both of my parents were born in Czechoslovakia, and I was raised on Bohemian cooking. The Easter meat loaf we serve is called Sekanina.

Quicke Brunelle (Belgium)

1 cup sifted all-purpose flour
1/2 teaspoon salt
1/3 cup cold butter
3 tablespoons cold water
1 (10-ounce) package frozen brussels sprouts, thawed and coarsely chopped
1/2 pound sliced bacon, cooked, drained and crumbled
1/2 pound grated Swiss cheese
2 eggs, beaten
1 cup heavy cream
Salt and pepper to taste
Paprika (optional garnish)

Sift flour and 1/2 teaspoon salt; cut in butter with pastry blender (or 2 knives) until evenly mixed. Add water gradually, tossing until evenly distributed. Press pastry into a ball; roll out between waxed paper to 1/8-inch thickness to fit a 9-inch pie plate. Line pie plate with pastry and flute outside edge. Arrange brussels sprouts, bacon and cheese in alternating layers in pastry.

Combine eggs and cream with salt and pepper to taste. Pour over brussels sprouts, bacon and cheese layers. Sprinkle with paprika if desired. Bake at 325 degrees for 45 minutes, or until filling is firm. Serves 6.

Little Baskets (Kosarkak)

2/3 cup butter
1 cup sifted flour
10 eggs, separated
1 cup sugar
1 1/3 cups ground *or* crushed nuts
2/3 cup chocolate bits

Combine butter and flour; blend in egg yolks. Separate mixture into nut-size portions and chill for several hours. Shape each portion into a ball. Roll thin and fit into very small buttered pie tins or shallow custard cups. Beat egg whites until stiff and fold in sugar, nuts and chocolate. Fill pastry-lined tins with mixture. Bake at 350 degrees for 20 minutes, or until golden brown. Serves 12–15.

Sauerbraten Meatballs

1 pound lean ground round
3/4 cup soft coarse bread crumbs
1/4 cup minced onion
Freshly ground black pepper, to taste
7 tablespoons lemon juice
2 tablespoons water
2 tablespoons margarine
2 1/2 cups beef broth
1/4 cup brown sugar
3/4 cup gingersnap crumbs
Poppy seed

Combine meat, bread crumbs, onion, pepper, water and 3 tablespoons of the lemon juice. Mix well and form into 1-inch balls.

Heat margarine in a skillet and brown meatballs. Remove from pan. To the drippings in the pan, add broth and remaining lemon juice. Bring to a boil; stir in sugar and gingersnap crumbs. Add meatballs to sauce and simmer, covered, for 10 minutes.

Stir and cook, uncovered, for 5 minutes longer. Serve over noodles and sprinkle with poppy seed. Serves 6.

Borscht

3 potatoes, cut in cubes
3 carrots, sliced
1 small onion, chopped
1/2 cup peas
1/2 cup green beans
1/2 cup beets, cut in cubes
Beet tops
1 tablespoon rice
Fresh dill and salt to taste
1 1/2 cups sour cream
3 eggs, hard-cooked

Place vegetables and rice in a large soup pot with a tight-fitting lid. Add enough water to cover top of vegetables. Add salt and dill. Cook slowly until rice and vegetables are tender. Add 1 1/2 cups sour cream. Heat a few minutes longer; add diced, hard-cooked eggs just before serving. You may need to add more water during the cooking process. Slow cooking helps bring out the flavors and keeps broth from boiling away.

New England Anadama Bread

3/4 cup boiling water
1/2 cup yellow cornmeal
3 tablespoons shortening
1/4 cup molasses
2 teaspoons salt
1 package yeast
1/4 cup warm water (105–115 degrees)
1 egg, beaten
2 3/4 cups flour

Stir together water, cornmeal, shortening, molasses and salt. Cool to lukewarm and add yeast dissolved in water; add egg. Add half of flour; when blended add other half. Knead about 5 minutes. Spread in a greased 9 x 5-inch loaf pan, patting in shape with floured hands. Let rise 1 1/2 hours. Bake in 375-degree oven for 50 minutes. Cover with aluminum foil after 20 minutes of baking time, then bake 30 more minutes. Cool on rack 10 minutes; remove bread from pan.

Sopaipillas

2 cups flour
1 1/2 teaspoons salt
1/2 teaspoon baking powder
1 1/2 teaspoons sugar
1 1/2 teaspoons shortening
1/8 cup warm water
1 tablespoon evaporated milk
Shortening for frying

Combine flour, salt, baking powder and sugar. Cut in 1 1/2 teaspoons shortening. Add water and milk to make dough. Divide dough into 12 balls. Roll each to 1/4-inch thickness; cut in half and fry in melted shortening at 450 degrees. Puffy sopaipillas are light, delicious fried dough triangles you find in New Mexico. Makes 24.

Caribbean Rice & Beans

3 1/2 cups coconut milk, canned
2 cups cooked coarsely choppedham
1 fresh hot pepper, seeded and chopped
2 cloves garlic, minced
3 slices bacon, coarsely chopped
3 tomatoes, peeled, seeded and chopped
1 tablespoon choppedfresh cilantro,
Salt and pepper to taste
2 cups long-grain rice
1 1/2 cups cooked kidney beans

In a saucepan combine 1/2 cup coconut milk, ham, hot pepper, garlic, bacon, tomatoes, cilantro, salt and pepper. Cook, stirring over low heat for 3–4 minutes, or until mixture is well-blended. Stir in rice, beans and remaining 3 cups coconut milk. Stir gently; cover and cook over low heat until rice is tender and liquid is absorbed.

Potato Dressing for Poultry (Kartoffel Spiess)

1 medium onion, diced
Giblets from poultry
1 tablespoon butter
4 cups mashed potatoes
2 teaspoons cloves
1 teaspoon salt

Brown diced onion and chopped giblets in butter; add to mashed potatoes. Add cloves and salt. Put into poultry and sew closed. Bake according to type of poultry used.

Crullers (Omaretti)

2 cups sifted flour
1/4 teaspoon salt
3 teaspoons baking powder
1/2 teaspoon mace
2 eggs
1/2 cup sugar
1 tablespoon vegetable oil
1/3 cup milk
Additional fat
Confectioners' sugar

Sift together the flour, salt, baking powder and mace. Beat eggs, sugar and oil until thick; stir in milk. Add flour mixture; beat until very smooth. Cover with towel; let stand 15 minutes. Heat additional fat to 370 degrees. Drop batter into it from tablespoon, a few at a time. Fry until browned, about 4 minutes. Remove with a slotted spoon; drain. Sprinkle with sugar, if desired. Makes 3 dozen.

Relishes & PRESERVES

Pumpkin Pickles

- **2 quarts raw pumpkin, cut into 1½–2-inch squares (skin and seeds removed)**
- **2 cups sugar**
- **1 cup water**
- **1 cup white vinegar**
- **½ cup cider vinegar**
- **2 cloves**
- **1 (3-inch) cinnamon stick, or to taste**

Place all ingredients, except pumpkin, in a 4-quart saucepan; bring to boil. Add pumpkin and boil until pumpkin becomes translucent. Refrigerate 48 hours. For a milder taste, remove seasonings after about 72 hours. If refrigerated, these pickles keep for 2–3 months.

Jalapeño Jam

- **1 cup chopped green bell pepper**
- **1 cup chopped jalapeño peppers**
- **1½ cups cider vinegar**
- **6 cups sugar**
- **½ teaspoon salt**
- **1 teaspoon cayenne pepper**
- **½ (6-ounce) bottle of pectin**
- **Several drops green food coloring**

Combine green pepper, jalapeño peppers and cider vinegar, half at a time, in blender. Purée until smooth. Combine purée, sugar, salt and cayenne pepper in saucepan. Bring to a boil. Cook for 2 minutes. Remove from heat. Add pectin.

Let stand for 5 minutes, stirring constantly. Add food coloring; mix well. Pour into hot sterilized jars, leaving ½-inch headspace; seal. Store in refrigerator. Makes 2 pints.

Dilled Okra

- **3 pounds okra, stems on**
- **Celery leaves**
- **6 cloves garlic**
- **6 large heads of dill and stems**
- **1 quart water**
- **2 cups cider vinegar**
- **½ cup canning salt**

Pack scrubbed okra into 6 sterilized pint canning jars. Into each jar put 1 garlic clove, 1 head, plus stem of fresh dill (or 2 tablespoons dill seed) and 3–4 celery leaves.

Make a brine of water, salt and vinegar; bring to a boil. Pour hot brine over okra, filling within ½ inch of top of jar. Seal and process in boiling-water bath for 5 minutes. Allow to age 1 month before opening.

Vidalia Onion Relish

- **10 cups chopped Vidalia onions**
- **2 large bell peppers, chopped**
- **1 hot pepper, chopped (optional)**
- **½ cup salt**
- **3 cups sugar**
- **3 cups cider vinegar**
- **2 teaspoons mustard seed**
- **2 teaspoons celery seed**
- **1 teaspoon turmeric**

Cover onions and peppers with ½ cup salt in ice water for 1 hour. Rinse and drain. Mix remaining ingredients in large pan and bring to a boil; add onions and pepper. Boil for 10 minutes. Pack in jars and process in water bath.

Short-Cut Chili Sauce

- **3 quarts peeled and chopped tomatoes**
- **3 cups chopped celery**
- **2 cups chopped onions**
- **1 cup chopped green pepper**
- **¼ cup salt**
- **2 cups granulated sugar**
- **¼ cup brown sugar**
- **1 teaspoon black pepper**
- **1½ teaspoons mixed pickling spices (tied in cheesecloth)**
- **1 cup white vinegar**

Combine tomatoes, celery, onions, green pepper and salt. Let stand overnight. Next day, drain in colander. *Do not press vegetables.* Place vegetable mixture in a large kettle and add granulated sugar, brown sugar, pepper and vinegar; add pickling spices tied in cheesecloth.

Bring to boil; reduce heat and simmer, uncovered, for 15 minutes. Place in hot jars; seal. Cold-pack for 10 minutes. Makes 5 pints.

Apple Jelly

- **2 teaspoons unflavored gelatin**
- **2 cups unsweetened apple juice**
- **1 cup sugar**
- **1½ tablespoons lemon juice**

Soften gelatin in ½ cup of the apple juice. Bring remaining 1½ cups juice to a boil. Remove from heat. Add softened gelatin, stirring to dissolve. Add sugar and lemon juice. Bring to a rolling boil. Ladle into clear half-pint jars and seal. Keep in refrigerator. Makes 2 half pints.

Salsa

6 pounds firm, ripe tomatoes (about 12)
1 pound onions (about 2)
1 pound green peppers (about 2)
1½ cups distilled white vinegar
1 large red pepper
1 tablespoon plus 1 teaspoon salt
2 teaspoons dry mustard powder
2 teaspoons granulated sugar *or* sugar substitute
2 teaspoons chili powder
1 teaspoon garlic powder
¾ teaspoon ground cumin
½ teaspoon ground black pepper
⅛ teaspoon crushed red pepper flakes

Peel, chop and seed tomatoes; allow to drain in a colander. Meanwhile, chop onions and peppers. In large pot over high heat, combine all ingredients; bring to a boil. Reduce heat to medium and cook, stirring occasionally for 45 minutes to 1 hour, or until very thick. Near end of cooking time, stir frequently to prevent sticking.

Spoon into hot sterilized jars, allowing ¼-inch headspace. Wipe rims with clean cloth dipped in hot water. Close according to jar manufacturer's instructions and process in boiling-water bath for 20 minutes. Makes 4 (8-ounce) jars.

Chili Sauce

4 quarts tomatoes (16 cups) chopped and peeled
2 cups chopped onions
1 cup chopped sweet red pepper
1 cup chopped green pepper
1 small hot red pepper
3 tablespoons salt
½ cup sugar
1 tablespoon white mustard seed
1 teaspoon cinnamon
1 teaspoon allspice
2½ cups vinegar

Combine vegetables, salt and sugar; cook until mixture begins to thicken. Add vinegar and spices in a bag; cook until mixture becomes a thick sauce. Pour into hot jars and seal immediately. Process 25 minutes. Remove carefully and cool. Store in dark place.

Hint: After vegetables have started cooking, mash down with potato masher. Add spice bag and cook until mixture starts thickening. Mash again. Pour off any liquid remaining after mashing vegetables. Add vinegar and cook mixture until thickened, stirring often. Taste! Remove spice bag and put in jars.

Green Tomato Relish

6 quarts (about 36–40 medium) green tomatoes, chopped
¼ cup salt
1½ quarts chopped onion
3 cups chopped green pepper
1½ cups chopped red sweet pepper
3 cups sugar
1½ quarts vinegar
2 tablespoons whole mixed pickling spices

Mix tomatoes and salt thoroughly. Let stand overnight; drain. In a large cooking pot, combine tomatoes with chopped onions, green and red peppers, sugar and vinegar. Put spices loosely in a thin, white cloth; tie top tightly and add to tomato mixture.

Bring mixture to a boil; boil gently with spices for 1½ hours, or until thickened, stirring frequently. Remove spice bag. Pour relish into hot, sterilized jars and seal with sterilized lids. Place in a boiling-water bath for 10 minutes. Remove and cool on rack. Store in a cool, dry, dark place. Makes about 6 pints.

Apple Butter

34 cups cored, sliced apples
1 cup vinegar
8 cups sugar
4 teaspoons cinnamon
1 teaspoon mace
1 teaspoon ground cloves

Do not peel. Add enough water to cook apples until soft. Press through sieve to make thick pulp; measure 16 cups. Add all ingredients and cook 1½ hours on low heat, stirring frequently to prevent scorching. Pour into sterilized jars. Seal while hot.

Zucchini Relish

10 cups ground zucchini, unpeeled
4 cups ground onions
2 cups ground cucumbers
1 green pepper, diced
1 ripe red pepper, diced
5 tablespoons salt
2¼ cups vinegar
4 cups sugar
1 teaspoon celery seed
1 teaspoon turmeric
1 teaspoon nutmeg
1 tablespoon cornstarch

Grind zucchini, onion, and cucumbers in blender or food processor. Start process with 1 cup water and equal portions of vegetables. In bowl combine ground vegetables and diced peppers. Sprinkle with salt and let stand 3 hours. Rinse and drain in cheesecloth bag.

In large kettle combine ground vegetable mixture with remaining ingredients. Cook slowly about 30 minutes until mixture is clear. Seal in hot jars at once. Makes 6 pints.

Beet Relish

1 quart diced, cooked beets (canned may be used)
1 quart diced, raw cabbage
1½ cups sugar
1 tablespoon salt
⅔ cup beet juice
⅓ cup vinegar
½ bottle horseradish *or*
1 (5-ounce) jar cream-style horseradish

Combine all ingredients and mix well. Make several days ahead and let stand in covered jar in refrigerator in order for flavors to blend—nice to take as gifts.

Tomato Butter

4 quarts stewed tomatoes
7 cups light brown sugar
1 tablespoon ground cloves
1 tablespoon cinnamon
1 teaspoon allspice

Combine ingredients and cook very slowly until thickened. Pour into hot jars and seal while hot.

Italian Peppers

2 gallons very hot peppers
2 (14-ounce) bottles ketchup
1 pint cider vinegar
1 cup granulated sugar
1 cup cooking oil
1 tablespoon salt

Cut caps from peppers and place in blender to chop coarsely (be sure to leave seeds in peppers). Mix remaining ingredients and heat to boil, stirring constantly; add peppers. Mix well; return to a boiling. Remove from heat; pack into sterilized jars and process open-kettle method for 25 minutes.

Note: These peppers are chunky and are like picanté sauce.

Homemade Blueberry Jam

2½ cups fresh *or* dry-pack frozen blueberries
3 cups sugar
⅓ cup orange juice
1 tablespoon lemon juice
½ bottle (3 ounces) fruit pectin

Wash berries. Crush blueberries in an enamel or stainless steel pan. Add sugar and fruit juices. Mix well. Bring to a full rolling boil. Boil hard 1 minute, stirring constantly. Remove from heat. Stir in pectin. Seal hot sterilized jars. Refrigerate. May be stored for 2 months. Makes 3 cups.

Nina's Rhubarb Marmalade

7 pounds ruby red rhubarb
6 pounds sugar
1 teaspoon salt
1 pound walnuts
2 oranges
1 lemon

Cut rhubarb, lemon and oranges into narrow strips, unpeeled; sprinkle with salt and sugar and let stand overnight in large, covered bowl. The next morning in an enamel or stainless steel kettle, cook over medium-low heat until mixture thickens. Add walnuts. Seal into sterile jars; cool and refrigerate.

Raspberry Rhubarb Jam

2 (10-ounce) packages frozen raspberries, thawed
1 pound rhubarb, cut in 1-inch pieces (4 cups)
5 cups sugar
1 (2½-ounce) package powdered fruit pectin

In Dutch oven, combine fruits. Stir in pectin. Place over high heat, stirring until mixture reaches a hard boil. Immediately stir in sugar. Bring to a full rolling boil and boil hard 1 minute, stirring constantly. Remove from heat. Using a metal spoon, skim off foam; stir and skim for 5 minutes. Quickly stir and ladle into 6 hot, scalded half-pint jars; seal.

Peach Butter

6 pounds fresh peaches
¼ cup fresh lemon juice
1 teaspoon cinnamon
3¼ cups sugar

Peel peaches; cut into fourths. Purée in blender. Combine 11 cups peach purée, lemon juice and cinnamon in large saucepan; mix well. Cook, uncovered, over medium heat for 2 hours, stirring frequently. Add sugar; mix well.

Cook mixture, uncovered, until of desired consistency, stirring frequently. Ladle into hot sterilized jars, leaving ½-inch headspace; seal with 2-piece lids. Process in boiling-water bath for for 10 minutes. May substitute nectarines for peaches. Makes 6 (8-ounce) jars.

Bread & Butter Refrigerator Pickles

3 medium-size cucumbers
1 cup vinegar
1 cup sugar
1 teaspoon salt
1 teaspoon dry mustard

Slice cucumbers ½ inch thick (do not peel). Combine sugar, vinegar, salt and mustard. Place cucumbers in liquid and simmer until transparent. Place in jar and refrigerate. Very tasty on sandwiches.

Vidalia Onion Jelly

4 pounds Vidalia onions, chopped
7½ cups sugar
¼ cup lemon juice
2 packets pectin
2 drops green food coloring
3 drops red food coloring
8 drops yellow food coloring

Place onions in large pan and add 4 cups water. Bring to rolling boil, lower heat and simmer 30 minutes. Remove from heat and strain through clean cloth into container. Measure 3½ cups juice. Place onion juice, lemon juice, sugar and food colorings in large pan.

Place pan over high heat, stirring constantly. Bring to a rolling boil and boil 1 minute. Add pectin; continue stirring; bring back to rolling boil and boil for 1 minute. Remove from heat and skim off foam. Pack into jars and process in hot-water bath.

Tomato Conserve

7 pounds ripe tomatoes, peeled and chunked
3 pounds brown sugar
2 cups apple cider vinegar
4 sticks cinnamon
2 tablespoons whole cloves
Cotton cloth bag

Tie cinnamon and cloves in bag with cotton string. In a large enamel kettle, simmer tomatoes, vinegar and sugar with the spice bag for 1 hour. Remove bag; ladle into hot sterile jars and seal. Cool and then store in cool place. Serve with meat or fish.

Pear Supreme

5 cups pears, chopped *or* ground
1 cup crushed pineapple
1 cup chopped maraschino cherries
½ cup maraschino juice
1 package pectin
5½ cups sugar

Bring ingredients to a hard boil. Add sugar. Cook 4 minutes. Pour into jars and seal.

Sweet & Perfect Green Tomato Pickles

8 quarts green tomatoes (10 pounds)
2 quarts peeled onions
1 cup salt
1 quart vinegar
4 cups sugar
6 tablespoons mixed pickling spices

Wash and cut tomatoes and onions into 1/8-inch slices; place in a bowl; sprinkle with salt. Cover and put on a heavy weight to hold down cover. Let stand overnight; wash and drain tomato mixture 3 times in cold water. Place in kettle; add vinegar and sugar.

Tie spices in cheesecloth bag and add. Simmer, uncovered, until tender, about 5 minutes; remove spice bag. Pour into clean hot jars; seal as directed. Process in water-bath canner for 30 minutes. Makes 6–7 pints.

Mom's Apple Butter

7 pounds apples, cored (need not be peeled)
1 cup cider vinegar
3 pounds brown sugar
2 tablespoons cinnamon

Cook apples until soft; press through a sieve. Add remaining ingredients and put in a roaster. Place in 350-degree oven; bake for 3 1/2 hours. Stir occasionally. Pour into hot jars. Seal at once.

Apple Jelly

5 cups sugar
4 cups apple juice
1 box powdered pectin

Measure sugar and set aside. Measure juice into a Dutch oven and stir in pectin. Quickly bring to a hard boil. Add all sugar and stir. Bring to a full, rolling boil, stirring constantly for 1 minute *(to an altitude of 3,000 feet).

Remove from heat and use a metal spoon to skim off foam. Pour to 1/2 inch from top of sterilized jelly jars. Cap and screw band on firmly. Process in boiling-water bath 5 minutes. Quick and easy jellies can be made from canned fruit juices.

*At altitudes of over 3,000 feet, increase boiling time 30 seconds for each 1,000 feet. My altitude is 7,000 feet and I must boil jelly 3 minutes to get proper consistency.

Excellent Microwave Sweet Pickles

1/2 teaspoon salt
1/4 teaspoon turmeric
1/4 teaspoon mustard seed
1/4 teaspoon celery seed
1/2 cup vinegar
1 cup sugar
2 cucumbers, thinly sliced (unpeeled)
1–2 onions, thinly sliced

In small bowl or measuring pitcher combine salt, turmeric, mustard seed, celery seed, vinegar and sugar. Mix cucumbers and onion in microwavable bowl. Pour vinegar mixture over cucumbers and onions.

Microwave, uncovered, on HIGH power for 5 minutes. Stir well; return to microwave for 5 minutes more. Cool; pour into quart jar and refrigerate. Pickles are ready to eat when thoroughly chilled. Makes 1 quart.

Frozen Peaches

Peaches, peeled and sliced
1 can frozen orange juice concentrate
2 cans water
1/4 cup sugar

Place prepared peaches in freezer boxes or containers. Mix together orange juice, water and sugar. Pour mixture over peaches in containers and freeze.

Note: It is a good idea to use 2 tablespoons of fruit fresh in water when you are slicing peaches, then drain that off before putting in containers. Keeps peaches from turning dark when opened after freezing. Keeps up to 3 years in freezer. These peaches are delicious.

Basic Barbecue Sauce

1 (8-ounce) can tomato sauce
3 tablespoons Worcestershire sauce
1/2 cup vegetable oil
1/4 cup cider vinegar
3 teaspoons mustard powder
3 tablespoons brown sugar
2 teaspoons chili powder
2 teaspoons sugar
1/2 teaspoon garlic powder
2 tablespoons dried, minced onion (*or* 1 1/2 teaspoons onion powder)
1/2 teaspoon salt
1/4 teaspoon black pepper

Combine all ingredients and let stand for at least 10 minutes. Use plain or customize with one of the following variations. Makes 2 1/4 cups.

Tex-Mex Barbecue Sauce

1/2 to 1 tablespoon chili powder
1/4 teaspoon ground cumin
1/4 teaspoon dried oregano
1 cup Basic Barbecue Sauce

Combine all ingredients in a small saucepan. Cook and stir over moderate heat until sauce boils; reduce heat and simmer 15 minutes. Makes 1 cup.

Fruity Barbecue Sauce

1/2 cup orange *or* unsweetened pineapple juice
1 cup Basic Barbecue Sauce
1 tablespoon honey
1/2 teaspoon fresh ginger root, minced
1 tablespoon lime juice
1 teaspoon cornstarch

Combine orange juice, honey, fresh minced gingerroot and barbecue sauce in small saucepan. Blend lime juice and cornstarch until smooth; add to sauce. Cook and stir over moderate heat to thicken; reduce heat and simmer 10 minutes. Makes 1 1/2 cups.

Meat
DISHES

Frankfurter Beef Loaf

- 2 pounds ground beef
- 4 medium-size frankfurters
- 1 cup bread crumbs
- 1 tablespoon chopped parsley
- 1 small onion, grated
- 1 egg, beaten
- 1 teaspoon salt (or less)
- 1/4 teaspoon pepper
- 4 slices bacon

Combine ground beef and bread crumbs. Season with grated onion, chopped parsley, salt and pepper. Moisten with beaten egg and shape into a loaf like any other meat loaf, but with the frankfurters first positioned lengthwise in the center. Press in pan and cover with divided ground beef mixture. Put bacon on top and bake in moderate oven at 350 degrees for 1 hour.

Invert pan and let fat drain. Turn loaf over and slice in 1-inch slices. Each slice will have a round of frankfurter through the center. This is a delicious meat dish; you may want to serve it with baked potatoes and buttered carrots, which may be cooked in the oven at the same time.

Veal-Rice Hot Dish

- 1 pound veal, cut in small cubes
- 1 large onion, finely chopped
- 1 cup celery, finely chopped
- 1/4 pound butter
- Cooked rice

Brown veal thoroughly in butter over medium heat; add onion and celery. Simmer until partially cooked. This dish is easy and quick to make!

Spicy New Orleans Chicken

- 1/2 cup onion, diced
- 1/2 cup celery, diced
- 1/2 cup margarine
- 3 pounds chicken pieces
- 2 tablespoons parsley
- 1 teaspoon thyme
- 1 bay leaf
- 1 garlic clove, minced
- 1 cup water

Sauté onion and celery in margarine. Add chicken pieces and brown lightly. Stir in seasonings and water, bringing to boil. Cover and simmer for about 1 hour.

Blue-Cheese Burgers

- 3/4 pound ground round steak
- 3/4 cup (3 ounces) crumbled blue cheese
- 2/3 cup soft bread crumbs
- 1/4 cup finely chopped green onion
- 2 tablespoons chopped cilantro
- 1 tablespoon chili sauce
- 1 1/2 teaspoons Dijon-style prepared mustard
- 1/8 teaspoon pepper

Combine all ingredients; mix well. Shape into 4 burgers*. Broil burgers 3 inches from heat source to desired degree of doneness. (5 minutes per side for medium.) Serve immediately. Serves 4.

*May be refrigerated up to 4 hours at this point.

Turkey Meat Loaf

- 1 pound ground turkey
- 1 cup bread crumbs
- 3 egg whites
- 2 medium tomatoes, finely chopped
- 1/4 cup green pepper, finely chopped
- 1/2 teaspoon horseradish
- 1/4 to 1/2 teaspoon salt (optional)
- 1 medium onion, finely chopped
- 1/4 to 1/2 teaspoon pepper (to taste)

Preheat oven to 375 degrees. Combine all ingredients and press into a 9 x 5-inch loaf pan. Bake 50–60 minutes. (Can be microwaved in covered glass pan for 15 minutes on MEDIUM-HIGH, then 5 minutes on HIGH.) Serves 6.

Dill-Sauced Meat Loaf

- 1 1/2 pounds ground beef
- 1/2 cup chopped onion
- 1/2 cup soft bread crumbs
- 1/2 cup dill pickle juice
- 1 egg
- 1 teaspoon salt
- 1/2 teaspoon pepper
- 1 cup ketchup
- 1/2 cup water
- 4 tablespoons sugar
- 2 teaspoons Worcestershire sauce
- 1 cup chopped dill pickle

Combine first 7 ingredients. Shape into a loaf and place in shallow baking dish. Combine remaining ingredients and pour over meat. Bake at 350 degrees for 1 1/4–1 1/2 hours, basting twice. Serves 6.

Tuna-Cheese Casserole

Chopped dill pickle adds zest.

- **2 tablespoons margarine**
- **10 saltine cracker squares (2/3 cup coarsely crushed crumbs)**
- **1 egg**
- **2 tablespoons milk**
- **1 cup coarsely grated cheddar cheese**
- **2 tablespoons chopped dill pickle**
- **1 (6–7-ounce) can tuna**

Preheat oven to 350 degrees.

Grease or spray with pan release a 7- or 8-inch pie plate.

In a small saucepan melt margarine. Crush crackers, a few at a time, in hand, to coarsely crush; add to margarine, toss to mix well; set aside.

In a medium bowl whisk egg to blend; whisk in milk. Grate in cheese. Chop and add pickle; add half of cracker crumbs.

Drain tuna (to do this wash top of can; open can but do not remove lid; press lid firmly against tuna while holding can upside down over sink). With fork flake tuna into egg mixture. Toss lightly to mix. Turn into prepared dish; sprinkle on remaining crumbs. Bake until heated through and crumbs begin to brown, about 20 minutes. Serves 2.

Lemony Stuffed Fish Fillets

- **2 pounds fresh *or* frozen fillets**
- **2 tablespoons butter *or* margarine**
- **1/4 cup *each* chopped onion, green pepper and celery**
- **2 cups bread cubes**
- **1 teaspoon grated lemon rind**
- **1 tablespoon lemon juice**
- **Dash salt and pepper**
- **1 teaspoon parsley flakes**
- **1 tablespoon butter, melted**
- **Snipped chives**
- **Parsley (garnish)**
- **Lemon slices (garnish)**

Arrange half the fillets in a greased casserole. Sauté onion, green pepper and celery in butter until tender. Stir in next 6 ingredients. Toss well.

Spoon stuffing over fillets; top with remaining fillets. Brush fillets with melted butter. Sprinkle with chives. Cover and bake at 450 degrees, allowing 10 minutes cooking time for each inch of thickness of fish. Uncover during last 5–7 minutes of baking time.

Cut through all layers into squares or pieces to serve. Garnish with parsley and lemon slices. Serves 6.

Hawaiian Fillets

- **1/4 cup brown sugar, packed**
- **1 tablespoon cornstarch**
- **1 (8-ounce) can pineapple chunks, packed in juice**
- **1/2 green pepper, cut into strips**
- **1/4 cup vinegar**
- **1 tablespoon soy sauce**
- **1 teaspoon snipped chives**
- **Dash garlic powder**
- **1 pound fresh skinless mahimahi, bluefish, perch or sole (1/2-inch thick)**
- **1/4 cup sliced almonds, toasted**

For sauce, combine sugar and cornstarch in a 1-quart microwave-safe dish. Drain pineapple, reserving juice. Stir juice into sugar. Stir in pepper, vinegar, soy sauce, chives and garlic powder. Microwave, uncovered, on HIGH for 2 1/2–4 1/2 minutes, or until bubbly; stir each minute. Cook 30 seconds more. Stir in pineapple chunks. Cover and keep warm.

Cut fish into 4 portions. Place in a 12 x 7 1/2 x 2-inch microwave-safe dish. Cover and cook on HIGH for 4–7 minutes, or until fish flakes. Turn dish after 4 minutes. Place fish on serving platter; spoon sauce over top and sprinkle with almonds. Serves 4.

Sloppy Joes

- **1 pound ground beef**
- **1 onion, chopped**
- **1 cup ketchup**
- **1 tablespoon sugar**
- **1 tablespoon vinegar**
- **1 tablespoon mustard**

Brown together ground beef and onions. Pour off fat and add remaining ingredients. Simmer 20 minutes. Spread on hamburger buns.

Cajun Shrimp

- **1/4 cup butter**
- **2 tablespoons flour (if frozen shrimp, use 3 tablespoons)**
- **1/2 cup green pepper, chopped**
- **3/4 cup chicken broth**
- **1 pound shrimp, uncooked, shelled and deveined**
- **1/2 cup celery, chopped**
- **1 tablespoon minced onion**
- **1/4 teaspoon garlic powder**
- **1/8 teaspoon coarse-ground black pepper**
- **1/8 teaspoon cayenne pepper**
- **Cooked rice**
- **Salt to taste**

Melt butter in medium-size skillet; add flour; cook and stir until bubbly. Add green pepper and celery. Cook, stirring constantly, for 5 minutes over medium heat. Remove from heat. Gradually add broth, stirring to blend. Add shrimp, minced onion, garlic powder, black pepper and cayenne pepper. Add salt to taste.Simmer, uncovered, for 10 minutes. Serve over rice. Serves 4.

Augustine Fish Fillets

- **2 tablespoons corn oil**
- **1 medium onion, chopped**
- **1/2 cup chopped pepper**
- **1 clove garlic, minced**
- **1/2 cup dry white wine**
- **3/4 pound white fish fillets**
- **1 large tomato, chopped**
- **2 tablespoons chopped pitted olives**
- **Dash of salt *or* hot pepper sauce**
- **2 tablespoons crumbled feta cheese**

In large skillet heat oil over medium heat. Add onion, pepper and garlic; sauté 3 minutes. Add wine; bring to boil. Push vegetables to the side and arrange fillets in center of skillet. Cover; cook 5 minutes.

Add tomato, olives and a dash or 2 of salt or hot pepper sauce if you desire. Sprinkle cheese over fish. Cover. Cook 3 minutes longer, or until fish is firm, but moist, and cheese is melted. Transfer fish to serving platter; top with vegetables and pan juices. Serves 4.

Savory Pepper Steak

- 1½ pounds round steak, cut in ½-inch-thick strips
- ¼ cup all-purpose flour
- ½ teaspoon salt
- ⅛ teaspoon pepper
- 1 (8-ounce) can tomatoes
- 1¾ cups water
- ½ cup chopped onion
- 1 small clove garlic, minced
- 1 tablespoon beef-flavored gravy mix
- 1½ teaspoons Worcestershire sauce
- 2 large green peppers

Coat beef strips with mixture of flour, salt and pepper. Brown meat in scant amount of hot grease. Drain tomatoes, reserving liquid. Add reserved liquid, water, chopped onion, garlic and gravy mix to meat. Cover; simmer until meat is tender, about 1¼ hours. Uncover; stir in Worcestershire sauce and green peppers (cut into strips). Simmer for 5 minutes.

If sauce is too thin, combine 1–2 tablespoons flour with an equal amount of cold water; stir into sauce. Cook and stir until thickened and bubbly. Add drained tomatoes (cut up); cook 5 minutes more. Serve over hot cooked rice. Serves 6.

Shrimp Crabcakes

- 1 pound crabmeat
- ¾ pound cooked shrimp, shelled and deveined
- 1 egg
- ¾ cup evaporated milk
- Salt and pepper to taste
- ½ cup minced scallions
- 1 tablespoon Dijon-style mustard
- ¼ teaspoon hot pepper sauce
- 1 teaspoon Worcestershire sauce
- ½ cup vegetable oil

Remove cartilage and shells from crabmeat, leaving lumps as large as possible. Place shrimp in processor or blender; add egg, milk, salt and pepper; purée as smooth as possible. Scrape sides of blender and transfer purée to mixing bowl.

Add crabmeat, scallions, mustard, hot pepper sauce and Worcestershire sauce. Stir gently but thoroughly to blend. Shape mixture into 10 cakes; sauté in 2 tablespoons of oil in a non-stick skillet for 3 minutes on each side. Serve with parsley butter. Serves 5.

Lamb & Pears

- 3 pounds boneless lamb, cut into bite-size pieces
- 2 tablespoons margarine
- 2 tablespoons vegetable oil
- 2 (1-pound) cans pear halves, sliced
- 3 tablespoons cider vinegar
- 1 tablespoon Worcestershire sauce
- 3 tablespoons brown sugar
- 3 teaspoons chopped green pepper
- 3 tablespoons cornstarch mixed with 1 tablespoon cold water
- 6 green onions, chopped
- 3–4 celery ribs, sliced
- ½ teaspoon ground nutmeg

Preheat oven to 350 degrees. In skillet brown lamb in margarine and oil. Place lamb in oven-proof casserole.

Drain pears, reserving liquid. In skillet, combine pear liquid, vinegar, brown sugar, sauce, cornstarch mixture and nutmeg. Cook over high heat, stirring constantly until thickened. Pour sauce over lamb and bake at 350 degrees for 1½ hours. Add green onion, celery, pepper and pears during final 15 minutes of cooking.

Pear Sausage Stuffing

- ½ pound ground pork sausage
- ¾ cup chopped celery
- ⅓ cup chopped onion
- ½ cup margarine
- 4 cups whole-wheat bread cubes
- 1 cup diced pears
- ½ teaspoon thyme, crushed
- ⅓ cup chicken broth *or* hot water

Brown sausage and drain. Remove from skillet. Sauté celery and onion in margarine for 6 minutes. Stir in sausage, bread, pears and thyme. Add broth or water; mix well. Place in greased 1-quart baking dish and bake, covered, at 350 degrees for 30 minutes. Makes 5 cups.

Pork & Pears

- 3 pork chops, ½-inch thick
- 1 tablespoon margarine
- ⅔ cup orange juice
- 2 tablespoons seedless (dark) raisins
- ½ teaspoon dry mustard
- ⅛ teaspoon allspice
- 1 (16-ounce) can pear halves, sliced and drained

Cook pork chops in margarine for 5 minutes, or until tender and lightly browned, turning once. Remove from skillet and keep warm. Add to the drippings in skillet orange juice, mustard and allspice, stirring to loosen brown goodies in bottom of skillet. Cook, stirring constantly. When sauce boils and thickens slightly, add pears and raisins. Pour sauce over pork chops.

Italian Meat Loaf

- 2 eggs, beaten
- ¾ cup bread *or* cracker crumbs
- ½ cup tomato juice
- 2 tablespoons parsley
- ½ teaspoon oregano
- ¼ teaspoon salt
- ¼ teaspoon pepper
- ½ teaspoon garlic powder
- 2 pounds ground beef
- 4 ham slices
- ½ cup mozzarella cheese, grated

Mix all ingredients, except ham and cheese, in a bowl. Line jelly roll pan with aluminum foil. Pat hamburger mixture onto foil. Layer sliced ham and half the cheese over hamburger. Roll up jelly roll fashion, using the foil to push roll. Remove foil from pan. Bake 45 minutes at 350 degrees. Sprinkle remaining mozzarella cheese on top and bake another 20 minutes.

Healthy Jo's (Healthy Exchange Version)

- 16 ounces ground turkey *or* beef (90 percent lean)
- 1 cup tomato sauce
- ½ cup chunky salsa
- Brown sugar substitute to equal 1 tablespoon

In large skillet sprayed with olive-flavored cooking spray, brown meat until done. Add tomato sauce, salsa and brown sugar replacement. Lower heat and simmer 15–20 minutes. Good served on 1 ounce (80 calories) hamburger buns. Serves 6 (⅓ cup each).

Seashore Clam & Shrimp Shells

- 1 (8-ounce) package small pasta shells, cooked and drained
- 2 tablespoons butter *or* margarine
- 1½ tablespoons olive oil
- ½ green bell pepper, seeded and sliced
- ½ red bell pepper, seeded and sliced
- 2 cloves garlic, minced
- 6 ounces small shrimp, cooked
- 12 ounces fresh clams, drained (reserve juice)
- 4 eggs, lightly beaten
- ¾ cup grated Romano cheese
- ⅓ cup chopped fresh parsley
- Salt and pepper to taste

In sauté pan heat butter and olive oil; add peppers and garlic; cook until peppers are tender.

Add cooked shells, shrimp and clams; heat thoroughly. Combine clam juice and beaten eggs; pour over shell mixture; toss. Add cheese, parsley, salt and pepper. Serves 4.

Wine-Braised Pork Chops

- 4 center-cut pork chops, very lean, 1 inch thick (approximately 12 ounces)
- 1 teaspoon crumbled dried sage leaves
- 1 teaspoon crumbled dried rosemary leaves
- 1 teaspoon finely chopped garlic
- Freshly ground pepper to taste
- 2 tablespoons margarine
- 1 tablespoon olive oil
- ¾ cup dry white wine, divided
- 1 tablespoon finely chopped parsley

Trim all fat from pork chops. Combine sage, rosemary, garlic and pepper. Press a little mixture firmly into both sides of each pork chop. In heavy 10–12-inch skillet, melt margarine with olive oil over moderate heat. When foam subsides, place chops in hot fat. Brown chops for 2–3 minutes on each side, turning carefully with tongs. When chops are golden brown, remove to a platter.

Pour off all but a thin film of fat from pan. Add ½ cup wine. Bring to a boil. Return chops to pan. Cover; reduce heat to low. Simmer chops, basting occasionally with pan juices, for 25–30 minutes, or until they are tender when tested with the tip of a sharp knife.

Transfer chops to heated serving platter. Add remaining ¼ cup wine to skillet. Boil briskly over high heat, stirring and scraping to loosen any browned bits. Continue cooking, uncovered, until liquid is reduced to a few tablespoons of syrupy glaze. Taste for seasonings and add parsley. Pour over pork chops and serve. Serves 4.

Beefsteak With Pizza Sauce

- 1 pound chuck steak, cut 1–1¼ inches thick
- 1 (28-ounce) can Italian plum tomatoes, crushed and undrained
- ¼ teaspoon oregano
- ¼ teaspoon basil
- ¼ teaspoon rosemary, crushed
- ¼ teaspoon marjoram
- ½ clove garlic, minced
- ½ tablespoon onion, minced
- Salt and pepper to taste
- 1 tablespoon olive oil
- 1 cup mozzarella cheese, grated

Arrange steak in a 10 x 6 x 2-inch baking dish. Spread tomatoes, all spices and oil over steak. Bake, uncovered, for 1¾ hours until tender. Remove from oven; place on a warmed platter; sprinkle mozzarella cheese over hot steak. Serves 3.

Mariner's Tuna Supreme

- 2 (10-ounce) packages frozen spinach, thawed
- 1 (10-ounce) can condensed cream of potato soup
- 2 (6½-ounce) cans tuna
- ¾ cup milk
- ¼ teaspoon nutmeg
- ⅛ teaspoon liquid hot sauce
- 4 tablespoons grated Romano *or* Parmesan cheese
- 1 cup soft bread crumbs
- 2 tablespoons butter, melted

Combine first 6 ingredients; place in an ovenproof casserole. Mix cheese and bread crumbs; sprinkle over casserole. Pour melted butter over all. Bake at 350 degrees until golden and bubbly. Serves 4.

Smoked Salmon Mousse

- ½ pound smoked salmon
- ½ pound cream cheese
- ⅓ cup chopped green onion
- ¼ cup finely chopped fresh dill
- Juice of ½ lemon
- Ground pepper to taste
- ½ teaspoon ground cumin
- Hot pepper sauce to taste
- 2 tablespoons white wine

Combine all ingredients in a food processor or blender. Blend to a fine purée. Spoon into a serving dish. Chill. Serve cool (not cold) with buttered toast, melba toast, crackers, chopped onion, drained capers and sliced cucumbers. Flavor improves when chilled overnight to allow flavors to blend. Let stand at room temperature to "warm up" before serving. Very quick and elegant. Great for drop-in company or a hostess gift.

Elegant Creamed Chicken

- 1 tablespoon butter
- 1 tablespoon flour
- ⅛ teaspoon salt
- ½ cup half-and-half
- ½ cup chicken broth
- Few shreds lemon peel
- 1 teaspoon lemon juice
- 1 egg yolk
- 1 to 1½ cups cooked chicken chunks
- 2 baked puff pastry patty shells

In medium saucepan melt butter. Whisk in flour; cook over medium heat 1 minute. Add salt; whisk in half-and-half and chicken broth, then lemon peel and juice. Whisk until boiling; reduce heat; simmer 1 minute.

In small bowl whisk egg yolk; whisk in about half hot sauce. Return to pan whisking egg mixture into remaining sauce. Cook over low heat, stirring gently with rubber spatula, until thickened slightly, about 2 minutes. (If made ahead, cool; cover; refrigerate. Reheat carefully so egg yolk does not curdle.) Add chicken; stir over low heat until warm. Serve over warm patty shells. Serves 2.

Glazed Pork Chops

4 (1-inch thick) loin pork chops
Salt and pepper
2 tablespoons (1/4 stick) butter
All-purpose flour
1/4 cup cider vinegar
6 tablespoons maple syrup
10 tablespoon dark brown sugar

Preheat oven to 450 degrees. Pat pork chops dry. Season meat with salt and pepper. Melt butter in large heavy skillet over high heat. Dredge chops in flour, shaking off excess. Add to skillet and cook until brown, about 4 minutes per side. Transfer to roasting pan. (Do not wash skillet.) Bake chops until thermometer inserted in thickest part registers 145 degrees, about 20 minutes.

Preheat broiler. Pour off drippings from skillet. Add vinegar to skillet and bring to a boil, scraping up any brown bits. Add maple syrup. Reduce heat to low. Cover and cook 10 minutes. Meanwhile, transfer chops to broiler pan. Pack 1 tablespoon brown sugar evenly on top of each. Broil pork until sugar is dark brown and glazed, turning pan to brown evenly, about 1 minute. Serve, passing sauce separately. Serves 4.

Pork Chops & Scalloped Potatoes

4 pork chops (cut 3/4 inch thick)
2 tablespoons oil
1 large onion, sliced and separated into rings
3 tablespoons butter *or* margarine
3 tablespoons flour
1 teaspoon salt
1/4 teaspoon pepper
1 cup milk
1 cup chicken broth
4 medium potatoes, peeled and thinly sliced
1 tablespoons chopped fresh parsley

Brown chops in oil about 3 minutes on each side; remove. Add onion rings to fat remaining in skillet. Sauté until tender. Remove from heat; reserve. Melt butter in medium saucepan. Stir in flour, salt and pepper. Cook 1 minute. Add milk and broth slowly. Cook, stirring constantly, until sauce thickens. Remove from heat.

Arrange sliced potatoes in buttered 11 x 7 x 2-inch baking dish. Top with reserved onion rings. Pour sauce evenly over potatoes and onions. Top with chops. Cover baking dish tightly with foil. Bake at 350 degrees for 1 hour. Uncover and bake 10 minutes longer. Sprinkle with parsley. Serves 4.

Ham Loaf

1 pound ground uncooked ham
1 pound ground fresh pork
2 eggs, beaten
1 1/2 cups Wheaties cereal
1/2 cup milk

Combine all ingredients and mix well. Pat into a 1 1/2-quart mold. Bake 1 1/2 hours at 350 degrees.

Sauce

1/4 cup brown sugar
1/4 teaspoon ground cloves
1 teaspoon mustard

Combine sugar, cloves and mustard; mix well. Spread on top of loaf.

Cherry Sauce

1 (No. 2) can tart cherries, drained (reserve liquid)
1/2 cup sugar
2 tablespoons cornstarch
1/4 teaspoon cloves
Red food coloring

Combine sugar, cornstarch and cloves; mix in saucepan with liquid from cherries. Cook, stirring constantly, until mixture boils and is thick. Add 1/4 teaspoon red food coloring and cherries. Serve on top of ham loaf. This was served at a church for a ladies' fashion show luncheon. It is very good.

Note: When serving a group, slice the loaf and spoon on sauce for each individual serving.

Easy Pork Fried Rice

1 1/2 tablespoons vegetable oil, divided
2 eggs, beaten
1 cup diced, fully cooked ham
1 cup finely chopped fresh mushrooms
1/2 cup thinly sliced green onions
3 cups cooked brown rice, chilled
1 tablespoon reduced-sodium soy sauce

Heat 1/2 tablespoon oil over medium heat in large skillet or wok. Add eggs and cook without stirring until set. Invert skillet over baking sheet to remove

Roast Chicken With Rosemary

1 cup plus 2 tablespoons virgin olive oil
1 bunch fresh rosemary
1 roasting chicken, about 5 pounds, rinsed well
Salt to taste
Freshly ground black pepper to taste (be generous)
2 large bulbs garlic

Preheat oven to 400 degrees. In a medium skillet, heat 1 cup olive oil to 300–325 degrees. Add rosemary sprigs, cooking until crisp, about 2 minutes, or until oil stops bubbling around rosemary. Place rosemary on paper toweling to drain. Remove rosemary leaves from stems, reserving 4 full sprigs for garnish. Allow oil to cool.

Place chicken in an ovenproof skillet. Salt and pepper the cavity and skin. Rub 1/4 cup rosemary oil across the skin. Rub heads of garlic with remaining plain olive oil and add to the skillet. Place on the lower rack of oven, cooking until garlic is tender, about 30 minutes.

Remove garlic and keep warm while continuing to cook chicken until done, about an additional 40 minutes, depending on the exact weight of your bird, or until an instant meat thermometer inserted in the thigh reads 160 degrees and the juices run clear.

Remove from oven. To keep skin crisp, allow chicken to cool to room temperature before covering. Pour cooking fat and juices into a glass measuring cup and retrieve the "jus." If the juices are caramelized in the pan, add 1/2 cup stock to reconstitute.

Transfer to a jar to safely transport to your picnic. At the picnic, present the chicken on a platter with the crisped rosemary and heads of garlic cut in half on the side. Carve the chicken. Serve with a splash of the "jus," crisped rosemary and half garlic head. Serves 4.

Pork Chops Divan

- 4 boneless center loin chops, cut 1 inch thick
- 1 tablespoon cooking oil
- 2 tablespoons butter *or* margarine
- 2 tablespoons flour
- 1½ cups milk
- ½ cup grated Parmesan cheese, divided
- ½ teaspoon ground nutmeg
- 1 tablespoon dry sherry
- ½ teaspoon Worcestershire sauce
- 1 large bunch fresh broccoli

Melt butter in a heavy saucepan . Add flour and stir to blend. Add milk. Cook and stir until sauce is thickened and smooth. Stir in 6 tablespoons Parmesan cheese, nutmeg, sherry and Worcestershire sauce. Set aside and keep warm. Heat oil in heavy skillet over medium-high heat. Brown chops on 1 side, about 3–4 minutes. Turn to brown other side.

Chop broccoli. Cook in salted water until tender; drain. Arrange chopped broccoli on serving platter. Pour 1 cup sauce over. Top with chops and garnish with additional sauce. Sprinkle with remaining Parmesan cheese. Serves 4.

Gourmet Meat Loaf

- 1 cup fresh *or* canned sliced mushrooms, drained
- ½ cup chopped onion
- 2 tablespoons butter *or* margarine
- ⅓ cup sour cream
- 1½ pounds ground beef
- ¾ cup oats (quick *or* old-fashioned), uncooked
- 1 egg
- 2 teaspoons salt
- ¼ teaspoon pepper
- 1 teaspoon Worcestershire sauce
- ⅔ cup milk

For filling, lightly brown mushrooms and onion in butter in medium-size skillet. Remove from heat; stir in sour cream.

For meat loaf, thoroughly combine all remaining ingredients. Place half of meat mixture in shallow baking pan. Shape to form an oval base. Lengthwise down the center make a shallow "well" for filling. Spoon filling into well. Shape remaining meat mixture over filling, making sure all filling is covered. Seal bottom and top meat mixtures together. Bake at 350 degrees for 1 hour. Let stand 5 minutes before slicing. Serves 6.

Roast Duck With Sausage-Apple Stuffing

- 1 (5-pound) duckling
- ½ pound bulk sausage
- 1 (8-ounce) package herb stuffing mix
- 1 cup chopped apple
- ½ cup chopped celery
- 1 (10½-ounce) can condensed cream of mushroom soup
- ¾ cup water
- 2 tablespoons chopped onion
- ⅛ teaspoon sage
- 1 tablespoon butter *or* margarine

Cook sausage. Pour off all but ¼ cup fat. Stir in stuffing mix, apple, celery, ¼ cup of soup and ½ cup water. Stuff into prepared duckling and fasten with toothpick or skewers. Place duckling, breast side up, in roasting pan. Roast at 325 degrees for about 2 hours. Baste occasionally. Meanwhile, in saucepan, cook onion with sage in butter until tender. Add remaining soup and water. Heat. Stir occasionally. Serve with duckling. Serves 4.

Sweet & Sour Chicken

- 3 tablespoons cooking oil
- 4 chicken breasts
- ¼ cup flour
- 1 (10-ounce) can pineapple chunks
- 3 tablespoons soy sauce
- 1 tablespoon sherry
- 1 teaspoon ginger
- Salt and pepper

Sauté chicken in oil until golden brown. Remove and place in slow cooker. Blend flour with the oil remaining in pan and cook for 1 minute. Drain juice from pineapple and make 1¼ cups by adding water. Add to the pan and bring to a boil, stirring until thickened. Add pineapple chunks, soy sauce, sherry, ginger, salt and pepper; return to a boil. Pour over chicken; cover and cook on high for 30 minutes, then low for 4 hours.

Pear Chicken Oriental

- 1 (29-ounce) can pears, reserve juice
- 1½ cups cooked chicken *or* beef (8 ounces) cut in strips
- 1 cup Chinese cabbage
- ½ cup bean sprouts
- 3 ounces Chinese pea pods, ½ cup, slightly cooked
- 1 cup torn lettuce
- Dressing (recipe follows)

Combine all ingredients, arranging pears and pea pods over vegetable-chicken mixture. Serve with this dressing.

Dressing

- 1 tablespoon oil
- 1 tablespoon white vinegar
- 1 teaspoon soy sauce
- Reserved pear juice

Mix well and serve on salad.

Curried Pork Chops & Apples

- ¼ cup flour
- 2 teaspoons salt
- 6 pork chops, cut ¾ inch thick
- 2 tablespoons lard *or* drippings
- 1 teaspoon curry powder
- ¼ cup ketchup
- 1½ cups apple juice
- 4 apples, quartered and cored
- ⅓ cup raisins

Combine flour and salt; dredge chops, reserving excess flour. Heat lard in skillet. Add chops and cook until browned. Pour off drippings. Combine reserved flour with curry powder. Blend in ketchup. Stir in apple juice and pour over chops. Cover tightly and cook slowly for 40 minutes. Add apples and raisins; continue to cook slowly, covered, for 15 minutes, or until chops are tender. Serves 6.

Pork Chop Spanish Rice

- 5 pork chops, 1/2 inch thick
- 2 tablespoons shortening
- 1 teaspoon salt
- 1/2 teaspoon chili powder
- 1/8 teaspoon pepper
- 3/4 cup long-grain rice
- 1/2 cup chopped onion
- 1/4 cup chopped green pepper
- 1 (28-ounce) can tomatoes, cut up
- 5 green pepper rings
- 1/2 cup shredded sharp process American cheese

Trim excess fat from chops. Slowly brown chops in hot shortening about 15–20 minutes. Drain off excess fat. Combine salt, chili powder and pepper. Sprinkle over chops. Add rice, onion and chopped green pepper. Pour tomatoes over all.

Cover and cook over low heat for 35 minutes, stirring occasionally. Add green pepper rings and cook 5 minutes longer, or until rice and meat are tender. Sprinkle with cheese. Serves 5.

Slow-Cooker Pot Roast

- 3–4 pounds pot roast
- 2 tablespoons shortening
- 1 teaspoon salt
- 1/4 teaspoon pepper
- 3 medium potatoes, pared and halved
- 3 medium carrots, cut into 2-inch pieces
- 2 medium onions, halved
- 1/2 cup water or beef broth

Brown meat on both sides in hot shortening in skillet. Place half of the vegetables in bottom of slow cooker. Season meat; place in slow cooker. Add remaining vegetables and liquid. Cover and cook on low 10–12 hours (or high 5–6 hours). Remove meat and vegetables carefully.
Variations: Add 1 teaspoon oregano, 1 teaspoon basil and 1 (8-ounce) can tomato sauce to basic recipe. Omit carrots, chopped onions and potatoes. Substitute 1 pound small peeled onions, 1 cup red wine and 1 cup sliced fresh mushrooms.

Herb Butter Basted Turkey Breast

- 1/2 cup (1 stick) butter, melted
- 1/4 cup fresh lemon juice
- 2 tablespoons minced green onion
- 2 tablespoons soy sauce
- 1 teaspoon sage
- 1 teaspoon thyme
- 1 teaspoon marjoram, crushed
- 1/2 teaspoon salt
- 1/4 teaspoon pepper
- 4–5 pounds frozen turkey breast, thawed

Combine butter, lemon juice, green onion, soy sauce, herbs and seasonings in a small saucepan; keep warm. Cook turkey breast on covered charcoal grill (kettle or wagon) or electric or gas grill with full cover, following manufacturer's directions for setting up grill.

Cook turkey breast approximately 2 1/4 hours, or until the internal temperature is 170 degrees. Brush with basting sauce frequently during cooking. Let turkey breast rest 15–20 minutes for easier carving. Pass remaining basting sauce with sliced turkey, or chill and slice. Serves 8.

Apricot Easter Ham

- 1 (12-pound bone-in) uncooked ham
- 1/2 quart apricot juice
- 1/2 quart apricot nectar
- Apricot Glaze (recipe follows)

In a deep baking pan pour apricot mixture over ham; bake 3 hours at 325 degrees. Baste with juice every half hour.

Apricot Glaze

- 1 cup dried apricots
- 1 cup water
- 1 tablespoon fresh lemon juice
- 6 tablespoons brown sugar
- 3 tablespoons honey
- 1/2 cup fresh orange juice

Combine all ingredients; cook until mixture comes to a boil. Simmer, uncovered, 13 minutes or until apricots are tender. Purée apricots with liquid. After ham has cooked 2 hours, paint top and sides with glaze every 15 minutes for the last hour. Remove from pan and place on a warmed platter; decorate with sprigs of fresh parsley and fresh herbs. Serves 20.

Sautéed Liver

- 1 1/2 pounds calf's liver, sliced 1/4 inch thick
- 2 tablespoons flour
- 1 1/4 teaspoons salt
- 1/4 teaspoon pepper
- 1/2 teaspoon paprika
- 2 tablespoons butter *or* margarine
- 1 onion, minced
- 1/3 cup dry white wine

Wash and dry liver; sprinkle with mixture of flour, salt, pepper and paprika. Melt butter or margarine in a skillet; sauté liver for about 3 minutes on each side. Transfer to a platter and keep warm.

Stir onion into butter remaining in the skillet; cook 2 minutes. Add wine and cook over high heat for 2 minutes. Pour over the liver. Serves 6.

Pork Loaf

- 2 pounds lean ground pork
- 1/4 cup ketchup
- 1 egg, slightly beaten
- 1 cup cracker crumbs
- 1 1/2 teaspoons salt
- 1/2 teaspoon pepper
- 3 tablespoons ketchup

Combine all ingredients, except for the 3 tablespoons ketchup, in a large bowl. Mix well. Press firmly into a 9 x 5 x 3-inch loaf pan. Spread 3 tablespoons ketchup over the top. Bake at 350 degrees for 1 hour.

Veal Loaf

- 1 1/2 pounds ground veal
- 1 1/4 pounds ground lean pork
- 1/4 teaspoon garlic salt
- 1/2 cup onion, chopped fine
- 2 cups bread cubes (4 slices)
- 1/4 cup shredded cheddar cheese
- 1 teaspoon salt
- 1/2 teaspoon pepper
- 2 eggs, beaten
- 3/4 cup milk

Combine all ingredients. Pack into a 9 x 5 x 2-inch loaf pan. Bake at 375 degrees for 1 1/4 hours. This is very good hot or cold.

Sirloin Chinese

- 1½ pounds sirloin steak, cut into ½-inch-wide strips
- 1 clove garlic, crushed
- 1 teaspoon paprika
- 1 tablespoon butter
- 1 cup sliced onions
- 2 green peppers, cut into slices
- 2 large tomatoes, sliced, *or* 1 can tomatoes
- 1 envelope *or* 1 cube beef bouillon dissolved in 1 cup boiling water
- ½ teaspoon teriyaki sauce
- 1 teaspoon soy sauce
- ¼ cup cold water
- 2 tablespoons cornstarch
- Salt and pepper to taste

Roll steak strips in paprika and let stand for 30 minutes. Heat butter and garlic in heavy skillet; sauté garlic until tender. Remove garlic and set aside. Place steak in skillet and brown quickly on all sides. Reduce heat to medium low; add garlic, onions and green peppers; simmer until vegetables are tender. Add tomatoes and beef bouillon; cover and simmer for 10 minutes. Dissolve cornstarch in cold water; add sauces and pour over mixture. Season to taste. Stir until thick and clear.

Simple Creamed Chicken

- 1½ tablespoons butter *or* margarine
- 1 tablespoon chopped onion
- 1½ tablespoons flour
- 1 cup milk (*or* half-and-half, if desired)
- ⅛ teaspoon salt
- Pepper to taste
- 1 to 1½ cups cooked chicken chunks
- 2 baked puff pastry patty shells

In medium saucepan melt butter or margarine. Add onion; cook just until transparent. Whisk in flour; cook over medium heat for about 1 minute. Whisk in milk, salt and pepper. Whisk until boiling. Cook on low, stirring often until it thickens slightly, about 5 minutes. (If making ahead, cook, cover and refrigerate.) Add chicken; stir over low heat until warm. Serve over warm patty shells. Serves 2.

Baked Chicken Reuben

- 2 chicken breasts, skinned and boned
- Salt and pepper
- 1–2 cups sauerkraut, lightly drained
- 1 large slice Swiss cheese, enough to cover chicken
- ¼ cup mayonnaise
- 1 tablespoon chili sauce *or* ketchup
- Paprika

Preheat oven to 325 degrees. Lightly grease a 1-quart baking dish. Place chicken breasts side by side in dish; sprinkle with salt and pepper. Spread sauerkraut evenly over chicken. Cover with cheese. Stir together mayonnaise and chili sauce or ketchup; spoon evenly over cheese. Sprinkle lightly with paprika. Bake, covered with foil, 45 minutes. Remove foil; bake 15 minutes longer. Serves 2.

Curry Marmalade Chicken

- ½ cup marmalade
- 2 tablespoons lemon juice
- 1 (2½–3-pound) chicken, cut up
- ½ teaspoon curry powder

Heat grill. In small bowl, combine marmalade, juice and curry powder; blend well. Set aside.

When ready to barbecue, place chicken, skin side down, on gas grill over low heat or on charcoal grill 4–6 inches from medium coals. Cook 45–60 minutes, or until chicken is fork-tender and juices run clear; turn often and brush frequently with basting sauce during last 15 minutes of cooking. Heat any remaining sauce to a boil; serve with chicken. Serves 4–5.

Salisbury Steak

- 1 pound lean ground beef
- ½ to ¾ cup cracker crumbs
- 1 egg
- ¼ cup chopped onion
- ½ teaspoon salt
- Black pepper to taste
- ½ cup water
- 1 can tomato soup

Combine ground beef, cracker crumbs, egg, onion, salt and pepper. Form into patties and put in skillet. Combine water and soup; pour over patties. Cover and simmer for 40 minutes. Delicious!!

Spiced Orange Pot Roast

- 4–5 pound beef chuck roast
- 1 tablespoon shortening
- ½ cup onion, finely chopped
- 1 clove garlic, minced
- 1 (8-ounce) can tomato sauce
- 2 cups orange sections, with juice
- 2 tablespoons sugar
- 1 tablespoon grated orange rind
- 1½ teaspoons salt
- ½ teaspoon nutmeg
- ½ teaspoon cinnamon
- ¼ teaspoon cloves
- Dash pepper

Brown meat slowly on both sides in shortening. Add onions and garlic. Cover and cook 20 minutes. Pour tomato sauce, orange sections, sugar and grated orange rind over meat. Sprinkle with salt and spices. Cover and cook slowly until meat is very tender, about 2 hours longer. Serves 6–8.

Liberty Bell Meat Sauce

- 1 pound hamburger meat
- 1 can process chunk meat
- 1 (32-ounce) jar pizza sauce
- 1 teaspoon parsley flakes
- 1 teaspoon oregano
- 1 teaspoon salt
- Pepper

Brown hamburger and drain. Add Spam, diced. Set aside. Combine the remaining ingredients and add meat. Slowly simmer about 30 minutes and serve hot over hamburger buns.

Turkey Au Gratin

- 1 (4.5–5.2-ounce) package broccoli rice au gratin rice mix
- 1 cup cubed smoked turkey
- 1 (2-ounce) jar pimientos
- 12 buttery crackers, crushed

Prepare rice mix in 2-quart saucepan according to package directions. Add turkey and pimiento; heat thoroughly. Transfer to serving dish; top with cracker crumbs. Serves 4.

Slow-Cooker Pork Chops, Italian-Style

- 3 pounds thinly sliced pork chops
- 2 tablespoons oil
- 1 (1-pound) can tomatoes
- 1 green pepper, diced
- 2 cloves garlic, mashed
- 1 onion, diced
- 1 teaspoon salt
- 1/4 teaspoon oregano
- 1 bay leaf
- 1/8 teaspoon hot red pepper flakes

In large skillet or slow-cooker, if it has a browning unit, brown chops on both sides in oil. Remove pork to slow-cooker. Combine all remaining ingredients and pour over pork in cooker. Cover pot and turn on low for 4–6 hours, or until chops are tender. Serves 6.

Yam 'N' Ham Loaf

- 1 pound smoked ham, ground
- 1/4 pound ground beef
- 1/4 pound ground pork
- 1/4 teaspoon salt
- 1/8 teaspoon pepper
- 1/4 cup minced onion
- 1 small green pepper, minced
- 1/2 cup chopped celery
- 1/3 cup quick-cooking dry oat cereal
- 1 egg, beaten
- 1/2 cup milk
- 3 1/2 cups mashed sweet potatoes *or* yams

Combine all ingredients, except sweet potatoes, and mix well. Arrange half of meat mixture in greased loaf pan. Cover with sweet potatoes and top with remaining meat mixture. Bake in 350-degree oven for about 1 hour. Makes 8 servings.

Citrus Pork Chops

- 4 pork loin butterfly chops, cut 3/4 inch thick
- 1 tablespoon oil
- 1/4 cup sliced scallions
- 1 tablespoon orange peel
- 1/2 cup orange juice
- 1/4 teaspoon dried basil

Heat oil in large skillet. Add scallions and orange peel. Sauté 3–4 minutes, or until onion is almost tender. Remove onion and orange peel. Set aside. Add pork chops and brown on both sides over medium heat. Add onion and orange peel. Add orange juice and basil. Cover and simmer for 10 minutes. Serves 4.

Herbed Pork Chops (Outdoor Grill)

- 4 pork loin chops, cut 1 inch thick
- 1 cup unsweetened pineapple juice
- 2/3 cup dry sherry
- 2 tablespoon brown sugar
- 1/2 teaspoon dried rosemary, crushed
- 1 clove garlic, minced

For marinade, combine all ingredients except chops. Mix well. Place chops in a shallow baking dish. Pour marinade over chops. Cover and refrigerate several hours or overnight, turning meat occasionally.

Drain chops, reserving marinade. Grill chops over medium coals for about 20 minutes. Turn chops and grill 15–20 minutes more, or until done, brushing occasionally with marinade. Serves 4.

Cajun Pork Chops

- 4 boneless pork chops, cut 1/2 inch thick
- 1 tablespoon paprika
- 1 teaspoon seasoned salt
- 1 teaspoon rubbed sage
- 1/2 teaspoon cayenne pepper
- 1/2 teaspoon black pepper
- 1/2 teaspoon garlic powder
- 2 tablespoons butter *or* margarine

Combine seasonings. Coat chops with seasoning mixture on both sides. Heat butter over high heat just until it starts to brown. Put chops in pan. Reduce heat to medium. Fry on both sides until dark brown, about 8–10 minutes. Serves 4.

Meat Loaf

- 2 pounds ground round steak
- 1 cup milk
- 2/3 cup uncooked oats
- 1/3 cup chopped green pepper
- 1/3 cup ketchup
- 1 egg, slightly beaten
- 2 teaspoons Worcestershire sauce
- 1 1/2 teaspoons salt
- 1/2 teaspoon poultry seasoning
- 1/4 teaspoon pepper

Preheat oven to 350 degrees. Mix ground meat lightly with remaining ingredients. Press meat mixture into an 8-inch square baking dish. Bake about 1 hour. Drain off pan juices. Refrigerate, covered, several hours or overnight. Cut into squares. Serves 6.

Baked Pork Chops in Tomato Sauce

- 4 pork chops
- 1 (8-ounce) can tomato sauce
- 1/2 cup water
- 2 cups finely diced celery
- 2 tablespoons sugar
- 1/2 teaspoon dry mustard

Brown pork chops. Place in shallow greased baking dish. Combine remaining ingredients and pour over chops. Bake at 350 degrees for 1 1/4 hours, or until tender. Serves 4.

BBQ Ham Steak

- 1/2 cup (1 stick) butter
- 2 cloves garlic, crushed
- 1/2 cup ketchup
- 1/2 cup water
- 1 1/2-to 2-pound fully cooked ham steak, about 1 inch thick

Melt butter in a medium-size saucepan. Add garlic and cook about 3 minutes. Remove from heat; stir in ketchup and water. Place ham steak in shallow pan. Pour sauce over ham. Cover and refrigerate 2 hours; turn ham after 1 hour.

Grill ham over medium-hot coals for 10–15 minutes per side, brushing with sauce occasionally. Heat remaining sauce; pass with ham. Serves 6–8.

Pies

FESTIVE

Southern Pecan Pie

- 3 tablespoons margarine *or* butter
- 1 teaspoon vanilla
- 3/4 cup sugar
- 3 eggs
- 1/2 cup chopped pecans
- 1 cup dark corn syrup
- Pinch of salt
- 1 (9-inch) unbaked pie crust
- 1/2 to 3/4 cup pecan halves

Preheat oven to 450 degrees. Cream butter with vanilla. Add sugar gradually; mix well. Add eggs, 1 at a time. Blend in chopped pecans, syrup and salt. Pour into pie crust and bake 10 minutes. Reduce heat to 350 degrees. Remove pie from oven and arrange pecan halves on top of filling. Return to oven and bake 30–35 minutes more. This is a traditional Southern favorite. Serves 8.

French Liqueur Pie

- 1/2 gallon vanilla ice cream
- 1 cup pecans, chopped and toasted
- Créme de menthe liqueur *or* syrup
- 2 (9-inch) chocolate cookie pie crusts
- Toasted pecan halves for decoration

Soften ice cream enough to stir in chopped pecans and créme de menthe to desired taste and color. Pour into cookie crusts; decorate tops with pecan halves. Cover with plastic wrap and freeze overnight. *Note:* Better to prepare the day before serving. Makes 2.

Fresh Rhubarb Pie

Crust

- 2 2/3 cups sifted flour
- 1 teaspoon salt
- 1 cup shortening
- 6 1/2 tablespoons cold water

Filling

- 1 1/2 to 2 cups sugar
- 1/3 cup flour
- 4 cups rhubarb, cut up
- 1 1/2 tablespoons butter

For crust, mix flour, salt and shortening with pastry blender. Add cold water gradually and stir with fork until you can shape it into a ball with your hands. Roll out 1/2 on floured surface, making 2 crusts.

For filling, mix sugar and flour together; mix lightly through the rhubarb. Pour into a 9-inch pastry-lined pan and dot with 1 1/2 tablespoons butter. Cover with top crust, which has slits cut in it. Rub milk over crust and sprinkle with sugar. Bake in a 350-degree oven for 1 hour, or until nicely browned.

Chocolate Pistachio Pie

- 2 (3 1/2-ounce) cans flaked coconut
- 4 (1-ounce) squares semisweet chocolate, melted
- 1/4 cup butter *or* margarine
- 1 quart pistachio ice cream, slightly softened

Heat oven to 375 degrees. Place coconut on jelly roll pan. Bake 5–10 minutes, stirring occasionally, until golden. In large bowl, using fork, combine toasted coconut, melted chocolate and butter until well-blended. Press mixture onto bottom and side of buttered 9-inch pie plate. Spread ice cream in pie crust. Cover. Freeze until firm, at least 1 hour.

Cracker Pie

- 3 egg whites
- 1/4 teaspoon salt
- 3/4 cup sugar
- 1 cup chopped pecans
- 18 plain crackers (unsalted tops), crushed
- 1 teaspoon vanilla
- 1/4 cup pineapple topping for ice cream
- 1 small container whipped topping

Beat egg whites with salt until almost stiff. Gradually add sugar and beat until stiff. Fold in nuts, cracker crumbs and vanilla. Mix well and pour into a well-buttered 9-inch pie pan. Bake in a 325-degree oven for 35 minutes. Cool completely. Fold pineapple topping into whipped topping; spread on pie and chill for 2 hours. Serves 6–8.

Kale Pie

- 2 cups cooked brown rice
- 3 eggs, beaten
- 1/4 cup milk
- 2 tablespoons chopped dill, chives *or* green onions
- 1/8 teaspoon nutmeg
- Salt and pepper to taste
- 1 pound cooked kale
- 1 cup crumbled feta cheese
- Margarine
- Bread crumbs

Mix rice, eggs, milk and spices. Layer in greased, or non-stick sprayed, casserole with kale and cheese. Top with bread crumbs and dot with margarine. Bake at 350 degrees for approximately 30 minutes.

Puff Pastry

- **3 cups all-purpose flour, sifted**
- **½ teaspoon salt**
- **¾ pound (3 sticks) unsalted butter, cut into 1½-teaspoon pieces**
- **10 tablespoons ice water**

Combine flour and salt on a table. Mix in butter until coated with flour. Make a trough or long well in flour. Add 2 tablespoons ice water to trough. With fingertips extended and palms upward, distribute water through flour by putting fingertips together while gently tossing flour. Continue technique, adding water 2 tablespoons at a time until dough just holds together without being sticky.

Flatten the dough into a rectangle with the palm of your hand in a downward motion. Refrigerate dough for 20 minutes.

On a floured surface, roll pastry into a rectangle 3 times longer than it is wide, ⅜-½ inch thick. Dust to remove any excess flour. Fold top third of the rolled dough over center third. Then fold bottom third of rolled dough over the center third to complete a "turn."

Rotate pastry clockwise 90 degrees and repeat the rolling and folding technique for a second turn. Wrap dough in plastic and refrigerate for 20 minutes.

Repeat rolling and folding technique for 2 additional turns. Wrap dough in plastic and refrigerate again for 20 minutes. Repeat the rolling and folding technique for 2 final turns, wrap in plastic, and refrigerate the dough for at least 20 minutes before rolling out for baking.

Refrigerate up to 3 days. If you freeze the dough, thaw it overnight in the refrigerator. Follow directions for Apple Tart. For other applications, flour and roll out dough to ⅛–¼-inch-thickness. Bake on a greased cookie sheet in a preheated oven at 400 degrees until golden, about 12 minutes. Makes 1½ pounds.

Lemon Sponge Pie

- **1 cup sugar**
- **3 tablespoons all-purpose flour**
- **1 teaspoon grated lemon rind**
- **2 tablespoons lemon juice**
- **1 large egg, separated**
- **2 tablespoons butter *or* margarine, melted**
- **1 cup milk**
- **Pinch salt**
- **1 (9-inch) unbaked pie shell**

Combine sugar and flour in a medium mixing bowl. Stir in lemon rind and juice; beat in egg yolk, then melted butter. Stir in milk. Beat egg white with salt until fairly stiff peaks form; then fold into lemon mixture until no streaks of white show. Pour into an unbaked pie shell. Bake in a moderate oven of 350 degrees for 40 minutes, or until crust is lightly browned and filling is puffy and light brown. Cool about 15 minutes before cutting. Good warm or cold. It is cakelike on top, with a layer of tart lemon custard underneath. Makes 1 (9-inch) pie.

Fourth of July Fresh Fruit Pie

- **1 (9-inch) graham cracker crumb crust**
- **1 (8-ounce) package cream cheese, softened**
- **1 (14-ounce) can sweetened condensed milk**
- **⅓ cup lemon juice**
- **1 teaspoon vanilla extract**
- **Strawberries, blueberries and banana slices (dipped in lemon juice), well-drained**
- **Light corn syrup (optional)**

In large mixer bowl, beat cream cheese until fluffy. Gradually beat in sweetened condensed milk until smooth. Stir in lemon juice and vanilla. Pour into pie crust. Chill 3 hours, or until set.

Just before serving, arrange well-drained fresh strawberries, banana slices and blueberries on top of chilled pie. Brush fruit with light corn syrup, if desired.

Coconut Cheese Pie

- **1½ tablespoons margarine, softened**
- **2⅔ cups flaked coconut**
- **4 eggs**
- **⅔ cup sugar**
- **1 (8-ounce) package cream cheese**
- **3 tablespoons lemon juice**

Spread butter evenly over bottom and sides of 9-inch pie pan. Press 1⅓ cups of coconut into butter, forming a shell. Place 1 cup of coconut, eggs, sugar, cream cheese and lemon juice in blender or food processor. Blend until smooth, about 1½ minutes; pour into coconut shell. Sprinkle remaining coconut in a ring around tip and in center.

Bake at 325 degrees for 30 minutes. (If coconut on top browns quickly, cover with a circle of aluminum foil). Serve warm or cool; refrigerate any remaining pie.

Crustless Chocolate Bourbon Pie

For a non-alcoholic pie use coffee instead of bourbon.

- **2 (1-ounce) squares unsweetened chocolate**
- **⅓ cup chopped pecans**
- **½ cup (1 stick) butter, softened**
- **1 cup sugar**
- **2 large eggs**
- **1 teaspoon vanilla**
- **2 tablespoons bourbon**
- **¾ cup flour, spooned lightly into cup**
- **½ teaspoon baking powder**
- **Few grains salt**

Preheat oven to 350 degrees. Place chocolate in custard cup and melt in preheating oven. I also spread pecans on small baking pan and toast lightly—4 minutes or so—while oven preheats.

Grease and flour a 9-inch pie pan; set aside. In a medium bowl beat butter until smooth; gradually beat in sugar. Add eggs 1 at a time; beat 1 minute after each addition. Beat in melted chocolate, vanilla and bourbon. Measure in flour, baking powder and salt; mix in on lowest speed. Stir in nuts. Pour into prepared pan.

Bake until cake tester comes out dry, about 30 minutes. Cool in pan on rack. Top will sink and crack a bit as it cools. Serve slightly warm, topped with whipped cream, ice cream (vanilla or coffee) or a dusting of confectioners' sugar. This freezes well. Serves 6.

Chocolate Almond Pie

Quick Coconut Crust

- **1/3 cup butter *or* margarine, melted**
- **2 2/3 cups coconut**

Combine margarine and coconut in medium bowl. Evenly press into an ungreased 9-inch pie pan. Bake in a 300-degree oven for 20–30 minutes, or until golden brown. Cool on wire rack.

Filling

- **2/3 cup slivered, blanched almonds**
- **1 (6-serving-size) package chocolate pudding and pie filling**
- **3 cups milk**
- **1/4 teaspoon almond extract**
- **1 cup frozen whipped topping, thawed**

Toast almonds in shallow pan in a 350-degree oven for 3–5 minutes, stirring once. Chop 1/2 cup of the almonds; reserve remaining almonds for garnish. Combine pie filling mix and milk in medium saucepan; blend well. Cook and stir over medium heat until mixture comes to a full boil.

Cool 5 minutes, stirring twice. Stir in chopped nuts and extract. Pour into pie crust and cover surface of filling with plastic wrap. Chill about 4 hours. Remove plastic wrap. Garnish with whipped topping and reserved nuts. Makes 1 (9-inch) pie.

Raspberry & Cream Pie

- **1 (9-inch) unbaked pie shell**

Filling

- **1/2 cup flour**
- **1 cup sugar (3/4 cup if raspberries are sweet)**
- **1 1/4 cups heavy cream**
- **Dash cinnamon**
- **4 cups fresh raspberries**

Preheat oven to 400 degrees. Blend flour, sugar, cream and cinnamon with a wire whisk or fork. Put raspberries in a large mixing bowl and pour cream mixture over them. Stir gently to coat raspberries. Spoon raspberries-and-cream mixture into pie shell. Bake for approximately 40 minutes, or until set. Serve at room temperature or slightly chilled. Refrigerate any remaining pie.

Glorious Grapefruit Ice Cream Pie

- **2 cups oatmeal cookies, finely crushed**
- **2 1/2 tablespoons sugar**
- **1/4 cup butter *or* margarine, melted**
- **1/2 cup sweet milk**
- **1/2 cup sugar**
- **1/2 cup frozen grapefruit juice concentrate**
- **1 pint vanilla ice cream, softened**
- **1 grapefruit**

Combine cookies and sugar; stir in melted butter or margarine. Press mixture onto bottom and up sides of a 9-inch pie plate; freeze. In a small mixer bowl, beat milk and 1/2 cup sugar about 2 minutes to dissolve sugar; add juice concentrate; mix well. Add ice cream by spoonfuls; beat on low speed of electric mixer until blended. Pour into prepared crust; freeze 4 hours or until firm. Peel, section and seed grapefruit. Garnish pie with grapefruit sections. Let stand 5 minutes before serving. Serves 8.

Glazed Peach Pie

- **1 (9-inch) pie shell, baked**

Filling

- **1 (8-ounce) package cream cheese**
- **2 tablespoons milk**
- **1/2 teaspoon almond extract**
- **2 tablespoons sugar**
- **2 (10-ounce) packages frozen peaches, thawed**

Glaze

- **1 tablespoon cornstarch**
- **1/4 cup sugar**
- **1 tablespoon lemon juice**
- **2/3 cup peach juice**
- **1 tablespoon margarine**

For filling, mix cream cheese, milk, almond extract and sugar. Spread into baked pie shell. Chill. Drain peaches, reserving juice; arrange slices on cream cheese.

To make glaze, combine cornstarch and sugar in saucepan. Add lemon juice and peach juice, stirring over medium heat until clear and thick. Add margarine and cook 2 minutes. When cool, pour glaze over peaches. Keep pie refrigerated until ready to serve.

Sweet Melon Seafoam Pie

- **1 baked pie shell, cooled**
- **1 tablespoon unflavored gelatin**
- **1/2 cup sugar**
- **1/4 teaspoon salt**
- **4 egg yolks, lightly beaten**
- **1/4 cup lime juice**
- **1/4 cup water**
- **1 teaspoon lime zest**
- **4 egg whites**
- **1/2 cup sugar**
- **1/2 cup whipping cream, whipped**
- **1 1/2 cups small sweet melon balls**
- **Toasted coconut for garnish**

Combine gelatin, 1/2 cup sugar and salt. Combine egg yolks, lime juice and water; add to gelatin mixture; cook until mixture comes to a boil. Remove from heat; add lime zest; chill until mixture becomes semi-firm. Beat egg whites and sugar to stiff peaks; fold in gelatin mixture; fold in whipped cream and melon balls; chill until firm.

To serve top each individual pie slice with whipped cream—wreath-style—and toasted coconut sprinkled on the whipped cream.

Pineapple Chess Pie

- **2 cups sugar**
- **3 tablespoons flour**
- **1/2 cup butter, softened**
- **4 eggs**
- **1 (8-ounce) can crushed pineapple**
- **1 teaspoon vanilla *or* 1/2 teaspoon lemon extract**
- **1 (9-inch) unbaked pastry shell**

Combine sugar, flour and butter; cream well. Add eggs, beating well. Stir in pineapple and extract. Pour mixture into an unbaked pastry shell. Bake at 350 degrees for 45 minutes or until knife inserted halfway between center and edge comes out clean. Cool thoroughly before serving. If you are a pineapple lover, you will love this pie.

Variation: For Hawaiian Pie, add 1 (3 1/2-ounce) can coconut to the Pineapple Chess Pie. Delicious!

Butterscotch Apple Pie

- 4 cups (about $1^1/_2$ pounds *or* 4 medium) Winesap apples, pared, cored and thinly sliced
- 1/2 cup brown sugar, packed (divided)
- Pastry for 1-crust (9-inch) pie
- 2 eggs
- 1 1/4 cups half-and-half
- 2 tablespoons cornstarch
- 1 teaspoon vanilla
- Dash salt

Toss apples with 1/4 cup brown sugar; arrange in unbaked pie crust. Bake at 375 degrees for 20 minutes, or until apples are almost tender. Remove from oven; reduce heat to 350 degrees and cool while preparing custard. Beat eggs and remaining brown sugar for about 2 minutes, or until thickened.

Add half-and-half, cornstarch, vanilla and salt; beat well. Pour over apples; gently move apples to evenly distribute custard. Bake at 350 degrees for 35–40 minutes, or until apples are tender when tested with a fork. Cover edge of pie with foil the last 15 minutes to prevent overbrowning. Serves 8.

Golden Grapefruit Chiffon Pie

- 1 1/3 cups gingersnap cookie crumbs
- 1/4 cup butter, melted
- 1 cup sugar, divided
- 1 envelope unflavored gelatin
- 1/2 teaspoon candied ginger, finely chopped
- 1/4 teaspoon grated grapefruit zest
- 3 eggs, separated
- 1 cup grapefruit juice
- 1/2 cup heavy cream, whipped
- Grapefruit sections, for garnish

Combine cookie crumbs, melted butter and 1/4 cup sugar; press into a 9-inch pie plate. Combine gelatin, 1/2 cup sugar, ginger and zest. Beat egg yolks with grapefruit juice; stir into gelatin mixture. Cook, stirring constantly, until gelatin dissolves; chill. Beat egg whites; add remaining 1/4 cup sugar; fold into cooled gelatin mixture; fold in whipped cream. Pour into prepared crust; chill until set. Garnish with additional whipped cream and grapefruit sections.

Cherry Dream Pie

- 1 (9-inch) unbaked pie shell
- 1 (3-ounce) package cream cheese
- 2 tablespoons milk
- 2 teaspoons sugar
- 4 drops almond extract
- 1 (3-ounce) package cherry-flavored gelatin
- 1 cup boiling water
- 1 (1-pound, 5-ounce) can cherry pie filling
- 1/2 cup heavy cream, whipped
- Slivered almonds

Line pan with pastry. Bake pricked pie shell in a preheated 450-degree oven for about 12 minutes. Cool. Combine cream cheese, milk, sugar and extract. Spread over bottom of baked crust. Dissolve gelatin in water. Cool until syrupy. Add cherry pie filling and chill until partially set. Pour into pie shell and chill until firm. Top with dollops of whipped cream and slivered almonds.

April Fools' Streusel Pie

- 1 (9-inch) pre-baked pie crust
- 2 cups water
- 3/4 cup sugar
- 1 tablespoon cream of tartar
- 1/4 teaspoon nutmeg
- 1/4 teaspoon cinnamon
- 22 whole round butter-flavored snack crackers
- 6 tablespoons unsalted butter, chilled
- 3/4 cup flour
- 6 tablespoons sugar
- 1/2 teaspoon cinnamon
- 1/8 teaspoon salt

Bring water, 3/4 cup sugar, cream of tartar, nutmeg and cinnamon to a boil in a 2-quart saucepan. Boil 5 minutes. Add crackers, but do not stir. Boil 2 minutes longer. Remove from heat and cool completely, about 1 hour.

For the streusel, cut butter in 5 pieces. Work into flour, sugar, cinnamon and salt using a food processor or pastry blender until it is the consistency of cornmeal. Pour cooled filling into pre-baked pie crust. Spread streusel evenly over top. Bake until lightly browned, about 30 minutes, in a preheated 350-degree oven.

Sour Cream Rhubarb Pie

- 3 tablespoons flour
- 1/2 teaspoon salt
- 1 1/4 cups sugar
- 1 egg, beaten
- 1 cup sour cream
- 1 teaspoon vanilla
- 1/2 teaspoon lemon extract (optional)
- 3 cups fresh rhubarb, cut into 1/2-inch pieces
- 1 (9-inch) pie shell, unbaked

Topping

- 1/3 cup sugar
- 1/3 cup flour
- Salt to taste
- 1 teaspoon cinnamon
- 1/4 cup butter, softened

Sift first 3 ingredients; add egg, sour cream, vanilla and lemon extract. Mix well. Add rhubarb. Pour into pie shell. Bake at 400 degrees for 15 minutes. Reduce heat to 350 degrees; bake 25 more minutes.

Mix topping ingredients. Sprinkle over pie. Return to oven for 15 minutes for topping to brown.

Picnic Rhubarb-Strawberry Pie

- 2 1/2 cups fresh rhubarb, cut into 1-inch pieces
- 1 pint strawberries, hulled and halved
- 2 (9-inch) unbaked pie shells
- 1 1/4 cups sugar
- 1/8 teaspoon lemon juice
- 4 tablespoons flour
- 1/2 teaspoon nutmeg
- 1/4 teaspoon cinnamon
- 1 1/4 teaspoons butter *or* margarine
- 2 eggs, beaten

Combine rhubarb and strawberries; place in pie shell. Combine sugar, lemon juice, flour, nutmeg and cinnamon; cut in butter.

Add beaten eggs; pour over fruit. Cut remaining pie shell into strips; arrange lattice-fashion on top of pie. Bake at 350 degrees for 1 hour, or until pastry is golden and flaky.

Neapolitan Ice Cream Pie

Pack in dry ice and take along.

Brownie Crust

- ½ cup (1 stick) butter
- 1 cup sugar
- 2 eggs, separated
- 2 (1-ounce) squares unsweetened chocolate, melted and cooled
- 1 teaspoon vanilla extract
- ½ cup all-purpose flour
- ⅛ teaspoon salt

Filling

- 2 pints strawberry ice cream, softened
- 1 cup whipping cream
- 2 tablespoons confectioners' sugar
- ½ teaspoon vanilla extract
- ¼ teaspoon almond extract
- ½ cup sliced almonds, toasted

Preheat oven to 325 degrees. For brownie crust, cream butter and sugar until light and fluffy. Add egg yolks; mix well. Stir in chocolate and vanilla. Blend in flour and salt. Beat egg whites until soft peaks form; fold into chocolate mixture.

Spread batter in a buttered 9-inch pie plate. Bake 30–35 minutes or until a wooden pick inserted in center comes out clean. Cool completely. Spread ice cream in "well" of crust. Return to freezer 2–3 hours, or until firm. Combine whipping cream, sugar and extracts; whip until stiff. Fold in almonds. Spread over ice cream.

Sour Cream Raisin Pie

- 1 (9-inch) baked pie crust
- 1 (4-serving) package sugar-free cook-and-serve vanilla pudding
- 1 cup skim milk
- ½ cup water
- 1 cup raisins
- ½ teaspoon vanilla
- 1¼ cups nonfat plain yogurt
- Sugar substitute to equal 2 tablespoons sugar
- 1 cup reduced-calorie whipped topping (8 calories per tablespoon)
- ½ teaspoon nutmeg

In medium saucepan, combine pudding mix, milk, water and raisins. Cook over medium heat, stirring constantly, until pudding comes to a boil, stirring constantly. Remove from heat. Stir in vanilla. Cool in pan for about 15 minutes. Add yogurt and sugar substitute. Pour into baked and cooled pie crust. Chill at least 3 hours. Combine whipped topping and nutmeg. Spread over chilled pie just before serving.

Cantaloupe Bavarian Pie

- 4 eggs, separated
- 1 cup sugar
- ½ teaspoon salt
- 1 package orange gelatin
- ¼ teaspoon cream of tartar
- 1½ cups diced cantaloupe, drained
- 1 tablespoon lemon juice
- 1 tablespoon grated lemon peel
- ½ cup orange juice
- 1 (10-inch) baked pie shell
- 1 cup whipping cream, whipped

Beat egg yolks slightly in top of a double boiler, then add ½ cup sugar, salt, lemon juice and grated peel. Cook, stirring frequently, until mixture coats the spoon; remove from heat. Bring orange juice to a boil and pour over gelatin. Stir until dissolved; blend egg mixture and gelatin mixture together; cool.

Beat egg whites with cream of tartar until stiff. Add remaining sugar gradually, beating until whites hold stiff glossy peaks. Fold in gelatin mixture; add cantaloupe, folding in carefully. Pile into pie shell and top with swirls of whipped cream. Chill for at least 4 hours before serving.

Applescotch Pie

- 5 cups thinly sliced tart apples (about 4 medium)
- 1 cup brown sugar
- ½ cup water
- 1 tablespoon lemon juice
- ¼ cup all-purpose flour
- 2 tablespoons granulated sugar
- ¾ teaspoon salt
- 1 teaspoon vanilla
- 3 tablespoons butter *or* margarine
- Pastry for 9-inch (2-crust) pie

In saucepan combine apples, brown sugar, water and lemon juice. Cover; cook over medium heat for 7–8 minutes, or until apples are just tender. Stir together flour, granulated sugar and salt; stir into apple mixture in saucepan. Cook, stirring constantly, until mixture thickens and boils. Boil and stir 1 minute. Remove from heat; stir in vanilla and butter. Cool to room temperature.

Heat oven to 425 degrees. Prepare pastry. Turn apple mixture into pastry-lined pie pan. Cover with slit crust; seal and flute. Cover edges with 2–3-inch strip of aluminum foil to prevent excessive browning. Remove foil last 15 minutes of baking. Bake 40–45 minutes.

Banana Blueberry Pie

- 1 can blueberries, drained (reserve juice)
- 2½ tablespoons cornstarch
- ½ cup sugar
- 2 tablespoons margarine
- 2 tablespoons fresh lemon juice
- 2 bananas
- Prepared whipped topping
- 1 (9-inch) pie crust, baked

Mix cornstarch and sugar; add to reserved juice and cook until thick, stirring constantly. Remove from heat. Add margarine and lemon juice. Add berries and cool. Line baked pie crust with sliced bananas. Pour cooled mixture over crust. Refrigerate until well-chilled. Top with whipped topping. Delicious!

Peach Cobbler

- 2 cups sliced peaches
- 1 cup sugar
- ½ cup margarine
- ½ cup sugar
- ¾ cup sifted flour
- ¾ cup milk
- 2 teaspoons baking powder
- ⅛ teaspoon salt

Combine peaches with 1 cup sugar; set aside. Melt margarine in a baking dish. Mix ½ cup sugar, flour, baking powder, milk and salt. Fold into margarine. Place peaches on top. Bake for 1 hour at 350 degrees, or until golden brown.

German Cherry Pie

2½ cups fresh *or* frozen sweet cherries, such as bings
6 tablespoons sugar
4 teaspoons cornstarch

Mix cherries and sugar and let stand 1 hour to make juice.

Crust

1½ cups flour
1½ teaspoons cinnamon
6 tablespoons sugar
⅛ teaspoon salt
½ cup butter
1 egg, beaten
½ teaspoon vanilla
½ teaspoon almond flavoring*
½ teaspoon cinnamon*

Combine dry ingredients; work in butter, egg and vanilla with hands until blended together. Press into a 9-inch pie pan and chill for 30 minutes. To complete filling, use half of cherry juice; thicken with cornstarch. Heat, stirring constantly for 2–3 minutes. Add remaining cherries to hot liquid. Pour into a chilled crust. Bake 50–60 minutes in a 350-degree oven.

*½ teaspoon almond flavoring and ½ teaspoon cinnamon may be added to filling along with vanilla for additional flavoring. Serve with whipped cream.

Zucchini Pie

2 tablespoons butter
1 cup light brown sugar
⅓ cup maple syrup
½ teaspoon *each* maple and lemon flavoring
½ teaspoon cinnamon
¼ teaspoon *each* salt, nutmeg and ground cloves
3 large eggs
½ cup coffee cream
¾ cup raw quick-cooking rolled oats
2 cups unpeeled grated zucchini (no seeds, outer rind only)
1 (9-inch) deep-dish unbaked pie shell

In large mixer bowl beat together the butter, syrup, sugar, flavorings, spices, eggs and cream until smooth and sugar dissolved. Stir in oats to moisten. Fold in zucchini. Pour evenly into pie shell. Bake in a 400-degree oven for 20 minutes. Reduce heat to 375 degrees and continue baking until center is firm, about 45 minutes. Cool completely before serving.

Grand Finale Sour Cream Apple Pie

1 egg, beaten
1 cup sour cream
1 teaspoon vanilla
¾ cup sugar
1 tablespoon flour
½ teaspoon salt
3 cups apples, sliced
1 (9-inch) unbaked pie crust

Topping

¼ cup margarine
1 teaspoon cinnamon
½ cup sugar
½ cup flour

Combine egg, sour cream and vanilla. Set aside. Mix sugar, flour and salt together. Mix into sour cream. Fold in apples and place in a pie crust. Bake at 375 degrees for 25 minutes, then turn oven to 325 degrees for an additional 25 minutes.

For topping, beat margarine until fluffy. Add remaining ingredients slowly and mix until crumbly. Sprinkle over pie and bake for another 15 minutes.

Angel Food Pie Filling

1 cup crushed pineapple
1 cup cold water
1 cup sugar
⅛ teaspoon salt
4 tablespoons cornstarch
2 eggs, separated
Whipped cream
Coconut *or* nuts

Beat egg yolks; add sugar, cornstarch and salt. Add pineapple and water. Cook in double boiler until thickened. Fold in beaten egg whites while mixture is still hot. Cool. Pour into baked pie shell. Cover with whipped cream. Sprinkle with coconut or nuts.

Frozen Butterscotch Pie

2 cups creme-filled chocolate sandwich cookie crumbs
⅓ cup butter, melted
1 (6-ounce) package butterscotch chips
1 (14-ounce) can sweetened condensed milk
1 (16-ounce) carton sour cream
⅓ cup amaretto liqueur
½ pint whipping cream

For crust, mix cookie crumbs and melted butter. Reserve 1½ cups; pat remaining crumbs into springform pan.

For filling, melt together chips and sweetened condensed milk. Cool to room temperature. Mix amaretto and sour cream; stir into melted chip mixture. Beat whipping cream to soft peaks and fold in.

On top of crumbs in springform, pour half of butterscotch mixture. Sprinkle 1 cup of reserved crumbs over top. Add remaining butterscotch mixture. Sprinkle ½ cup crumbs over the top. Cover and freeze 6 hours.

Apple Tart

Another excellent way to use patty shells—for dessert. This was adapted from a recipe in Gourmet, *October 1991.*

2 frozen puff pastry patty shells
1 medium apple (I use Golden Delicious)
1 tablespoon sugar
¼ teaspoon cinnamon
1 tablespoon cold butter
2 tablespoons jelly *or* jam (currant, cherry or apricot)
Vanilla ice cream

Preheat oven to 400 degrees.

Let patty shell pastry thaw on counter just until pliable; gently roll each to about a 5-inch circle; transfer to baking sheet (air-flow style is best). Peel, core and thinly slice apple; arrange slices on pastry circles in overlapping rows. Combine sugar and cinnamon; sprinkle over apples; dot with bits of butter. Bake until apples are tender and pastry golden, about 25 minutes. Transfer to rack to cool; immediately spread on jelly or jam to glaze. Serve with ice cream. Serves 2.

Chewy Cherry Coconut Tarts

Crust

- ½ cup butter, softened
- ½ cup brown sugar, lightly packed
- 1 egg yolk
- 1 cup flour

Filling

- 2 egg whites
- ½ cup brown sugar, lightly packed
- ½ cup shredded coconut
- ⅓ cup chopped maraschino cherries, drained
- ¼ cup finely chopped nuts
- 1 teaspoon vanilla

Combine all crust ingredients, mixing to a smooth dough, using hands, if necessary. Press into 12 muffin cups to form tart shells.

For filling, beat egg whites to stiff peaks. Stir in remaining ingredients. Mix well. Spoon into prepared shells. Bake at 325 degrees on lower oven rack for 18–23 minutes, or until golden. Cool. These tarts freeze well.

Little Jack Horner Plum Pudding Pie

- 1 (9-inch) unbaked pie shell
- 1 cup unsifted flour
- 1 teaspoon ground cinnamon
- ¼ teaspoon salt
- ¼ teaspoon ground cloves
- ⅓ cup butter *or* margarine
- ⅓ cup dark corn syrup
- ¼ cup chopped candied fruit
- 1½ cups prepared mincemeat
- ½ cup chopped walnuts
- 3 eggs, separated

In large bowl, mix together flour, cinnamon, salt and cloves. Cut in butter with pastry blender or 2 knives until coarse crumbs form. Mix corn syrup and candied fruit. Stir fruit mixture, mincemeat and walnuts into flour mixture. Beat egg whites until soft peaks form when beater is raised.

Beat egg yolks until thick and lemon-colored; stir into flour mixture. Fold in egg whites. Pour into pastry shell. Bake in a 350-degree oven for about 1 hour, or until cake tester inserted in center comes out clean. Serve warm. Decorate with whipped cream or whipped topping and candied cherries or bits of candied fruit.

Squash Pie

- 1½ cups cooked, mashed squash
- 1 cup rich milk, cream or half-and-half
- 1 tablespoon flour
- ¾ cup sugar
- 2 egg yolks
- 1 teaspoon vanilla
- 1 tablespoon butter
- 1 (9-inch) unbaked pie shell

Cook an acorn squash in light salt water just like you would potatoes. Drain and mash the squash only.

Mix all ingredients and warm until butter melts. Pour into unbaked pie shell. Bake for 15 minutes at 400 degrees, then reduce temperature to 350 degrees and bake 30–35 minutes, or until set. Top with meringue.

Sour Cream Raisin Pie

- 2 eggs
- 1 cup sugar
- 1 cup thick sour cream
- 1 cup raisins, chopped
- ¼ teaspoon nutmeg
- ¼ teaspoon salt
- 1 tablespoon lemon juice
- 1 (9-inch) unbaked pastry shell

Beat eggs, add sugar and beat until light. Whip sour cream and fold into egg mixture. Add raisins, nutmeg, salt and lemon juice; mix. Pour mixture into pastry shell and bake in very hot oven (450 degrees) for 10 minutes. Reduce temperature to moderate (350 degrees) and bake 20 minutes longer. Makes 1 (9-inch) pie.

Fresh Kumquat Pie

- 1 (9-inch) baked pie shell
- ¼ cup cornstarch
- 1½ cups water
- 1 cup sugar
- Pinch salt
- 3 eggs, separated
- ⅓ cup kumquat purée
- 1 teaspoon lemon juice
- 1 tablespoon margarine

In heavy saucepan combine water, sugar, cornstarch, salt and egg yolks. Place over medium heat and bring to a boil. Stir constantly. Boil 2 minutes and remove from heat. Add lemon juice, puréed kumquats and margarine. Pour mixture into a baked pie shell. Top with whipped cream.

Quickie Peanut Butter Pie

- ⅓ cup chunky peanut butter
- ½ cup confectioners' sugar
- 1 large package chocolate pudding (or make your own)
- ½ cup chopped, salted Virginia-type peanuts
- Prepared crust

Cut peanut butter and confectioners' sugar together. Cook chocolate pudding. Stir in half of peanut butter mixture. Cool 8 minutes, stirring frequently. Stir in half of remaining peanut mixture and chopped peanuts. Pour half of this filling in pie shell; sprinkle with remaining peanut mixture. Pour in remainder of filling. Chill 3 hours. Serve with whipped cream on top.

Raisin Rhubarb Pie

- 1 (Double) 9-inch pie crust
- 3 cups rhubarb, cut into 1-inch pieces
- 1½ tablespoons dark raisins
- 1½ tablespoons golden raisins
- ⅓ cup extra-fine soft bread crumbs
- 1 cup sugar
- ¼ teaspoon nutmeg
- ¼ teaspoon salt

Mix rhubarb, raisins, bread crumbs and sugar. Put into a pastry-lined pie plate; sprinkle with nutmeg and salt.

Cover with a top crust or lattice crust. Bake at 400 degrees for 15 minutes; reduce heat to 350 degrees; bake for 30 minutes longer.

Sandwich TASTIES

Taco Meat Patties

1½ pounds ground beef
1 small onion, chopped (¼ cup)
1 teaspoon Worcestershire sauce
1 teaspoon salt
¼ teaspoon pepper
1 (1¼-ounce) envelope taco seasoning mix
¾ cup water
1 small avocado *or* 1 medium-size tomato, sliced
1 cup shredded cheddar cheese

Mix meat, onion, Worcestershire sauce, salt and pepper. Shape mixture into 6 patties (¼ inch thick). Brown patties in large skillet over medium heat; turn 1 time. Remove patties and set aside. Pour fat from skillet. Mix seasoning mix and water in same skillet; heat to boiling, stirring constantly. Reduce heat; return patties to skillet and turn each to coat with sauce. Peel avocado and cut into 6 rings or use sliced tomato. Cover and simmer 10 minutes. Sprinkle with cheese; cover and heat until cheese is melted, about 2 minutes. Serve sauce over patties on heated hamburger buns. Makes 6.

California Carousel

2 ounces fresh mushrooms
½ medium green pepper
½ medium tomato, thinly sliced
4 thin slices Bermuda onion
4 slices Muenster cheese
1 cup fresh sprouts, washed and drained
2 whole-wheat pita bread
⅛ teaspoon garlic powder
1½ tablespoons real mayonnaise

Cut top section off pita bread to make a pocket. Mix mayonnaise and garlic powder; spread on inside of pockets on both sides. Chop mushrooms and green pepper into bite-size pieces. Slice tomato and onion. Combine mushrooms, green pepper and sprouts; mixing well. Fill each pocket with mixture of mushrooms, peppers and sprouts. Insert slices of tomato, onion and cheese. Serves 2.

Chicken on a Bun

2 (7-ounce) cans chicken
¼ cup chopped, stuffed olives
¾ cup diced celery
¾ cup chopped pickles
2 tablespoons chopped onion
½ cup mayonnaise
8 hamburger buns
Butter
16 slices American cheese

Combine chicken, olives, celery, pickles and onion; add mayonnaise. Slice buns into halves; spread with butter. Spread chicken mixture on buns; top with 1 slice cheese. Place buns on a greased cookie sheet. Bake at 350 degrees for 10–15 minutes, or until cheese is melted. Makes 16 sandwiches.

Korean Beef Patties

1 pound ground beef
4 tablespoons soy sauce
1 tablespoon toasted sesame seeds, crushed
1 tablespoon toasted sesame oil
2½ tablespoons chopped green onion
1 tablespoon garlic, minced
Black pepper to taste

Combine all ingredients. Form into 4 balls and flatten into patties. Broil, grill or pan-fry until done. Serves 4.

Delicious Tomato Club Sandwiches

12 slices sandwich bread
2 medium tomatoes, thinly sliced
8 slices bacon, crisply fried
2–3 dill pickles, thinly sliced
Mustard-Cheese Sauce (recipe follows)

Remove crusts from bread; toast on both sides. For 4 sandwiches, place 2 slices tomato on each of 4 slices toast. Cover with second slice toast. Place 2 strips of bacon and 3 thin slices pickle on second slice toast. Cover with third slice toast. Pour hot Mustard-Cheese Sauce over top. Serve immediately. Serves 4.

Mustard-Cheese Sauce

2 tablespoons butter *or* margarine
2 tablespoons flour
½ teaspoon salt
¼ teaspoon dry mustard
Dash pepper
1 cup milk
1 cup cut-up process sharp American cheese (4 ounces)

Melt butter over low heat in saucepan. Blend flour and seasonings. Cook over low heat, stirring until mixture is smooth and bubbly. Remove from heat and stir in milk. Heat to boiling; boil 1 minute. Remove from heat. Stir in cheese until melted. This is the greatest sandwich ever! Your family and guests will love it.

Muffuletta Sandwich

½ cup chopped Spanish olives
½ cup chopped pitted, ripe olives
½ cup chopped, drained hot and spicy garden mix
¼ cup finely chopped fresh parsley
½ cup olive oil
3 tablespoons lemon juice
1 clove garlic, minced
⅛ teaspoon pepper
1 teaspoon dried oregano leaves, crushed
1 loaf (about 1 pound) round Italian bread
4 ounces boiled ham, sliced
4 ounces provolone cheese, sliced
4 ounces salami, sliced
Olives for garnish

In medium bowl, combine first 9 ingredients; mix well. Cover; refrigerate at least 4 hours or overnight. Cut bread in half lengthwise. Hollow out center of each half, leaving 1-inch-thick shell. Save crumbs for another use.

Stir olive mixture well. Spoon half of the mixture into bread shell. Top with ham, provolone, salami and remaining olive mixture. Cover with remaining bread shell; press down lightly. Wrap in plastic wrap; refrigerate until serving time, at least 2 hours.

To serve: Cut into 8 wedges. Garnish with olives. Serves 4.

Chicken Salad Sandwiches

4 hard-cooked eggs, chopped
1 cup cooked chicken, diced
1 teaspoon lemon juice
½ teaspoon salt
¼ teaspoon paprika
¼ to ⅓ cup mayonnaise
12 slices white *or* whole-wheat bread

Combine eggs and chicken. Add lemon juice, salt and paprika to mayonnaise. Stir ¼ cup into egg mixture. Add more mayonnaise to taste. Spread chicken salad on 6 slices of bread, cover with remaining slices; pat down. Cut sandwiches in half. Serves 6.

Reuben Burgers

1 pound ground beef
1 small onion, finely chopped
1 (4½-ounce) can corned beef spread *or* deviled ham
⅛ teaspoon garlic salt
⅛ teaspoon pepper
¼ teaspoon salt
1 (8-ounce) can sauerkraut, drained
5 slices Swiss cheese

Mix all ingredients, except sauerkraut and cheese. Shape mixture into 5 patties about ¾ inch thick. Set oven control at broil (550 degrees). Broil patties 4 inches from heat, turning once, to desired doneness (10–15 minutes). Top each patty with sauerkraut and a cheese slice. Broil until cheese is light brown. Good served on toasted rye bun or pumpernickel buns. Makes 5 patties.

Knife & Fork Tunaburgers

1 egg
1 (7-ounce) can tuna, drained
½ cup bread crumbs
½ cup mayonnaise
1½ tablespoons onion, finely chopped
½ tablespoon green pepper, finely chopped
1½ tablespoons sweet pickle relish
Vegetable oil
4 hamburger buns, split
1 (10¾-ounce) can cream of celery soup
1 (14-ounce) can small green peas, drained
Paprika (for garnish)

Combine first 7 ingredients; form into 4 patties. Brown on both sides in vegetable oil; remove; set aside. In saucepan combine cream of celery soup and green peas. Heat through. Make open-face sandwiches; spoon creamed peas over both halves on plate; dust with paprika.

Easy Barbecue

4 cups chopped, cooked beef
3 cups chopped chicken *or* turkey (white meat)
2 cups ketchup
2 medium onions, chopped
½ cup vinegar
1 tablespoon Worcestershire sauce
Dash hot sauce
Salt and pepper to taste
3 tablespoons brown sugar
1 (13¾-ounce) can chicken broth
2 tablespoons corn-oil margarine

Sauté onions in margarine. Add meats and other ingredients. Cook on simmer for 30 minutes, stirring often. Add water, if needed. Serve on toasted buns.

Yummy Taco Hot Dogs

⅓ cup chili sauce
1 teaspoon minced hot chili pepper *or* few drops red pepper sauce
5 frankfurters
5 frankfurter buns, partially split, buttered and toasted
⅔ cup shredded lettuce
⅓ cup shredded natural cheddar cheese

Combine chili sauce and hot chili pepper. Drop frankfurters into boiling water, reduce heat and cook 5–8 minutes; drain. Place frankfurters in toasted buns. Spoon chili sauce mixture over frankfurters. Top with shredded lettuce and cheese. Serve immediately. Makes 5 servings.

Cheesy Corned Beef Barbecue Sandwiches

1 (12-ounce) can corned beef
6 slices bread, toasted
½ cup ketchup
2 teaspoons horseradish
2 teaspoons mustard
2 teaspoons vinegar
2 teaspoons finely chopped onions
6 slices cheddar cheese

Chill corned beef; cut lengthwise into 6 slices. Place a slice of corned beef on each slice of toast. Combine ketchup, horseradish, mustard, vinegar and onion. Spread half of sauce over corned beef. Top each sandwich with slice of cheese. Broil 6 inches from heat until cheese melts. Serve remaining sauce with sandwiches. Serves 6.

Salad BOWL

Hot Bacon Potato Salad

- 1/2 pound bacon, diced
- 3/4 cup chopped onion
- 1/3 cup chopped green pepper
- 6 cups chopped *or* sliced potatoes
- 3/4 cup mayonnaise (not salad dressing)
- 1/3 cup chopped pimiento
- 1/4 cup sugar
- 1 teaspoon salt
- 1/8 teaspoon pepper

Cook bacon, onions and green pepper until bacon is crisp. Drain, reserving a small amount of drippings. Add remaining ingredients. Mix thoroughly and gently. Bake in casserole for 20 minutes at 350 degrees to blend flavor. Keep warm on serving tray or in a small slow cooker.

This is a different kind of potato salad. It is very tasty and easy to make. You will want to double the recipe if you have a large family.

Hot Potato Salad

- 8 medium to large potatoes, cooked, peeled and diced
- 1/2 pound American cheese, diced
- 1/2 cup chopped celery
- 1/2 cup chopped onion
- 1 cup mayonnaise
- Salt and pepper to taste
- 1/2 pound bacon, fried
- 1/2 cup sliced stuffed olives

Combine potatoes, cheese, onion, celery and mayonnaise. Add salt and pepper to taste. Put into a 9 x 13-inch pan. Top with chopped bacon and olives. Bake 1 hour at 325 degrees. May be made early and refrigerated until time to bake. Serves 8–10.

Vegetable Gelatin Mold

- 2 envelopes unflavored gelatin
- 3 1/2 cups tomato juice
- 2 tablespoons prepared Caesar salad dressing
- 1/2 cup thinly sliced carrots
- 1/2 cup cauliflower
- 1/2 cup cooked peas
- 1/4 cup thinly sliced radishes
- 1 tablespoon sesame seed
- Sour cream

In saucepan, sprinkle gelatin over 1/2 cup tomato juice to soften. Heat until gelatin is dissolved, stirring often. Add remaining 3 cups tomato juice and salad dressing. Refrigerate until mixture mounds slightly when dropped from a spoon.

Fold remaining ingredients into gelatin mixture. Pour into 6-cup mold. Cover and refrigerate until set, about 2 hours. Unmold and serve with sour cream. Makes 3 cups or 10 servings.

Salmon Rice Salad

- 2 cups cooked white rice, cooled
- 1 cup celery, thinly sliced
- 1/2 cup sliced green onions
- 1/2 cup sweet pickle relish
- 1 cup mayonnaise *or* Ranch salad dressing
- 1/2 teaspoon black pepper
- 2 (6-ounce) cans pink salmon
- 1/2 cup chopped red *or* green pepper
- 1 cup frozen peas, thawed
- Lettuce leaves

Combine all ingredients, except lettuce, and toss gently. Chill. Serve on lettuce leaves.

Potato Salad

- 6 medium-size potatoes (about 3 pounds), pared, thinly sliced
- 1 cup (4 ounces) Swiss cheese, cut into thin strips
- 6 strips bacon, cooked and crumbled
- 1 1/2 cups dairy sour cream
- 3 tablespoons tarragon wine vinegar
- 1 tablespoon chopped fresh chives
- 1 tablespoon sugar
- 1 tablespoon prepared mustard
- 1 teaspoon salt
- Dash cayenne pepper

Place potato slices in 3 inches of boiling, salted water in Dutch oven. Return to boiling; reduce heat. Simmer, uncovered, over medium heat 5 minutes, or until potatoes are tender. Drain; rinse with cold water.

Place potatoes, cheese and bacon in a large bowl. Combine sour cream, vinegar, chives, sugar, mustard, salt and pepper. Spoon sour cream mixture over potato mixture; stir gently to combine. Refrigerate, covered, several hours or overnight to allow flavors to blend. Makes 8 cups.

Turnip Toss

- 3 cups shredded turnips
- 1 1/2 cups shredded carrots
- 1/2 cup raisins
- 1/2 to 3/4 cup mayonnaise
- 1 tablespoon lemon juice

Combine all ingredients and toss well. Cover and chill if desired. Serves 6–8.

Pineapple-Lime Snow Salad

- 1 (10-ounce) can crushed pineapple
- Water
- 1 (6-ounce) package lime gelatin
- 1 (8-ounce) carton whipped topping
- 1 (32-ounce) carton small-curd cottage cheese
- 1 (11-ounce) can mandarin oranges, drained
- 1 cup pecans *or* walnuts, finely chopped
- 1/2 cup flaked coconut
- Maraschino cherries for garnish

Drain pineapple; reserve syrup; set aside. Combine syrup and water to measure 1 cup; heat in saucepan to a boil. Add lime gelatin; cook until gelatin is dissolved; remove from heat; add 1 cup cold water; set aside. In large bowl combine pineapple, whipped topping, cottage cheese, mandarin oranges, pecans and coconut; mix well. Add lime gelatin to fruit and cottage cheese mixture. Turn into a 13 x 9-inch dish; cover; refrigerate until set. Cut into squares; garnish with maraschino cherries.

Confetti Chicken Slaw

- 2 cups shredded green cabbage
- 1 cup shredded red cabbage
- 1 1/2 cups chopped cooked chicken *or* turkey
- 1 (8-ounce) can sliced water chestnuts, drained
- 1 (6-ounce) package frozen snow peas *or* pea pods, thawed and drained
- 1/4 cup julienne-cut carrots
- 1/4 cup sliced green onions
- 1 cup salad dressing *or* mayonnaise
- 1 (5-ounce) can chow mein noodles *or* lettuce leaves

In a large bowl, combine green and red cabbage, chicken, water chestnuts, snow peas, carrots and green onions. Add dressing gently to coat. Cover and refrigerate 1 hour. Serve slaw on a bed of chow mein noodles or spoon each serving of slaw onto a lettuce leaf. Serves 6–8.

Tuna Macaroni Salad

Best if made a day ahead.

- 1/2 cup elbow macaroni, uncooked
- 1/4 cup mayonnaise
- 1/4 teaspoon dry mustard
- 1 1/2 teaspoons lemon juice
- 2 tablespoons water
- 1 teaspoon capers, if desired
- 1/4 cup chopped green pepper
- 1 green onion
- 1 (6–7-ounce) can tuna
- Salt and pepper to taste
- Dash of paprika

Cook macaroni in salted water according to directions on package; drain. Meanwhile, in a medium bowl, stir together mayonnaise, dry mustard, lemon juice, water, capers and green pepper. With scissors snip in green onion, including part of top.

Lightly drain tuna; flake in with fork. Add macaroni; toss lightly to mix. Taste; add salt and pepper as needed. Add paprika for color. Cover; chill. Serves 2.

Layered Tuna Salad

- 3 cups greens (bite-size leaf lettuce, iceberg lettuce or spinach)
- 1/2 cup frozen peas, thawed
- 1 (6–7-ounce) can tuna, drained
- 2 hard-cooked eggs, cut into wedges
- 1/2 cup grated cheddar *or* Swiss cheese
- 1/3 cup Dressing (recipe follows)

On each plate layer half of ingredients as follows: cover plate with greens; sprinkle on peas; add chunks of tuna and wedges of egg; sprinkle on cheese; spoon dressing over all. Serves 2.

Dressing

- 3 tablespoons mayonnaise
- 1 1/2 tablespoons sour cream
- 1 teaspoon Dijon-style mustard
- 2 teaspoons vinegar *or* cider vinegar
- 1 teaspoon water
- 1 tablespoon chopped fresh parsley *or* 1 teaspoon dill *or* both

Whisk ingredients together. If made ahead, cover and refrigerate. Makes 1/3 cup.

Southwest Salad

Salad Dressing

- 1/2 teaspoon grated orange rind
- 1/4 cup fresh-squeezed orange juice
- 1/2 cup vegetable oil
- 2 tablespoons sugar
- 3 tablespoons red wine vinegar
- 1 tablespoon lemon juice
- 1/4 teaspoon salt

Salad

- 3 heads Boston lettuce, washed and chilled
- 1 small cucumber, thinly sliced
- 1 avocado, peeled and sliced crosswise
- 1 small red onion, sliced and separated into rings
- 1 (11-ounce) can mandarin oranges, drained, *or* fresh orange sections

Combine salad dressing ingredients; mix well and set aside. Arrange lettuce, cucumber, avocado, onion and oranges on individual plates. Drizzle salads with dressing just before serving. Serves 6.

Zippy Perfection Salad

- 2 envelopes unflavored gelatin
- 1/4 cup sugar
- 1 teaspoon salt
- 1 1/2 cups boiling water
- 1 1/2 cups cold water
- 1/2 cup vinegar
- 2 tablespoons lemon juice
- 2 cups cabbage, finely shredded
- 1 cup celery, chopped
- 1/4 cup green pepper, chopped
- 1/4 cup pimiento, diced
- 1/3 cup stuffed green olives, sliced

Thoroughly mix gelatin, sugar and salt. Add boiling water and stir to dissolve gelatin. Then add cold water, vinegar and lemon juice. Chill until partially set. Add remaining ingredients. Pour into an 8 1/2 x 4 1/2 x 1 1/2-inch loaf pan. Chill until firm. Just before serving time, unmold and garnish salad with more olives and carrot curls.

Colorful Coleslaw

- 4 cups thinly sliced green cabbage*
- 1 cup thinly sliced red cabbage
- 1 cup thinly sliced carrots
- 1 cup blanched pea pods
- 1 cup pineapple tidbits
- 1/2 cup chopped celery
- 1 cup whipping cream
- 1/2 cup dairy sour cream
- 1/4 cup fresh lemon juice
- 2 tablespoons sugar
- 4 teaspoons Dijon-style prepared mustard
- 1/4 teaspoon salt
- 1/4 teaspoon pepper

Combine vegetables and fruit in large mixing bowl; cover and chill. About 1 hour before serving, combine whipping cream, sour cream, lemon juice, sugar, mustard, salt and pepper in a small, chilled mixer bowl. Beat until almost stiff. Fold whipped cream mixture into cabbage mixture. Cover and chill. Makes 10 cups.

**Note:* Four cups prepared slaw mix from produce department of grocery store may be substituted.

Winter White Gelatin

- 1 (8-ounce) package cream cheese, softened
- 1/2 cup granulated sugar
- 1/2 teaspoon vanilla *or* almond extract
- 1/2 cup milk
- 1 envelope unflavored gelatin
- 1/4 cup cold water
- Boiling water
- 1 cup whipped topping
- Fruit *or* berries for decoration (strawberries are great)

Blend cream cheese, sugar and vanilla or almond extract. Gradually add milk. Set aside. Dissolve gelatin in cold water. Add boiling water to make 1 cup. After slightly cooled, stir into cream cheese mixture. Chill until slightly thickened and fold in whipped topping. Chill in 1 1/2-quart mold. Unmold and garnish before serving.

Chilled Pasta, Roasted Garlic & Tomatoes

- 3/4 pound pasta, your choice
- 1/2 cup virgin olive oil
- 1 head garlic roasted until tender, peeled and minced
- 8 medium tomatoes, peeled, seeded and diced
- 1/4 cup chopped fresh basil
- Salt to taste
- Freshly ground black pepper, to taste
- 3/4 cup grated Parmesan cheese
- 4 sprigs fresh basil

In a large amount of boiling water, cook pasta until tender. Transfer to a strainer; drain, and rinse with tepid water. Transfer to a bowl. Add 1/4 cup olive oil and toss to coat pasta. Refrigerate to chill.

In a medium-size bowl, combine remaining olive oil with garlic, tomatoes and basil. Season with salt and pepper. Add pasta and toss to mix well. Place in a sealed container for traveling to the picnic. For the picnic, distribute pasta to the serving platter. Top with grated Parmesan cheese. Garnish with basil sprigs and serve. Serves 4.

Glistening Garden Salad

- 1 (3-ounce) package lemon gelatin
- 1 (3-ounce) package lime gelatin
- 2 cups boiling water
- 1 1/2 cups cold water
- 3 tablespoons lemon juice
- 1 cup shredded carrots
- 1 cup finely chopped, unpeeled cucumber
- 1/4 cup sliced celery
- 1 1/2 teaspoons prepared horseradish
- Lettuce leaves (optional)
- Mayonnaise (optional)

Dissolve gelatin in boiling water; add cold water, lemon juice and horseradish. Chill until partially set. Fold in vegetables. Pour into 5 1/2-cup mold or in dish equivalent to mold size. Chill until set. Unmold onto lettuce leaves or cut in squares. Serve with mayonnaise, if desired. Serves 8.

Fruit Salad

- 1 can apricot pie filling
- 1 can mandarin oranges, drained
- 1 can pineapple tidbits, drained
- 1 cup miniature marshmallows
- 2 bananas, sliced

Combine ingredients; chill. This is so simple, you will love it!

Parmesan Italian Dressing

- 1 envelope Parmesan salad dressing mix
- 1/4 cup water
- 2 tablespoons vinegar
- 2/3 cup mayonnaise *or* salad dressing
- 2 teaspoons anchovy paste

Shake salad dressing mix with water in a covered jar. Add vinegar, mayonnaise and anchovy paste. Shake until blended.

Apricot Salad

- 1 (29-ounce) can apricot halves
- 1 (1-pound 4-ounce) can crushed pineapple
- 1 (6-ounce) box apricot *or* orange gelatin
- 2 cups boiling water
- 1 cup reserved juice
- 3/4 cup miniature marshmallows
- Topping (recipe follows)

Drain apricots and pineapple, reserving juice. Dissolve gelatin in 2 cups boiling water. Stir in reserved juice. Chill until slightly congealed. Fold in fruits and marshmallows. Pour into an 11 x 7-inch pan. Chill until firm.

Topping

- 1/2 cup sugar
- 3 tablespoons flour
- 1 egg, slightly beaten
- 2 tablespoons butter
- 1 cup reserved fruit juice
- 1 cup whipped topping

Cook juice, sugar, flour and egg over low heat until thickened. Stir in butter. Cool. Fold in whipped topping and spread over the set gelatin salad. Refrigerate until serving. Cut into squares to serve.

Vegetable Gelatin Salad

1 (3-ounce) package lemon gelatin
1 tablespoon sugar
1 cup boiling water
1/2 cup fresh grapefruit juice
1 tablespoon vinegar
1/2 cup shredded cabbage
1/3 cup diced celery
1/3 cup grated carrots
1 tablespoon minced onion
2 tablespoons chopped green pepper
1/3 teaspoon salt
1/4 teaspoon pepper *or* paprika

Dissolve gelatin and sugar in boiling water. Add grapefruit juice and vinegar. Pour into a 9 x 13-inch dish. Add remaining ingredients, mixing well. Refrigerate until firm, about 4 hours. Serves 15.

Oriental Seafood Salad

1 pound fresh *or* frozen seafood (use a combination of fish and shrimp, scallops or lobster)
2 tablespoons oil, divided
2 green onions, chopped
1/4 teaspoon ground ginger
3/4 cup chicken broth
1/4 cup ketchup
2 tablespoons cider vinegar
2 tablespoons dry sherry
1 teaspoon sugar
Dash pepper
Dash hot pepper sauce (Tabasco)
2 teaspoons cornstarch
1 tablespoon water
Lettuce leaves

If frozen, thaw seafood. Cut into 1-inch pieces.

Heat 1 tablespoon of the oil in a large frying pan or wok. Add seafood and stir-fry gently until cooked through. Remove to a large bowl and set aside. Into same pot or wok, add remaining 1 tablespoon oil; sauté onion and ginger for 1 minute. Stir in next 7 ingredients; heat to boiling.

Combine cornstarch and water; pour into broth mixture and cook 1 minute, or until slightly thickened. Pour sauce over seafood. Cover and refrigerate at least 4 hours or overnight.

To serve, arrange lettuce leaves on serving plate. Place seafood mixture in a mound on lettuce. Serves 4.

Sweet-Sour Salad Dressing

1 3/4 cups oil
1/3 cup vinegar
1 small onion, grated
1 clove garlic, crushed
1 teaspoon dill weed
1/2 teaspoon tarragon
1/2 teaspoon celery seed
1/2 teaspoon ground ginger
1 teaspoon paprika
1/2 cup sugar
1 teaspoon salt
1/2 teaspoon mustard
1 tablespoon lemon juice

Blend all ingredients in blender until well-mixed. Store in refrigerator until serving.

Cranberry Relish Mold

2 (3-ounce) packages cherry gelatin
1 teaspoon unflavored gelatin
2 cups boiling water
1 (16-ounce) can whole-berry cranberry sauce
1 (7-ounce) can crushed pineapple, drained
1/4 cup chopped celery
Fresh cranberries (for garnish)
Mayonnaise

Dissolve cherry and unflavored gelatins completely in boiling water. Let cool slightly; then stir in cranberry sauce, drained pineapple and celery. Pour into a glass serving bowl or 6-cup mold that first has been rinsed under cold water; chill until firm.

At serving time, dip mold briefly in a pan of hot water to loosen and unmold onto chilled plate. Garnish with fresh cranberries. Top each portion with a small dollop of mayonnaise. Serves 8–10.

Sweet Potato Salad

1 pound sweet potatoes *or* yams
Water to cover potatoes
2 green onions, sliced
1/2 cup mayonnaise
1/4 cup chopped, toasted pecans
1 stalk celery, diced
1 tablespoon lemon juice
Parsley for garnish (optional)

Prepare potatoes and cube them. Place in pot of water to cover. Simmer until tender, about 30 minutes. Drain well and cool. In small bowl combine potatoes with onions and celery. Mix mayonnaise and lemon juice. Blend into potato mixture. Sprinkle with pecans.

Serve immediately or cover and refrigerate 1 hour. Sprinkle with parsley, if desired.

Fruit Fantasy

3 egg yolks
2 teaspoons apple cider vinegar
1 tablespoon margarine
2 cups pitted white cherries
2 cups pineapple chunks
2 tablespoons sugar
2 tablespoons pineapple syrup
Dash salt
1 cup cream, whipped
2 cups small marshmallows
2 oranges, cut in pieces

Cook egg yolks, sugar, salt, vinegar, pineapple syrup and margarine in pan until thick. Cool. Fold in whipped cream, cherries, marshmallows, pineapple and oranges. Chill.

Salad

1/2 small head red cabbage, finely chopped *or* shredded
1/2 cup golden raisins *or* chopped apple
2/3 cup applesauce
1/4 teaspoon salt
2–3 teaspoons prepared horseradish

Combine ingredients and mix together. Cover and refrigerate at least 1 hour. Serves 4.

French Salad Dressing

- 1 can condensed tomato soup
- 3/4 cup rice vinegar
- 1 cup salad oil
- 1 cup ketchup
- 1/2 cup sugar
- 2 teaspoons paprika
- 2 teaspoons dry mustard
- 1 teaspoon salt (if desired)
- 1 tablespoon Worcestershire sauce
- 2 cloves garlic, minced finely *or* crushed
- 3 tablespoons onion flakes
- 3 tablespoons parsley flakes

Stir ingredients together. Enjoy your salad!

Sweet Potato Salad

- 3 cups sweet potatoes, cooked and cut in bite-size chunks
- 1 1/2 cups celery, sliced diagonally
- 1 cup pineapple chunks, fresh *or* canned
- 1/2 cup chopped pecans
- 1/4 cup orange juice
- Salt to taste
- Curry Mayonnaise (recipe follows)

Cook potatoes just until tender (do not overcook). Peel when slightly cooled, then cut up. Mix gently with remaining salad ingredients and chill until ready to serve. May be served individually on lettuce leaves topped with Curry Mayonnaise, or served in a large bowl with dressing on the side. Serves 6.

Curry Mayonnaise

- 2 teaspoons curry powder
- 2 teaspoons orange peel, grated
- 1 cup mayonnaise
- 2 tablespoons cream, if needed

Combine ingredients and mix thoroughly. If thick, add 2 tablespoons cream to thin.

24-Hour Fruit Salad

- 3 cups Royal Anne cherries, halved and pitted
- 2 cups pineapple, crushed
- 2 (11-ounce) cans mandarin oranges
- 2 1/2 cups miniature marshmallows
- 1/2 cup almonds, blanched

Dressing

- 2 eggs
- 2 tablespoons sugar
- 1/4 cup cream
- Juice of 1 lemon
- 1/2 teaspoon lemon flavoring
- 1 cup whipping cream

Drain all of the fruit; mix with marshmallows and almonds. Let stand while preparing dressing. To prepare dressing, beat eggs and gradually add sugar, 1/4 cup cream, lemon juice and flavoring. Cook in top of double boiler, stirring constantly, until thick. Cool. Fold in 1 cup heavy cream, which has been whipped. Fold into fruit mixture very gently. Chill for 24 hours before serving.

Stuffed Pear Salad

- 1 can pear halves (7–8)
- 1/2 cup crushed pineapple, drained
- 1 (3-ounce) package cream cheese
- 1 tablespoon chopped pecans
- 1 tablespoon chopped maraschino cherries

Place pear halves on paper towels to drain excess moisture. Place cream cheese, pecans and cherries into bowl. Drain crushed pineapple well, then add to other ingredients. Stir until mixed thoroughly. Stuff pear halves with about 1 tablespoon of mixture. Use all the mixture. There should be enough to stuff about 7–8 pear halves. Serve on bed of lettuce leaves.

Relished Rice Salad

- 3 cups cold, cooked rice
- 1/2 cup sweet pickle relish
- 4 hard-cooked eggs, chopped
- 1/2 cup finely chopped onion
- 2 tablespoons chopped pimiento
- 1 1/2 cups mayonnaise
- 1 hard-cooked egg, sliced (garnish)

Combine first 6 ingredients; toss. Chill thoroughly. Garnish with egg slices.

Summer Cauliflower Salad

- 1 medium head cauliflower
- 3 stalks celery, chopped
- 1/4 cup chopped green pepper
- 1/3 cup Italian salad dressing
- 1/4 teaspoon salt
- 5 green onions, chopped
- 1/4 cup sliced pimiento-stuffed olives
- 1/3 cup salad dressing *or* mayonnaise
- 1 teaspoon sugar
- 1/4 teaspoon pepper

Separate cauliflower into florets; cut into bite-size pieces. Combine cauliflower, onions, celery, olives and green pepper in a large bowl; set aside. Combine remaining ingredients; mix well; pour over vegetables. Toss gently; cover and chill 3–4 hours. Serves 8.

Raspberry Pineapple Salad

- 2 cups boiling water
- 2 (3-ounce) packages raspberry-flavored gelatin
- 1 (16-ounce) package frozen raspberries, partially thawed
- 1 (8 1/4-ounce) can crushed pineapple, drained

Add boiling water to gelatin and stir until dissolved. Add raspberries immediately; separate berries with a fork and mix gently. Add pineapple and mix; pour into lightly oiled 6 1/2-cup ring mold and chill. Unmold and garnish with greens and fruit. Serves 8.

Western Dressing

- 1 cup mayonnaise
- 1/2 cup dairy sour cream
- 1/3 cup parsley, snipped
- 3 tablespoons chives, snipped
- 3 tablespoons tarragon vinegar
- 3 tablespoons anchovy paste
- 1 tablespoon lemon juice
- Dash pepper

Blend mayonnaise with dairy sour cream. Add remaining ingredients and stir well. Chill.

Flo's Broccoli Cabbage Salad

- 2 cups shredded cabbage
- 1 head fresh broccoli, cut into florets
- 1 small onion, diced
- 1 cup diced celery
- 1/4 teaspoon salt
- 1/4 teaspoon herbs-and-spices seasoning
- 1 tablespoon vinegar
- Mayonnaise (enough to moisten salad)
- 1/2 pound bacon, fried, drained and crumbled

Combine cabbage, broccoli, onion and celery. Sprinkle salt and seasoning on mixture and mix well. Add vinegar and mix well. Add mayonnaise. Place in a serving dish; refrigerate until ready to serve. Add crumbled bacon to top of salad. Serves 4.

Barbecue Bean Salad

- 1 (1-pound) can (2 cups) cut green beans, drained
- 1 (1-pound) can cut wax beans, drained
- 1 (1-pound) can kidney beans, drained
- 1/2 cup green pepper, chopped
- 1 medium onion, sliced
- 3/4 cup sugar
- 2/3 cup vinegar
- 1/3 cup salad oil
- 1 teaspoon salt
- 1 teaspoon pepper

Combine vegetables; toss lightly. Combine sugar, vinegar and salad oil; pour over vegetables. Add salt and pepper; toss lightly. Chill overnight. Before serving, toss again to coat with marinade. Serves 6–8.

Caesar Salad

- 1 head lettuce
- 1 head romaine
- 2 cups white bread crumbs
- 3/4 cup olive oil
- 1 clove garlic (mashed)
- 1/4 cup lemon juice
- Salt and pepper
- 1 tablespoon Worcestershire sauce
- 1/4 cup Parmesan cheese, grated
- 1/4 cup bleu cheese, crumbled

Tear greens into a large salad bowl. Fry bread crumbs and garlic in 1/4 cup olive oil until golden brown. Drain on paper towels. Combine lemon juice with remaining oil, salt, pepper and Worcestershire sauce. Mix the cheeses with greens. Pour dressing over. Add croutons and toss again lightly.

Sweet 'n' Sour Slaw

Dressing

- 1 cup mild honey
- 1 cup wine vinegar
- 1/2 cup finely chopped onion
- 1 teaspoon celery seed
- 1 teaspoon salt

In small saucepan, combine all ingredients and bring to a boil. Reduce heat and simmer for 5 minutes. Cool.

Vegetables

- 1 large head cabbage, finely chopped (about 4 cups)
- 1 cup diced green pepper
- 1 cup diced celery

Pour enough dressing over prepared vegetables to coat thoroughly; toss. Cover and chill several hours or overnight to blend flavors. Serves 10–12.

Corned Beef Salad

- 3 small packages lemon gelatin
- 3 cups hot water
- 4 tablespoons vinegar
- 2 cups mayonnaise
- 1 green pepper, finely chopped
- 1 can corned beef, broken in pieces
- 2 cups chopped celery
- 2 tablespoons grated onion

Combine gelatin, hot water and vinegar; let set until syrupy. I usually beat the mayonnaise a few seconds with electric mixer, then add corned beef and beat a few minutes to break up beef. Add remaining ingredients. You may add a little garlic, if desired. Use a 13 x 9 x 2-inch pan.

Holiday Lime Salad

- 1 large box lime gelatin
- 1 cup hot water
- 2 cups miniature marshmallows
- 2/3 cup mayonnaise
- 1/2 cup cold water
- 3 stalks celery, diced
- 1 cup chopped maraschino cherries
- 1 cup chopped nuts
- 1 apple, diced
- 1 small can crushed pineapple
- 2 bananas, thinly sliced

Dissolve gelatin in hot water, then add marshmallows; stir to melt marshmallows. Add cold water, and when cooled, add cherries, mayonnaise, celery, apple, pineapple, nuts and bananas. Mix in a 13 x 9 x 2-inch glass dish. Place in refrigerator until set.

Purple Lady Salad

- 1 (6-ounce) package red raspberry gelatin
- 1 cup hot water
- 1 large can crushed pineapple, undrained
- 1 can blueberry pie filling
- 1 (8-ounce) container frozen whipped topping, thawed

Dissolve gelatin in hot water. Add pineapple and pie filling. Chill until thick; fold in whipped topping. Looks attractive in a clear glass bowl. Let stand in refrigerator until set.

Citrus Orange Salad

- 2 (6-ounce) packages orange gelatin
- 2 cups boiling water
- 1 (6-ounce) can frozen orange juice concentrate
- 1 (8-ounce) can mandarin oranges with juice
- 1 (1-pound, 4-ounce) can crushed pineapple with juice

Dissolve gelatin in boiling water. Add remaining ingredients; stir to combine and let set. If desired, pour into mold.

Star-Studded Hot Potato Salad

1 cup onion, diced
1 tablespoon butter
$1/2$ cup vinegar
$1/2$ cup mayonnaise
1 teaspoon sugar
1 teaspoon salt
1 teaspoon parsley
1 cup bacon, cooked and crumbled
Pepper
4 cups potatoes, cooked and diced

Sauté onion in butter about 2 minutes. Stir in all other ingredients, except potatoes and bacon. Fold in potatoes carefully and sprinkle with bacon. Heat through another 2–3 minutes and serve.

House Roquefort Dressing

$1/2$ teaspoon garlic powder
$1/3$ cup cider vinegar
1 cup salad oil
1 cup mayonnaise
1 teaspoon salt
$1/3$ teaspoon white pepper
$1/4$ teaspoon paprika
$3/4$ teaspoon dry mustard
1 teaspoon sugar
$1/3$ cup evaporated milk
$1/3$ cup lemon juice
5 ounces Roquefort cheese, grated

Mix garlic powder and vinegar. Add oil gradually to mayonnaise, mixing well after each addition. Add seasonings and mix well. Add milk gradually, mixing or beating well after each addition; then add the lemon juice and vinegar in the same manner. Add cheese and mix. Makes $3^1/2$ cups dressing.

Vinaigrette Dressing

1 tablespoon sugar
1 teaspoon salt
1 teaspoon paprika
1 teaspoon mustard
$1/4$ teaspoon pepper
$1/4$ cup mild vinegar
$3/4$ cup salad oil
$1/8$ teaspoon onion juice
6 green olives, finely chopped
2 small dill pickles, finely chopped
1 tablespoon chives, minced
1 tablespoon pimiento, minced
2 hard-cooked eggs, finely chopped

Combine all ingredients in a covered jar and shake. Chill. Shake again before using. Keep refrigerated.

Spring Salad Mold

2 beef bouillon cubes
1 (3-ounce) package lemon gelatin
1 cup boiling water
2 tablespoons tarragon vinegar
$1/2$ teaspoon salt
1 cup dairy sour cream
$1/2$ cup cucumber, unpared and chopped
$1/4$ cup green pepper, finely chopped
$1/4$ cup radishes, sliced
2 tablespoons green onion, sliced

Dissolve bouillon cubes and gelatin in boiling water. Add vinegar and salt. Chill until mixture is partially set. Add sour cream; beat smooth. Add remaining ingredients. Pour into a 3-cup mold. Chill until mixture is firm. Serves 6.

Sea Leg Salad

1 small package sea legs or crabmeat
1 bunch scallions, sliced
$1/2$ to 1 cup celery, thinly sliced
Fresh parsley
Salt and pepper
1 can water chestnuts
$1/4$ cup cashews
1 tablespoon vinegar
4–5 tablespoons mayonnaise
1–2 tablespoons sugar

Mix vinegar, mayonnaise and sugar; set aside. Combine remaining ingredients and pour vinegar mixture over. Refrigerate for a few hours before serving. Serve with tomato and cucumber for garnish.

Parmesan Blue Cheese Dressing

2 cups mayonnaise *or* salad dressing
1 (8-ounce) can seasoned tomato sauce
$1/4$ cup Parmesan cheese, grated
1 ounce blue cheese, crumbled
2 tablespoons cooking sherry
2 cloves garlic, minced
1 teaspoon paprika

Mix all ingredients together. (For a smoother dressing, blend in blender 10–15 seconds.) Chill. Serve over lettuce and tomatoes. Makes $3^1/4$ cups.

Cucumber Salad

1 (3-ounce) package lemon gelatin
$1^1/4$ cups boiling water
$3/4$ cup salad dressing *or* mayonnaise
1 cup cottage cheese
$3/4$ cup shredded cucumber
2 tablespoons grated onion
$1/3$ cup slivered almonds (optional)

Combine gelatin and water; set in refrigerator to cool while preparing remaining ingredients. Blend other ingredients thoroughly and add to gelatin. Refrigerate until firm.

Salad Dressing

1 small onion, cut up
1 cup mayonnaise
$1/3$ cup salad oil
$1/4$ cup ketchup
$1/2$ teaspoon paprika
1 cup grated cheese
2 tablespoons sugar
2 tablespoons vinegar
1 teaspoon prepared mustard
$1/2$ teaspoon salt
$1/4$ teaspoon celery seed
Dash pepper

Put all ingredients, except cheese, in blender. Cover and blend until smooth. Remove from blender and stir in cheese. Cover and chill. Serve over tossed vegetable greens. Makes $2^1/2$ cups.

Blueberry Gelatin Salad

1 large package grape *or* raspberry gelatin
1 tablespoon sugar
1 large can crushed pineapple, undrained
1½ cups boiling water
1 can blueberry pie filling

Topping

1 (8-ounce) package cream cheese, softened
1 cup sour cream
½ to ¾ cup confectioners' sugar
1 teaspoon vanilla
½ cup chopped pecans

Dissolve gelatin and sugar in boiling water. Add pineapple and blueberry filling. Pour into dish. Chill until firm. Mix well all topping ingredients, except pecans. Spread over gelatin mixture. Sprinkle with chopped nuts.

Pistachio Fruit Salad

1 (12-ounce) container non-dairy whipped topping
2 packages pistachio pudding mix
1 (13-ounce) can crushed pineapple
1 can fruit cocktail
1 can mandarin orange segments
1 small bottle maraschino cherries
Iceberg lettuce leaves
Few mandarin orange segments

Mix together pineapple with pudding and pineapple juice. Drain orange segments and fruit cocktail. Blend remaining ingredients, except cherries and lettuce, with whipped topping. Chill in refrigerator overnight and serve on Iceberg lettuce leaves, with orange and cherry garnish.

Yogurt Curry Dressing

1 cup yogurt
1 tablespoon prepared mustard
1 teaspoon seasoned salt
½ teaspoon curry powder

Combine all ingredients and chill. Makes 1 cup.

Favorite Vegetable Salad

1 (3-ounce) package orange gelatin
1 cup salad dressing (at room temperature)
1 cup cottage cheese
1 cup grated carrots
1 cup chopped celery
1 small onion, chopped

Dissolve gelatin in 1 cup boiling water. Add salad dressing. Cool 15 minutes. When cool add cottage cheese and vegetables. Turn into an 8 x 8 x 2-inch square pan. Cut in squares after chilled. Takes about 45 minutes. This is very easy to make, nutritious and great for lunch or dinner.

Mixed Fruits With Strawberry Citrus Dressing

¾ cup vegetable oil
6 tablespoons red wine vinegar
1½ tablespoons frozen orange juice concentrate, thawed
1½ tablespoons honey
1 cup fresh strawberries, stemmed
3 tablespoons mayonnaise
Assorted sliced fruits (strawberries, melons, bananas, peaches, apples, oranges, cherries, grapes)

Combine first 6 ingredients in container of electric blender. Blend until smooth. Refrigerate in covered container. Serve over sliced fruits. Serves 6–8. Makes 1½ cups dressing.

Thousand Island Dressing

3 hard-boiled eggs, chopped
3 stuffed green olives, chopped
2 tablespoons cheddar cheese, grated
2 tablespoons onion, chopped
½ cup salad dressing
2 tablespoons green peppers, chopped

Mix together all ingredients and serve.

Kidney Bean Salad

1 (No. 2) can kidney beans
¼ cup salad dressing
1 cup chopped celery
3 tablespoons minced onion
½ cup sweet pickle relish
½ teaspoon prepared horseradish
¼ teaspoon chili powder
Bacon bits
Hard-cooked eggs

Drain beans. Combine salad dressing and next 5 ingredients. Toss together lightly with beans. Chill a few hours in refrigerator. Serve on lettuce leaf; garnish with bacon bits and sliced, hard-cooked eggs. Serves 4–6.

Mexican Salad

1 bunch green onions, chopped
4 tomatoes, diced
1 head lettuce, broken
½ pound cheddar cheese, grated
1 avocado, diced
1 bag tortilla chips
1 pound ground beef
1 can kidney beans, drained
½ teaspoon salt
8 ounces French dressing (1 cup)

Brown ground beef; drain and cool. Prepare lettuce, tomatoes, onions, cheese, avocado and kidney beans. Toss with meat. Add salt and salad dressing. Refrigerate. When ready to serve, add tortilla chips.

Sauerkraut Salad

1 can chopped sauerkraut
1 cup chopped onion
1 cup chopped celery
1 cup chopped green peppers
¼ cup oil
½ cup sugar
½ cup vinegar
1 cup shredded carrots for color, if desired

Combine sauerkraut, onion, celery and pepper. Combine oil, sugar and vinegar; bring to boil. Remove from heat and pour over sauerkraut mixture. Add carrots before serving.

Roast Peppers & Radicchio Salad

- 1/4 cup balsamic vinegar
- 3/4 cup extra virgin olive oil
- Salt to taste
- Coarsely ground black pepper to taste
- 2 large red peppers, roasted, peeled, seeded and torn into bite-size pieces
- 1 head radicchio
- 1 cup picked basil leaves, torn into pieces

In a small bowl, whisk together vinegar and oil. Add salt and pepper to taste. Carefully peel off leaves from head of radicchio. Select best 8 large leaves and line serving platter. Tear remaining leaves into bite-size pieces. In a medium-size bowl, combine peppers, radicchio and basil leaves. Add dressing and toss. Transfer to a sealed container for traveling to the picnic.

For the picnic, arrange the larger whole radicchio leaves on serving platter. Position pepper and Radicchio Salad in the center of the platter. Top with additional black pepper, if desired. Serves 4.

St. Patrick's Day Molded Lime-Cucumber Salad

- 1 (3-ounce) package lime-flavored gelatin
- 1 teaspoon salt
- 3 tablespoons cider vinegar
- 1 teaspoon grated onion
- 2 cups sour cream
- 1/4 cup mayonnaise
- 1 large cucumber, finely shredded and well-drained
- Lettuce leaves

In medium bowl, stir gelatin and salt. Add 2/3 cup boiling water and stir until gelatin is dissolved. Stir in vinegar and onion. Refrigerate until mixture mounds slightly when dropped from a spoon, about 40 minutes. With wire whisk or hand beater, beat in sour cream, mayonnaise and cucumber until well-mixed. Pour into 6-cup mold. Refrigerate several hours until set. To serve, unmold onto serving plate. Tuck lettuce leaves around salad. Serve with dressing of your choice. Serves 8.

Apple, Broccoli & Peppers With Basil Vinaigrette

- 2 medium (about 1 pound) Newtown Pippin apples, cored and sliced
- 2 cups cooked broccoli florets
- 1 *each* medium red and yellow sweet pepper, seeded and cut into bite-size pieces
- 2 green onions, diagonally sliced
- Basil Apple Vinaigrette (recipe follows)

Combine all ingredients; toss in Basil Apple Vinaigrette. Serves 4–6.

Basil Apple Vinaigrette

Combine 2 tablespoons *each* olive oil and apple juice, 1 tablespoon vinegar, 2 teaspoons chopped fresh basil* and 1 small clove minced garlic; mix well. Makes 1/4 cup.

*One-half teaspoon crushed dried basil may be substituted.

Garlic Salad Dressing

- 2 cups mayonnaise
- 1/3 cup buttermilk
- 1/3 cup vegetable oil
- 1/4 cup water
- 1 1/2 tablespoons garlic powder
- 1 tablespoon vinegar
- 1 1/2 teaspoons lemon juice
- 1 1/2 teaspoons honey
- 3/4 teaspoon dry mustard
- 1/2 teaspoon salt

Combine mayonnaise and buttermilk; mix well, using a wire whisk. Stir in remaining ingredients. Cover and refrigerate at least 8 hours. Makes 3 cups.

Olive Dressing

- 1/2 of 3-ounce package cream cheese, softened
- 1 cup Italian dressing
- 1/4 teaspoon paprika
- 1/3 cup chopped, stuffed green olives

Beat together cream cheese and Italian dressing until smooth. Stir in paprika and olives. Mix well.

Raspberry Gelatin

- 1 (6-ounce) *plus* 1 (3-ounce) packages raspberry gelatin
- Lemon-lime soda
- 1 medium can crushed pineapple
- 2 (10-ounce) packages frozen raspberries, thawed, undrained
- 1/4 cup chopped nuts
- Whipped topping

Mix gelatin and 2 cups hot water. Do not add cold water. Drain pineapple and add lemon-lime soda to make 2 cups liquid. Add to gelatin. Add pineapple, raspberries and nuts. After gelatin has set, top with whipped topping.

Raspberry-Wine Mold

- 1 (16-ounce) can raspberries
- 1/2 cup red wine
- Water
- 2 (3-ounce) packages raspberry-flavored gelatin

Drain raspberries into 2-cup measure; add 1/2 cup red wine and water to make 2 cups. Prepare raspberry gelatin, using berry-wine-water mixture. Pour into individual molds. Add raspberries to molds when gelatin has cooled; refrigerate. When firm, invert onto serving plates. Serves 4–6.

Good Blender Dressing

- 2 cups salad oil
- 1 cup sugar
- 2/3 cup vinegar
- 1/2 teaspoon pepper
- 1 teaspoon salt
- 1 tablespoon dry mustard
- 2 eggs
- 1 small onion, cut up

Place all ingredients in blender; blend well. Pour into covered container and store in refrigerator.

Beef Salad Vinaigrette

- 2 stalks celery
- 5 sour cornichons
- 1 red onion
- 2 medium tomatoes
- 4 cups freshly boiled beef, cut into 1/2-inch cubes
- 1 clove garlic, finely minced
- 2 tablespoons finely chopped parsley

Sauce

- 1 tablespoon Dijon mustard
- 2 tablespoons red wine vinegar
- Salt *and* pepper
- 2/3 cup peanut, vegetable *or* corn oil, chilled

Trim and cut celery and cornichons in julienne strips. Peel onion. Cut in half and slice as thinly as possible. Peel and seed tomatoes. Cut in half and cube. Place beef, celery, onion, tomatoes, cornichons, garlic and parsley in large mixing bowl.

To make sauce, place mustard, vinegar, salt and pepper in a chilled mixing bowl. Gradually add oil, stirring rapidly with a whisk. Pour over salad. Toss and serve. Serves 4–5.

Roasted Red Pepper Dressing

- 3/4 cup (2 small) roasted red bell peppers*
- 2/3 cup plain yogurt
- 2 teaspoons balsamic vinegar
- 1/2 teaspoon garlic pepper
- 1 tablespoon minced parsley

Place red peppers, yogurt, vinegar and garlic pepper in blender or food processor. Blend or process until smooth. Transfer to small bowl. Stir in parsley. Cover and chill at least 2 hours. Makes 1 cup.

*To roast red bell pepper halves, place on pan, skin side up. Broil 2–3 inches from heat source. Watch carefully, turning until skins are black all over. Remove from heat; transfer to sealable food-safe plastic bag. Let steam 15–20 minutes. Remove from bag; peel off and discard blackened skin.

If desired, bottled roasted red bell peppers may be substituted. Rinse; drain and dry peppers. Proceed as recipe directs, adding 1/2 teaspoon sugar with ingredients in blender or food processor.

Fruited Chicken Salad

- 3 cups chopped cooked chicken
- 1 (20-ounce) can pineapple tidbits, drained
- 1/4 cup finely chopped onion
- 1 cup chopped celery
- 1 cup green grape halves
- 1/8 teaspoon seasoned salt
- 1 tablespoon lemon juice
- 1/2 cup toasted almonds
- 1/2 to 1 cup mayonnaise

Combine chicken, pineapple, onion, celery, grapes, seasoned salt, lemon juice and almonds in bowl; mix well. Add enough mayonnaise to moisten to desired consistency. Chill until serving time. Serves 8.

Creamy Parmesan Herb Dressing

- 3/4 cup cottage cheese
- 1/2 cup buttermilk
- 1/4 cup grated Parmesan cheese
- 1/2 teaspoon Italian seasoning
- 1/8 teaspoon black pepper
- 1 tablespoon chopped green onions
- 1 tablespoon chopped sun-dried tomatoes, if desired

Place cottage cheese, buttermilk, Parmesan cheese, Italian seasoning and pepper in food processor or blender. Blend or process until smooth. Transfer to small bowl. Stir in onions and sun-dried tomatoes, if desired. Cover and chill. Makes 1 1/2 cups.

Flaked Fish Salad

- 1 1/2 cups cod *or* haddock, broiled *or* lightly sautéed
- 1/2 cup finely chopped celery
- 2 hard-cooked eggs, diced
- 3 tablespoons Russian dressing
- 1/4 teaspoon celery seed
- 2 tablespoons fresh lemon juice
- 1/4 teaspoon seasoned salt
- 1 tablespoon chopped fresh parsley
- 1 tablespoon chopped onion
- Shredded ice-cold lettuce

Flake fish; add celery and diced eggs. Blend together remaining ingredients, except lettuce. Combine with fish mixture thoroughly, but lightly. Cover; chill; serve heaped on cold crisp lettuce. Serves 4.

Cinnamon Apple Almond Salad

- 1 cup whole, unroasted almonds
- 2 tart green apples
- 2 red apples
- 2 cups sliced celery
- 1/2 cup mayonnaise
- 1/3 cup yogurt
- 1/3 teaspoon grated orange peel
- 1/2 teaspoon ground cinnamon
- Mixed greens

Heat oven to 350 degrees. Spread almonds in shallow pan and toast for 15 minutes, stirring once or twice. Cool. Core and chop apples; combine almonds, apples and celery. Blend mayonnaise, yogurt, orange peel and cinnamon. Fold in mayonnaise mixture and serve on greens. Serves 4–6.

Dill-icious Cucumber Dressing

3/4 cup plain nonfat yogurt
1/2 cup chopped cucumber
1 tablespoon dill weed
2 teaspoons sugar
2 teaspoons lemon juice
1/8 teaspoon pepper

Blend and serve. A great complement to green, vegetable and chicken salads.

(10 calories and 0 grams fat per tablespoon)

Frozen Fruit Salad

16 ounces frozen melon balls
1 fresh pineapple, peeled, cored and chunked
1 cup red seedless grapes
1 cup green seedless grapes
3 cups strawberries, sliced
3 bananas, sliced
4 teaspoons artificial sweetener
1 cup water
12 ounces frozen orange juice concentrate, thawed

Place all fruits in large serving bowl. Combine sweetener, water and orange juice concentrate; pour over fruit and freeze. Serves 12. (108 calories per serving)

Chinese Beef Salad

3 pounds flank steak
1 (12-ounce) bottle Italian dressing
1 green pepper, cut into strips
2 cups bean sprouts
1 (11-ounce) can mandarin orange segments, drained

Place steak in shallow pan. Pour dressing over steak to coat well. Let marinate in refrigerator 24 hours. Drain. Bake at 350 degrees for 1 hour, or until steak is tender and done as desired. Cut into 1-inch cubes. Toss with green pepper strips, bean sprouts and mandarin orange segments. Serves 8.

Summer Salad

1 package macaroni rings
½ cup chopped celery
½ cup chopped onions
1 cup diced cucumbers
1 cup shredded carrots

Dressing

½ teaspoon pepper
¼ cup vinegar
½ cup sugar
¾ cup salad dressing

Cook macaroni; cool. Add celery, onions, cucumbers and carrots. Mix dressing ingredients; refrigerate overnight. You may also add diced ham, cheese or olives, if desired.

Sunshine Spinach Salad

Bright with flavor, color and texture, this spinach salad is sure to become a favorite.

4 cups spinach, trimmed, torn in pieces and chilled
3 oranges, peeled and sliced
1 avocado, peeled and sliced
1 small red onion, thinly sliced
1 cup raisins
½ cup slivered almonds, toasted
1 tablespoon sesame seed, toasted
Salt and pepper

Dressing

¼ cup oil
¼ cup wine vinegar
1 tablespoon sugar
1 teaspoon grated orange peel
½ teaspoon tarragon
Dash nutmeg

Combine all salad ingredients, except salt and pepper. Combine all dressing ingredients; blend well. Pour dressing over salad; add salt and pepper to taste. Gently toss and serve. Serves 4–6.

Waldorf Rice Salad

2 cups cold cooked natural brown rice
1 cup cubed apple (1 medium)
½ cup halved red grapes
⅓ cup chopped celery
⅓ cup lemon yogurt
⅓ cup reduced-calorie mayonnaise
¼ cup chopped pecans

In medium bowl, combine rice, apple, grapes and celery. In small bowl, combine yogurt and mayonnaise; blend well. Pour yogurt mixture over rice mixture; toss gently. Sprinkle with pecans. Serves 4.

Honey Spinach Salad

This salad is a delight made unusual with honey.

3 slices bacon
3 tablespoons honey
2–3 tablespoons lemon juice
2 tablespoons grated cheddar cheese
2–3 tablespoons vinegar
2 teaspoons grated lemon peel
¼ cup chopped apples or pears
1 hard-cooked egg, sliced
Spinach
Lettuce
Bean sprouts

Cut bacon in small pieces and fry until crispy. Add vinegar, honey, lemon juice and grated lemon peel; simmer for about 2 minutes. Mix spinach, lettuce, bean sprouts, and apples or pears. Pour bacon mixture over salad greens. Toss lightly. Garnish with grated cheese and hard-cooked egg. Serves 4.

Cilantro Dressing

1 cup tomato juice
1 tablespoon oil
1 clove garlic, minced
½ teaspoon pepper
1 teaspoon fresh minced cilantro
¼ teaspoon chili powder
Crushed red pepper, to taste

Blend and serve with mixed vegetable salads.

(11 calories and 1 gram fat per tablespoon)

Parmesan Dressing

1 cup plain nonfat yogurt
2 tablespoons grated Parmesan cheese
2 tablespoons skim milk
¼ teaspoon paprika
1 clove garlic, minced
Pepper to taste

Blend ingredients and serve. Perfect for pasta salads.

(12 calories and 0 grams fat per tablespoon)

Cashew-Shrimp Salad

- 3/4 cup vegetable juice cocktail
- 1 tablespoon soy sauce
- 1 teaspoon oil
- 1/2 teaspoon grated lemon peel
- 1/2 teaspoon grated fresh ginger
- 3/4 pound medium shrimp, cooked, shelled and deveined
- 1 1/2 cups cucumber slices, cut in half
- 1 large carrot, cut into matchstick-thin strips (1 1/4 cups)
- 3 green onions, sliced (1/2 cup)
- 1/4 cup coarsely chopped dry-roasted cashews (1 ounce)
- Lettuce leaves
- 4 slices French bread

In medium bowl combine vegetable juice cocktail, soy sauce, oil, lemon peel and ginger. Add shrimp, cucumbers, carrot and green onions; toss to coat well. Cover; refrigerate until serving time, at least 2 hours.

Before serving, add cashews; toss to coat well. To serve: On 4 lettuce-lined salad plates, arrange shrimp mixture.

Summer Steak Salad

- 1 tablespoon Vinaigrette Dressing (recipe follows)
- 2 cups thinly sliced strips of grilled *or* broiled steak
- 1/2 sweet onion, thinly sliced
- 6 cherry tomatoes, halved
- 1 tablespoon drained capers

Prepare dressing; set aside. In a medium bowl combine steak strips and onion slices. Dribble in dressing, tossing with a fork, until there is a thin film of dressing on meat. If made ahead cover and refrigerate. Just before serving add tomatoes and capers; toss lightly. It will probably need a little more dressing to coat the tomatoes. Serves 2.

Basic Vinaigrette Dressing

This dressing is a good basic vinaigrette, so whatever is left can be used on greens or other salads.

- 3 tablespoons olive *or* other salad oil *or* a combination
- 1 tablespoon vinegar
- 1/2 teaspoon salt
- 1/2 teaspoon dry mustard
- 1/4 teaspoon pepper, freshly ground, if possible
- 1 clove garlic, split

In small bowl whisk together oil, vinegar, salt, dry mustard and pepper. When slightly thickened add garlic clove; set aside. Cover to store. Makes about 1/4 cup.

Pear Chef's Salad

- 1 quart torn salad greens
- 2 fresh pears, cored and sliced
- 1 cup julienne cooked ham
- 1 cup cooked chicken chunks
- 1 cup shredded cheddar cheese
- 1 small cucumber, scored and sliced
- 4–6 radish roses (optional)
- Vinaigrette Dressing (recipe follows)

Line shallow salad bowl with torn greens. Arrange pears, ham, chicken, cheese and cucumber on greens. Garnish with radish roses. Serve with Vinaigrette Dressing. Serves 4–6.

Vinaigrette Dressing

- 1/3 cup vinegar
- 1/3 cup oil
- 2 tablespoons minced parsley
- 2 teaspoons grated lemon peel
- 1 teaspoon crushed thyme

Combine ingredients and mix well. Makes about 3/4 cup.

Fruited Chicken Salad

- 1 1/2 cups chopped, cooked chicken *or* turkey
- 1 cup chopped, unpeeled apple
- 3/4 cup chopped celery
- 1/2 cup chopped walnuts
- 1 (3-ounce) package cream cheese, softened
- 1/2 cup sour cream
- 3 tablespoons pineapple juice
- 1/4 teaspoon salt
- 1/8 teaspoon white pepper

Combine first 4 ingredients. Combine cream cheese and remaining ingredients; mix well. Add to chicken mixture, stirring well. Cover and chill. Serves 6.

Cole Slaw

- 1 head stonehead cabbage (or any very crisp head)
- 1 onion, diced
- 1 rib celery, diced
- 7 slices lean bacon
- 1/4 cup sugar
- 1/2 teaspoon salt
- 1/2 teaspoon celery seed
- 1/4 teaspoon black pepper
- 1/2 cup apple cider vinegar

Grate cabbage and refrigerate. Fry bacon crisp; add onion and sauté. Discard all but 1/2 cup of bacon grease. Crumble bacon. To bacon, onion and bacon grease add the celery, sugar, salt, celery seed and pepper. Add vinegar and simmer over very low heat to dissolve sugar. Stir well. Keep warm until ready to serve; pour over crisp cabbage and toss well. Serve at once. Serves 4-6.

Gazpacho Beef Salad

- 12 ounces cold, poached beef, thinly sliced
- 2 medium tomatoes, cut in thin slices
- 1 medium cucumber, peeled and cut in thin slices
- 1 medium red bell pepper, seeded, cut into 1/4-inch–wide strips
- 1 cup thinly sliced celery
- 1 small red onion, peeled, halved lengthwise and cut crosswise in thin slices

Dressing

- 1/2 cup spicy-hot canned vegetable juice cocktail
- 1/4 cup finely chopped kosher dill pickles
- 2 tablespoons red wine vinegar
- 2 tablespoons olive oil
- 1/2 teaspoon finely minced garlic

Arrange beef and vegetables on a serving platter. Combine dressing ingredients in a small jar with a tight lid; shake well. Pour 2 tablespoons on beef. Serve with remaining dressing to spoon over each portion. Serves 4.

Summer Beef & Fruit Salad

1 pound beef steak
½ cup plain yogurt
1 tablespoon lemon juice
1 tablespoon honey
1 clove garlic, finely chopped
⅛ teaspoon curry powder
⅛ teaspoon salt
1 cup seedless grapes, sliced in half lengthwise
1 cup julienned jicama
½ medium cantaloupe, diced
2 bunches watercress, cleaned and tough stems removed

Trim fat from steak. Broil 4 inches from heat, 5–7 minutes per side to desired doneness. Slice steak across grain into thin slices.

Combine yogurt, lemon juice, honey, garlic, curry powder and salt in small bowl. In larger bowl, combine grapes, jicama and cantaloupe.

For each serving, arrange ¼ of steak slices and ¼ of fruit mixture on bed of watercress. Serve with yogurt dressing on side. Serves 4.

Peanut Apple Salad

1 tablespoon flour
½ cup sugar
1 egg
2 tablespoons apple cider vinegar
1 (8-ounce) can crushed pineapple, drained (reserve juice)
4 cups (1 pound) red *or* green sliced apples, unpeeled
1 (8-ounce) container non-dairy whipped topping
3 cups salted Spanish peanuts

To make salad dressing, combine flour and sugar; mix well. Beat egg; add to flour-sugar mixture. Add vinegar and reserved pineapple juice. Cook in small pan on low heat, stirring constantly, until thick; cool.

Combine pineapple and apples in bowl. Pour cooled dressing over fruit. Fold in whipped topping. Before serving, sprinkle peanuts on top; otherwise they tend to get soft. Serves 10.

Summer Salad With Smoked Seafood

Seafood alternatives: smoked scallops, shrimp, trout, bluefish, mullet, whiting, oysters and mussels

6 tablespoons vegetable oil
4½ tablespoons red wine vinegar
1½ tablespoons sugar
¾ teaspoon dried tarragon
¼ teaspoon salt
⅛ teaspoon pepper
4 drops hot sauce
4 cups torn romaine lettuce *or* mesculun
4 cups torn bibb lettuce *or* mesculun
3 cups honeydew melon balls *or* cantaloupe *or* a combination of both
½ cup sliced almonds, toasted
½ pound smoked salmon, cut into thin strips
½ red onion, thinly sliced and separated into rings

Combine first 7 ingredients in a jar with a tight-fitting lid; cover and shake well (or use your favorite bottled salad dressing).

Combine remaining ingredients in a large bowl. Add dressing; toss well. Serve immediately. Serves 6.

Chicken Pasta Salad

8 ounces macaroni shells, cooked
3 cups cubed, cooked chicken
1 cup chopped cucumber
1 cup chopped celery
¾ cup chopped green olives
1 medium onion, chopped
½ cup mayonnaise
½ cup Italian dressing
2 tablespoons lemon juice
1 tablespoon Dijon mustard
1 teaspoon pepper
½ teaspoon salt

Combine macaroni, chicken, cucumber, celery, olives and onion. Toss gently.

Combine remaining ingredients and pour over chicken-macaroni mixture. Serves 6.

Chili-Spiced Beef & Rice Salad

1 pound well-trimmed boneless beef top sirloin steak, cut 1 inch thick
2 teaspoons Spicy Seasoning Mix, divided (recipe page 54)
2 cups spicy cooked rice*
1 medium orange, peeled *or* red apple, cut into ¾-inch pieces
2–3 green onions, thinly sliced
¼ cup coarsely chopped walnuts, toasted

Heat 10-inch non-stick frying pan over medium heat for 5 minutes. Meanwhile rub 1 teaspoon Spicy Seasoning into both sides of beef steak. Panbroil steak 12–14 minutes for rare (140 degrees) to medium (160 degrees), turning once. Season with salt, if desired.

Meanwhile, combine rice, orange or apple, onions and walnuts. Carve steak into ¼-inch-thick slices. Arrange beef and rice mixture on individual plates, or serving platter. Serves 4.

*Cook ⅔ cup rice according to package directions; add 1 teaspoon Spicy Seasoning Mix to water before cooking.

Fruit Salad Trifle

6 (¾-inch thick) slices purchased pound cake
3 medium ripe nectarines, sliced and pit removed
1 cup fresh raspberries
1 (3½-ounce) package instant vanilla pudding mix
2¼ cups raspberry yogurt drink
Nectarine slices
Fresh raspberries
Fresh mint

Cut each slice of pound cake into ¾-inch cubes. Place half on bottom of 2-quart straight-sided, clear glass bowl. Cover with half of nectarine slices and half of raspberries.

Prepare pudding according to package directions using yogurt drink instead of milk. Spoon half of prepared pudding over fruit. Repeat layers. Cover with plastic wrap. Refrigerate 2–3 hours. Garnish with nectarine slices, raspberries and mint just before serving. Serves 6–8.

Tuna Noodle Nicoise

Sounds like a lot of ingredients and work; however, it is a complete meal. I just add toasted French bread and dessert—ice cream is easy!

For less-experienced cooks I have included a work organization plan as part of the directions—the salad actually goes together quickly.

Dressing

1/4 cup salad oil (olive oil is good)
2 1/2 tablespoons wine *or* cider vinegar
2 tablespoons yogurt
2 tablespoons mayonnaise
1/4 teaspoon salt
Pepper to taste

Salad

1/4 pound fresh green beans (or cooked leftovers)
1 1/4 cups dry noodles
1 fully ripe tomato, chopped
4–6 black olives, sliced
1 (6-ounce) can tuna, drained
1 tablespoon capers

Bring salted water to boiling and cook beans if necessary. In another pot of salted water cook noodles.

Meanwhile, prepare salad dressing. Into a small bowl or cup measure oil, vinegar, yogurt, mayonnaise, salt and pepper. Whisk until blended and thick; set aside.

Chop tomato and olives; open and drain tuna. Drain cooked beans; set aside. Drain noodles; rinse with warm water; drain; return to pan and stir in about 1–2 tablespoons dressing.

Spread noodles in a shallow serving dish—about 8-inch size. Arrange tomato pieces, beans, olives, tuna and capers in single layers over noodles. Dribble on 1–2 tablespoons dressing. Cover and refrigerate the dressing and salad until serving time. Pass dressing to spoon over individual servings.

Taco Salad

3 cups corn chips, crushed
1/2 head iceburg lettuce, shredded
3 tomatoes, quartered
1 (8-ounce) can refried beans
1/2 cup onions, diced
1 cup cheddar cheese, grated
1/2 cup prepared salsa (optional)
1/2 cup sour cream (optional)

Crush corn chips and place on 2 serving dishes. Top with a bed of iceburg lettuce and tomatoes; set aside. Heat refried beans thoroughly and spoon on the salad. Sprinkle on cheddar cheese, onions and salsa; top with sour cream. Makes 2 servings.

Spiced Banana Relish

1 tablespoon cloves
1 teaspoon nutmeg
3 cinnamon sticks
1 1/2 teaspoons allspice
2 cups cider vinegar
1/2 cup sugar
16 ripe bananas

Tie spices in a cheesecloth bag. Combine vinegar and sugar in a saucepan. Add spice bag and simmer until mixture starts to thicken. Peel and cut bananas in 1/2-inch slices. Add to syrup and simmer for 2 minutes. Remove spice bag and pack in hot sterilized jars. Seal immediately. Process for about 10 minutes. Makes 4 pints.

Oriental-Style Dressing

1/4 cup red wine vinegar
3 tablespoons soy sauce
1 tablespoon oil
1/2 teaspoon ginger
1/4 teaspoon pepper
1 clove garlic, minced
1/2 teaspoon toasted sesame seed

Blend and use with chicken and beef stir-fry salads.

(25 calories and 2 grams fat per tablespoon)

Classic Italian Dressing

1/2 cup red wine vinegar
2 tablespoons olive oil
2 cloves garlic, minced
1 tablespoon chopped green onion
1 tablespoon chopped fresh parsley
1 teaspoon Italian seasoning
1/4 teaspoon salt
1/8 teaspoon sugar
Fresh pepper, to taste
2 teaspoons Dijon mustard

Blend and chill. Goes well with vegetable salads and salads featuring small portions of meat. (47 calories and 4 grams fat per tablespoon)

Orange Vinaigrette

1/4 cup white wine vinegar
1/4 cup orange juice
2 teaspoons sugar
2 tablespoons minced onion
2 teaspoons oil
2 teaspoons Dijon mustard
1/8 teaspoon pepper

Blend and serve with fruit or green salads.

(27 calories and 2 grams fat per tablespoon)

Gingered Yogurt Dressing

1 (8-ounce) container plain nonfat yogurt
2 tablespoons pineapple juice
1/2 teaspoon ginger
1/2 teaspoon dry mustard
1/4 teaspoon garlic powder

Blend ingredients and chill. Goes well with fruited chicken salads.

(9 calories and 0 grams fat per tablespoon)

Mixed Apple & Green Toss

4 cups assorted salad greens, torn in pieces and chilled
1 red apple, sliced
1 green apple, sliced
1/2 cup whole almonds, toasted
1/3 cup sliced green onions
1 cup crumbled bleu cheese (optional)

Dressing

1/4 cup oil
1/4 cup balsamic vinegar
1 tablespoon sugar
2 teaspoons prepared mustard

Combine all salad ingredients except bleu cheese. Combine all dressing ingredients; blend well. Pour dressing over salad; toss well. Sprinkle with bleu cheese, if desired. Serve immediately. Serves 4–6.

Triple Cheese "Terrine"

2 (8-ounce) packages cream cheese, softened
2 tablespoons milk
½ cup freshly grated Parmesan cheese
2 tablespoons chopped fresh parsley
1 teaspoon basil
½ teaspoon oregano
½ teaspoon thyme
¼ teaspoon pepper
1 clove garlic, crushed
6 (1-ounce) slices provolone cheese, about 1/8-inch thick
2 ounces thinly sliced prosciutto
Coarsely ground black pepper
Fresh herbs
Thinly sliced French *or* Italian bread
Cantaloupe and honeydew melon slices

Combine cream cheese, milk, Parmesan cheese, herbs, garlic and spices. Beat until light and fluffy.

Brush 8½ x 4½-inch loaf pan lightly with melted butter. Line with plastic wrap. Spread ½ cup cream cheese mixture in bottom of pan. Top with 3 slices provolone, trimming cheese to fit pan. Top with another ½ cup of cream cheese mixture. Layer with prosciutto, then another ½ cup of cream cheese mixture. Top with remaining provolone and cream cheese mixture. Cover pan with plastic wrap. Refrigerate overnight.

About 1 hour before serving, unmold loaf onto serving plate. Sprinkle top with pepper. Garnish with fresh herbs. Serve sliced with bread and melon. Serves 8–10.

Apple Pineapple Relish

1½ quarts cored and diced apples
1 (8½-ounce) can crushed pineapple
1 cup brown sugar
¼ cup chopped candied ginger
¾ to 1 cup vinegar
½ teaspoon curry powder
¼ teaspoon crushed dried red pepper

Combine apples, pineapple, brown sugar, ginger, vinegar, curry powder and dried pepper. Cook rapidly for about 25 minutes, or until thickened. If mixture becomes too dry, add ¼ cup water. This is great served with lamb, ham, turkey or pork, and also may be used as a glaze over meat loaf or ham slices before heating. Only 27 calories for each tablespoon. Makes 3½ cups.

Pasta Nicoise

1 (8-ounce) package uncooked pasta spirals
2 cups broccoli florets
1 (7-ounce) can tuna, packed in water, drained
2 green onions, chopped
1 red pepper, chopped
1 cup diced celery
¼ cup chopped parsley
¼ cup olive oil
3 tablespoons lemon juice
3 tablespoons white vinegar
1 garlic clove, minced
1 tablespoon anchovy paste

Cook spirals according to directions; add broccoli the last 3 minutes of cooking time; drain and set aside. Toss tuna, onions, pepper and celery with pasta and broccoli. Combine remaining ingredients; pour over pasta salad and toss to coat. Refrigerate. Add dressing just before serving (279 calories per serving). Serves 6.

Fruit Kabobs

1 tablespoon cornstarch
⅛ teaspoon ground cinnamon
¼ cup lemon juice
¼ cup orange juice
3 tablespoons honey
1 medium apple, cut into 1-inch cubes
1 (8-ounce) can pineapple chunks, drained
1 (8-ounce) can mandarin orange sections, drained
1 medium banana, cut into ½-inch slices
6 (6-inch) wooden skewers

In 2-cup measure mix cornstarch, cinnamon, lemon juice, orange juice and honey. Microwave at HIGH for 1½–3½ minutes, or until thick, stirring once or twice.

Alternate apple, pineapple, orange and banana on skewers to fill each skewer. Brush with glaze. Refrigerate. Brush with glaze again before serving. Serves 6.

Stuffed Fresh Peaches

8 small ripe peaches
2 tablespoons lemon juice
2 tablespoons sugar
1 tablespoon chopped golden raisins
2 tablespoon slivered almonds, divided
¾ cup ricotta cheese

Peel peaches and cut in half, removing pits. Keep halves paired. Rub peach halves with lemon juice and sprinkle with sugar. Stir raisins and 1 tablespoon almonds into ricotta. Heap mixture into half of each peach and cover with second half to re-form peach. Stand peaches upright, letting the halves separate slightly at the top to show a mound of filling. Sprinkle with remaining almonds. Serves 8.

Soups & STEWS

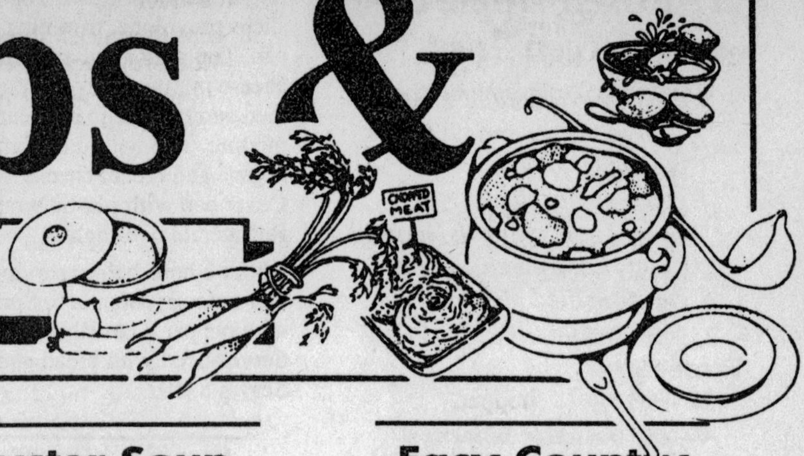

Autumn Corn & Pumpkin Chowder

- 1/2 cup butter *or* margarine
- 2 onions, chopped
- 1/2 cup all-purpose flour
- 7 ears corn, kernels cut off
- 1 1/2 cups cooked pumpkin
- 2 cups chicken broth
- 1/4 teaspoon salt
- 1 cup cubed cooked ham
- 1/4 teaspoon allspice
- 2 cups light cream

In a deep pot melt butter; cook onions. Add next 5 ingredients; simmer 10 minutes; add ham. Pour half the chowder into food processor or blender; mix until smooth. Return to soup pot; simmer 25 minutes. Add allspice and cream; serve hot with crisp crackers or toast points. Serves 7.

Creamy Peanut Butter Soup

- 6 cups milk
- 1 tablespoon beef bouillon granules
- 3 tablespoons butter *or* margarine
- 2 tablespoons flour
- 6 tablespoons creamy peanut butter
- 1 teaspoon celery salt
- 1/4 teaspoon Worcestershire sauce
- 1/8 teaspoon honey
- 1/2 teaspoon onion, grated
- 1/8 teaspoon pepper

Heat milk; add remaining ingredients; heat slowly until thickened, stirring constantly. Serve with saltines or small cheese crackers.

Oyster Soup for 100

- 18 quarts oysters
- 7 gallons milk
- 2 cups butter
- 2 teaspoons pepper

Just cover the oysters with water in large kettles; bring to boil; simmer until the edges curl. Skim off any foam. Stir in the butter and hot milk. At serving sprinkle with pepper. It will take 10 boxes of oyster crackers to complete the meal.

Chili Chicken

- 1 large finely chopped onion
- 1 cup finely chopped green pepper
- 1 clove crushed garlic
- 1 tablespoon chili powder
- 1/4 teaspoon dried oregano
- 1 teaspoon cumin powder
- 2 tablespoons oil
- 1/2 cup tomato purée (not paste)
- 1/2 ounce unsweetened chocolate, grated
- 1 cup chicken broth
- 1/3 cup slivered, blanched almonds
- Salt and pepper to taste
- 4 cups coarsely chopped, cooked and boned chicken

In a saucepan over moderate heat, sauté onion, pepper, garlic, chili powder, oregano and cumin in hot oil until vegetables are tender. Add tomato purée and chocolate; cook over low heat, stirring constantly, until chocolate melts. Add chicken broth; cook 5 minutes. Pulverize almonds and stir in slowly. Season. Add chicken; simmer for 10 minutes. Serve over steamed rice. Serves 6–8.

Easy Country Fresh Veggie Soup

- 1 (32-ounce) jar sauerkraut, drained
- 1 1/2 cups sliced carrots
- 1 cup sliced celery
- 1/2 cup chopped onion
- 2 (10-ounce) cans condensed beef broth *or* consommé
- 4 cups water
- 4 cups tomato juice
- 2 tablespoons chopped parsley
- 1 tablespoon sugar
- 1 bay leaf
- 1/2 teaspoon salt
- 1/4 teaspoon pepper
- Sour cream (optional)

Combine all ingredients, except sour cream, in large saucepan. Mix well. Bring to a boil. Cover and simmer for 1 1/4–1 1/2 hours or until vegetables are tender. Serve with a dollop of sour cream, if desired. Serves 8.

Tater-Patch Stew

- 1 pound ground beef, browned
- 1 cup chopped cabbage
- 2 cups stewed tomatoes
- 1 cup frozen peas
- 1 beef bouillon cube
- 2 medium onions, sliced
- 1/2 cup diced celery
- 1 cup diced potato
- 1 cup water
- 1/4 teaspoon garlic powder

Combine all ingredients, except peas and potato, in a slow cooker. Simmer on low for 7 hours. Add potato 2 hours before serving; add peas 15 minutes before serving. Serves 6.

Seafood-Cheddar Stew

- 2½ cups rich fish stock
- 1 cup plus 2 tablespoons clam juice
- ¼ pound scallops with juice, chopped
- ¼ pound uncooked shrimp, shelled, deveined and chopped
- ¼ pound cooked crabmeat, shredded
- 2 green onions, white part only, chopped
- 1 celery stalk, chopped
- 2 tablespoons fresh parsley, chopped
- 1½ tablespoons chopped pimientos
- 3 tablespoons butter
- 5 tablespoons all-purpose flour
- 3 tablespoons dry vermouth (optional)
- ¼ cup half-and-half *or* evaporated milk
- ¾ cup whipping cream
- 1⅛ teaspoon dried dillweed
- ¾ teaspoon dried thyme, crumbled
- ½ teaspoon freshly ground pepper
- ¼ teaspoon freshly grated nutmeg
- Salt to taste
- ¾ cup grated cheddar cheese

Combine stock, clam juice, scallops and their juice, shrimp, crabmeat, onions, celery, parsley and pimientos in heavy large saucepan; simmer 30 minutes. Melt butter in heavy small saucepan over low heat. Whisk in flour and stir 3 minutes. Blend in vermouth. Remove from heat. Whisk in half-and-half. Stir into seafood mixture. Blend in cream, dillweed, thyme, pepper and nutmeg. Season with salt. Add cheese and stir until melted. Simmer 10 minutes. Serves 4.

Mexican Corn Soup

- 3 tablespoons butter
- ⅓ cup chopped green pepper
- ¼ cup sliced green onion
- 1 large clove garlic, minced
- 5 tablespoons all-purpose flour
- ¼ teaspoon oregano
- ¼ teaspoon pepper
- 2–3 drops red pepper sauce
- 3 cups condensed chicken broth
- 1½ cups red salsa, mild to medium
- 1 bay leaf
- 2 cups (8 ounces) shredded Monterey Jack cheese
- 1 (12-ounce) can vacuum-packed corn, drained
- Tortilla chips
- Cilantro

Melt butter in 3-quart saucepan. Sauté green pepper, onion and garlic until tender, about 5 minutes. Stir in flour and seasonings. Gradually stir in broth and salsa. Add bay leaf. Bring to boiling, stirring constantly. Boil and stir 1 minute. Mix in 1½ cups cheese and corn; stir until cheese is melted. Remove bay leaf. Garnish each serving with tortilla chips, remaining shredded cheese and cilantro. Makes 7 cups.

Green-Chili Stew

- 2 pounds lean stew beef, cut into cubes
- 1 tablespoon salad oil
- 1 cup chopped onion
- 1 clove garlic
- 1 (1-pound) can tomatoes
- 1 cup beef stock
- 1 (4-ounce) can green chilies
- 1 teaspoon salt
- 2 tablespoons fresh coriander (optional)
- Black pepper, freshly ground

Heat oil in large skillet. Put in beef chunks and sauté until browned on all sides. Stir in onions; cook until wilted and beginning to take on color. Stir in garlic. Next, add beef stock and stir well to get all browned bits loose from bottom of pan.

Add tomatoes and salt. If chilies are whole, slit and remove seeds; then chop. Add chilies and coriander to pan. Grind in fresh black pepper to taste; cover and lower heat to simmer. Cook until meat is tender, about 1½ hours. Serve in soup bowls. Put a mound of hot boiled rice in each bowl, if desired.

Nautical Chowder

- ½ cup chopped onion
- ½ cup sliced celery
- ¼ cup butter
- 3 cups diced, peeled raw potatoes
- 2 cups water
- 2 tablespoons flour
- 2 cups milk
- 2 teaspoons salt
- ½ teaspoon fine herb blend
- ⅛ teaspoon pepper
- 1 (1-pound) can pink salmon *or*
- 2 (7-ounce) cans tuna, drained and flaked
- Chopped parsley
- Lemon juice

Sauté onion and celery in butter until tender and lightly browned. Add potatoes and water. Simmer until potatoes are just tender, about 15 minutes. Blend flour into ½ cup milk. Add to remaining milk and stir into potato mixture. Add salt, herbs and pepper.

Cook until soup is smooth and slightly thickened. Add fish and allow to heat. Garnish with chopped parsley and serve with a few drops lemon juice for each serving. Serves 6–8.

Chicken Chowder

- ¼ cup chopped onion
- ½ teaspoon curry powder
- 2 tablespoons oil
- 2 tablespoons flour
- 4 cups chicken broth
- 2 tomatoes, chopped
- 2 apples, pared and chopped
- ½ cup sliced carrots
- ¼ cup chopped green pepper
- 2 tablespoons parsley
- 1 tablespoon lemon juice
- 1 teaspoon sugar
- ½ teaspoon salt
- Dash pepper
- 1½ cups yellow squash, pared and chopped
- 1 cup diced, cooked chicken

In large saucepan, cook onion and curry powder in hot oil until onion is tender, but not brown. Blend in flour. Stir in chicken broth, tomatoes, apples, carrots, green pepper, parsley, lemon juice, sugar, salt and pepper; bring mixture to boiling, stirring occasionally. Lower heat; cover and simmer 15 minutes. Stir in squash and chicken; simmer 15 minutes more or until squash is tender. Serve over rice. Serves 6–8.

Wedding Soup

- 5 pounds chicken wings (or other chicken parts)
- 2 pounds finely ground beef
- 2 medium onions, chopped
- 4 large pieces celery
- 15 peppercorns
- 2 teaspoons poultry seasoning *or* savory
- 2 lemons
- Grated Parmesan cheese
- 2 tablespoons salt
- Salt and pepper to taste
- 3 (10-ounce) packages chopped frozen spinach (or precooked fresh spinach)

Into a large pot filled with 6 quarts water, place chicken wings, 1 onion, 2 tablespoons salt and 8 peppercorns. Cook about 1 hour; add other peppercorns, 1 onion, celery and seasonings. Cook another 1/2 hour, or until chicken is done.

While chicken is cooking, season ground beef with salt and pepper; roll meatballs very small (about the sizc of marbles), to which you add a little salt and ground pepper. Remove chicken, celery, onions and peppercorns from broth and bone chicken. Set aside and cover chicken. Add meatballs to simmering broth. When balls are cooked, add spinach and bring to slow boil. Add boned chicken to meatballs and spinach. When ready to serve, add thin slice lemon to bowl and sprinkle with Parmesan cheese. Serves 12.

Sausage Cheddar Chowder

- 3 cups water
- 2 chicken bouillon cubes
- 1 (12-ounce) package smoked sausage, thinly sliced
- 2 cups thinly sliced carrots
- 2 cups thinly sliced celery
- 1 teaspoon onion salt
- 1/2 cup ground oat flour*
- 2 cups milk
- 1 1/2 cups (6 ounces) shredded cheddar cheese

Combine water and bouillon cubes in a 4-quart kettle. Bring to a boil over medium heat, stirring occasionally until bouillon cubes are dissolved; reduce heat. Stir in meat, celery, carrots and onion salt. Cover; simmer 10 minutes. Bring to a boil; gradually add milk and oat flour, stirring constantly. Reduce heat and simmer 10 minutes, stirring occasionally. Remove from heat. Add cheese; mix until cheese is melted. Makes 8 (1 cup) servings.

*Oat flour; Place 1 1/4 cups quick or old-fashioned oats, uncooked, in blender or food processor. Cover; blend 60 seconds. Store in a tightly covered container in a cool dry place up to 6 months. May also be used for breading, thickening or gravies, dredging or browning.

Wild Rice Soup

- 1 cup uncooked wild rice
- 3 cups boiling water
- 2 strips smoked bacon
- 1/4 cup chopped onion
- 3/4 cup sliced celery
- 1/2 cup sliced carrots
- 1 (14 1/2-ounce) can chicken broth
- 2 (10 3/4-ounce) cans cream of mushroom soup
- 2 soup cans milk
- 1 (4-ounce) can mushrooms, *plus* liquid
- 1 teaspoon seasoned salt
- Pepper to taste

Combine rice and boiling water in large saucepan; simmer, covered, 50–60 minutes. Drain off excess liquid; set rice aside. Fry bacon until crisp; remove bacon and sauté onion, celery and carrots in small amount of bacon fat. Combine broth, soup, milk, mushrooms, salt and pepper, reserved crumbled bacon, sautéed vegetables and wild rice. Simmer, covered, 1 hour. Serves 8.

Mexican Potato Soup

- 4 cups chopped, peeled potatoes
- 1/2 cup chopped onion
- 2 tablespoons margarine
- 2 tomatoes, seeded and chopped
- 2 tablespoons margarine
- 4 cups hot water
- 6 chicken bouillon cubes
- 1 pound chopped ham
- 1 1/2 cups sour cream

Cook potatoes in water to cover in saucepan for 12–15 minutes; drain. Sauté chopped onion in 2 tablespoons margarine in skillet. Remove onion with slotted spoon. Sauté tomatoes in 2 tablespoons margarine in skillet. Add onion, tomatoes, hot water, bouillon, ham and sour cream to potatoes. Simmer for 15 minutes; do not boil. Serves 6.

Creamy Lettuce Soup

- 2 tablespoons butter
- 1/2 cup chopped green onions
- 16 cups leaf lettuce, torn in pieces
- 3 cups chicken broth
- 1/8 teaspoon black pepper
- Salt to taste
- 2 (3-ounce) packages cream cheese

Sauté onions and lettuce in a large saucepan in butter until lettuce is limp, about 2 minutes. Add broth and pepper; simmer 5 minutes. Season to taste with salt. Purée soup in blender or food processor until smooth. Return soup to pot to reheat. Dice cream cheese; add to soup. Heat soup until cream cheese is melted. Serve. Delicious!

Sausage Chowder

- 2 1/2 cups diced potatoes
- 1/2 cup chopped celery
- 1 medium onion, chopped
- 1/2 pound sausage meat *or* links
- 2 1/2 tablespoons flour
- 3 1/2 cups milk
- Salt and pepper to taste

Cook potatoes, celery and onion in a small quantity of boiling salted water until tender; do not drain. Cut sausage in small pieces and fry slowly; pour off most of the fat, leaving 2–3 tablespoons. Add flour to sausage and mix well. Add milk all at once and cook, stirring constantly, until thickened. Add potatoes. Season with salt and pepper. Reheat slowly. If held for a period of time, keep hot in a double boiler. Serves 6.

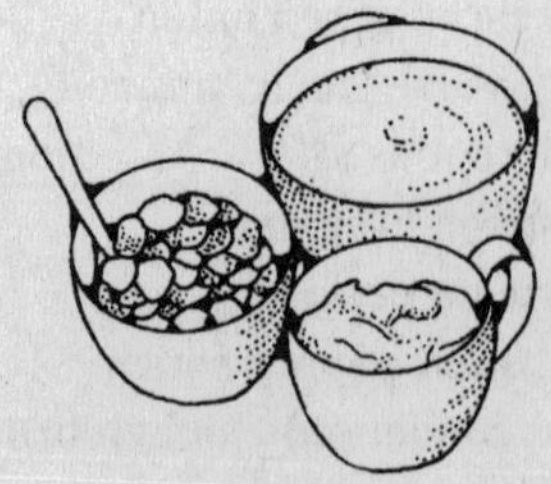

Tasty TRIMMERS

Squash Strips

- 1 pound crookneck squash, cut in 1/4-inch-thick strips
- 1 pound zucchini, cut in 1/4-inch-thick strips
- 1/4 cup chopped green onions
- 1/2 teaspoon dried leaf basil *or*
- 1 1/2 teaspoons fresh chopped basil
- 1/4 teaspoon dried leaf thyme
- Dash white pepper
- Pimiento strips
- Fresh basil sprig, if desired

Place crookneck squash and zucchini in a 1 1/2-quart microwave-safe casserole. Sprinkle with green onions, basil, thyme and pepper. Cover tightly. Microwave on 100 percent power (HIGH) for 3 minutes. Stir; re-cover. Microwave on 100 percent power (HIGH) for 3–4 minutes more, or until squash is tender. Garnish with pimiento strips and basil sprig, if desired. Serves 8. (46 calories per serving)

Low-Calorie Orange Dessert Cups

- 1 orange, sliced in half
- 1/4 banana, peeled and sliced
- 1/2 apple, peeled, cored and diced
- 1/2 tablespoon cinnamon
- 2 tablespoons low-fat yogurt

Remove fruit from orange rind, leaving rind intact. Separate orange sections and cut into small pieces. In a small bowl, combine orange pieces, banana, apple, cinnamon and yogurt. Mix well. Fill orange-rind halves with fruit mixture. Wrap and chill. (98 calories per serving)

Tarragon Chicken

- 1 chicken, 3–4 pounds, cut up, skin and visible fat removed *or*
- 3 whole chicken breasts, split, skinned, trimmed of fat
- 1 medium onion, peeled and thinly sliced
- 3–4 shallots, peeled and cut into thirds (optional)
- 2 tablespoons vegetable oil
- 1/4 cup dry white wine *or* vermouth
- 1 teaspoon dry tarragon
- 1/2 teaspoon black pepper

Preheat oven to 350 degrees. Wash chicken and pat dry. Place in a shallow baking pan. Sprinkle onions and shallots around and under chicken pieces. Pour oil and wine or vermouth over chicken. Sprinkle with tarragon and black pepper. Cover baking pan tightly with foil. Bake 45 minutes. Remove foil. Turn oven up to 375 degrees. Bake, uncovered, for an additional 15 minutes. If desired, garnish with fresh watercress. Serves 6. (153 calories per serving)

Baked Tomatoes

- 2 tomatoes, cut in halves
- 1 tablespoon oil
- 1/2 teaspoon chopped parsley *or*
- 1/4 teaspoon dry parsley flakes
- 1/4 teaspoon oregano
- 1/4 teaspoon basil

Place tomato halves in a lightly oiled baking dish. Drizzle oil over tomatoes and sprinkle with remaining ingredients. Bake in a 350-degree oven for 20–30 minutes. Serves 4. (45 calories per serving)

Special Sweet Potatoes

- 2 (4-ounce) sweet potatoes, peeled and diced
- 1 tablespoon water
- 1 (8-ounce) can crushed pineapple packed in unsweetened pineapple juice drained
- 1/8 teaspoon ground ginger
- 1/8 teaspoon ground nutmeg
- 2 teaspoons margarine

In a 1-quart microwave-safe casserole, combine sweet potatoes, water and pineapple. Sprinkle with ginger and nutmeg. Cover tightly. Microwave on 100 percent power (HIGH) for 4 minutes. Stir; re-cover. Microwave on 100 percent power (HIGH) 4–6 minutes more, or until potatoes are tender. Dot with margarine. Serves 4. (158 calories per serving)

Sautéed Carrots

- 1 pound carrots, peeled and grated
- 1 tablespoon fresh lemon juice
- 2 tablespoons frozen apple juice concentrate, thawed
- 1 teaspoon margarine *or* 1 1/2 teaspoons non-fat "butter" granules
- Poppy seeds (garnish)

In a non-stick skillet, combine carrots, lemon juice and apple juice concentrate. Place over medium-high heat and sauté about 3 minutes, stirring constantly. Add margarine or "butter" granules and stir to coat evenly. Garnish with poppy seeds and serve hot. (44 calories per serving)

Tarragon Lemon Chicken

4 (4-ounce) skinless, boneless chicken breast halves*
2 tablespoons all-purpose, unbleached flour
2 tablespoons finely chopped fresh tarragon *or* 1 tablespoon dried
1/4 teaspoon nutmeg
1/2 teaspoon cinnamon
1/8 teaspoon white pepper
2 tablespoons lemon-flavored margarine
1/4 cup freshly squeezed lemon *or* lime juice
1 medium-size red bell pepper, seeded and cut into julienne strips
Fresh tarragon sprigs for garnish, if desired
Lemon slices for garnish, if desired

Trim all visible fat from chicken. Combine flour, tarragon, nutmeg, cinnamon and white pepper in a plastic or paper bag; insert chicken, 2 pieces at a time. and shake bag until chicken is well-coated.

Over medium-high heat (350 degrees on electric frying pan) heat margarine until hot. Add chicken; cook 6-7 minutes on each side or until browned. Add lemon juice and bell pepper; reduce heat and simmer 10 minutes, or until chicken is fork-tender. Transfer chicken to platter; spoon sauce over. Garnish with tarragon sprigs if desired; border platter with lemon slices. Serves 4. (198 calories per serving)

*For chicken that will be more moist and more tender inside and crispier and crustier outside, soak pieces in cold water to cover 1 hour before coating. Remove from water; do not dry. Place wet pieces in the bag and shake.

White Bean Dip

1/2 pound Great Northern white beans
6 cloves garlic
Olive oil *or* non-stick cooking spray
1/2 large red pepper, minced
1 small red onion, minced
3 tablespoons lemon juice
2 tablespoons parsley leaves
1 teaspoon salt
Assorted vegetable sticks
Toasted pita wedges

Place beans and enough water to cover beans in pan; bring to boil. Boil 3 minutes; remove from heat. Cover and let stand for 1 hour. Drain and rinse. Return to pan; add 4 cups water and garlic cloves. Bring to boil; cover and simmer for 1 hour, or until beans are tender. Drain.

Meanwhile, coat skillet with cooking spray. Sauté pepper and onion 5 minutes until tender. When beans are cooked, place in processor with lemon juice, parsley and salt; pulse until well-blended. Remove to bowl; stir in pepper mixture. Serve with vegetable sticks and pita wedges. Serves 12. (70 calories per serving)

Easy Sugar-Free Apple Pie

Calorie-reduced pastry (2-crust 9-inch pie)

2 1/2 cups unsifted all-purpose flour
2 tablespoons salad oil
1 teaspoon salt
1/3 cup lite margarine
6 tablespoons ice water

Combine flour and salt in bowl. Cut in margarine and oil until coarse crumbs form. Sprinkle in water, 1 tablespoon at a time, tossing with fork until dough forms. Form into 2 balls. Roll out on floured surface for 2-crust pie.

Filling

1 (6-ounce) can frozen unsweetened apple juice
6 cups sliced, peeled apples
1 tablespoon cornstarch
1 tablespoon cinnamon

Mix cornstarch and apple juice concentrate in saucepan. Cook, stirring until clear. Stir in apples and cinnamon. Pour into pastry-lined pie plate; top with other crust. Fold under edge of crust and form a ridge; flute edge. Bake at 375 degrees for 45 minutes, or until nicely browned. Serves 8. (86 calories per serving)

Cold Cucumber Soup/Zucchini Soup

Basic Light White Sauce

1 tablespoon corn oil
1 tablespoon finely chopped onion
1 tablespoon cornstarch
1/4 teaspoon salt
Dash pepper
1 cup skim milk

In 1-quart saucepan warm oil over medium heat. Add onion, stirring frequently; cook 1–2 minutes or until tender. Stir in cornstarch, salt and pepper until thoroughly blended. Remove from heat. Gradually stir in milk until smooth. Stirring constantly, bring to boil over medium heat and boil 1 minute. Makes 1 cup.

Cold Cucumber Soup

Follow recipe for Basic Light White Sauce. Stir in 1 cup chicken bouillon and 1 teaspoon dried mint flakes with milk. Cool sauce. Place sauce, 2 cucumbers, peeled, seeded, diced (2 cups) and 1/2 cup parsley sprigs in blender; cover. Blend on high speed 30 seconds, or until smooth. Cover; refrigerate until chilled. If desired, serve with lowfat plain yogurt.

Cold Zucchini Soup

Follow recipe for Cucumber Soup. Instead of cucumbers and parsley, use 2 cups diced zucchini. Makes 3 cups. (70 calories per serving)

Vegetable Medley

4 medium carrots, diagonally sliced (2 cups)
2 cups fresh broccoli florets
2 medium crookneck squash *or* zucchini, sliced (2 cups)
1/2 teaspoon seasoned salt
Dash white pepper

Arrange vegetables in concentric rings on a round microwave-safe platter: carrots around outside of platter, then broccoli and squash in center. Cover tightly. Microwave on 100 percent power (HIGH) for 5–7 minutes, or until vegetables are tender-crisp. Sprinkle with seasoned salt and white pepper. Serves 6. (51 calories per serving)

Asparagus With Lemon Sauce

- 1 pound fresh asparagus, washed
- 3 tablespoons water
- 1 tablespoon margarine
- 1 tablespoon all-purpose flour
- 1/2 cup skim milk
- 1/2 teaspoon ground ginger
- 1 teaspoon grated lemon peel
- 2 teaspoons lemon juice
- Lemon slices

Snap off and discard tough stalk ends of asparagus. Arrange spears, with buds toward center, in a shallow microwave-safe dish. Sprinkle with water. Cover tightly. Microwave on high for 3 minutes. Rearrange, moving outside spears to center of dish. Re-cover; microwave on high for 3 minutes more, or until almost tender. Let stand 5 minutes.

In a 1-cup glass measure, microwave margarine on high for 45–50 seconds, or until melted. Stir in flour. Microwave on high for 1 minute, or until bubbly. Stir in milk and ginger. Microwave on high for 1 minute. Stir; microwave on high for 1–1 1/2 minutes more, or until thickened. Stir in lemon peel and juice.

Drain asparagus; arrange on a microwave-safe platter. Pour lemon sauce evenly over asparagus. Microwave on high for 50 seconds, or until heated through. Garnish with lemon slices. Serves 4. (74 calories per serving)

Tomato-Cheese Topper

- 3/4 cup vegetable juice
- 1/4 cup chopped green pepper
- 1 tablespoon all-purpose flour
- 1 teaspoon Worcestershire sauce
- Dash hot pepper sauce
- 4 ounces pasteurized process cheese spread, cubed
- Hot potato skins *or* baked potatoes

In 1-quart saucepan, stir together juice, green pepper, flour, Worcestershire and hot pepper sauce. Over medium heat, heat to boiling, stirring often. Reduce heat to low; stir in cheese until melted. Spoon over potato skins or baked potatoes. Makes 1 cup. (26 calories per tablespoon)

Breakfast Omelet

- 1 medium (5 1/2-ounce) red thin-skinned potato, scrubbed and pierced
- 4 eggs, beaten
- 1/2 cup chopped green onions
- 1/2 cup sliced, fresh mushrooms
- 1/4 teaspoon dried leaf basil
- 1/8 teaspoon dried leaf oregano
- Salt to taste
- 1 teaspoon margarine
- 1 tomato, seeded and chopped

Place a paper towel on bottom of microwave oven. Microwave potato on high for 3 minutes. Cool and dice (do not peel). In a medium bowl, combine potato, eggs, green onions,mushrooms, basil, oregano and salt. Set aside. In a 9-inch pie plate, microwave margarine on high for 20 seconds, or until melted.

Swirl dish to coat. Pour egg mixture into pie plate. Adjust power level to medium. Microwave 3–6 minutes, or until edges look slightly set. Using a rubber spatula, gently lift edges of omelet, allowing uncooked egg to flow underneath. Sprinkle with tomato. Microwave on medium 3–5 minutes more, or until set, but still moist. (Serves 4, 138 calories per serving.)

Tuna Oriental

- 1/2 green pepper, cut in 1/4-inch strips
- 1 small onion, thinly sliced
- 2 teaspoons oil
- 1/3 cup pineapple juice
- 1 1/2 teaspoons cornstarch
- 2/3 cup drained pineapple chunks (canned in juice)
- 1 tablespoon sugar
- 1 tablespoon vinegar
- 1 (6 1/2-ounce) can unsalted tuna, drained and flaked
- 1/8 teaspoon pepper
- Dash Tabasco sauce

Cook green pepper and onion in oil, leaving slightly crisp. Mix pineapple juice with cornstarch; add to green pepper and onion mixture. Cook, stirring gently until thickened. Add remaining ingredients. Cook 5 minutes, stirring occasionally. May be served over rice. Serves 3. (185 calories per serving)

Shrimp Kabobs

- 1 medium green bell pepper, seeded and cut in 12 pieces
- 2 small onions, each cut in 6 wedges
- 12 medium mushrooms
- 12 cherry tomatoes, stemmed
- 1 pound uncooked large shrimp, shelled and deveined (about 18–20)
- 1/4 cup light soy sauce
- 1/2 cup dry white wine
- 1 teaspoon sugar
- 1/2 teaspoon garlic powder
- 1/2 teaspoon ground ginger

Combine bell pepper, onion, mushrooms, tomatoes and shrimp in bowl. In a 2-cup glass measure, combine soy sauce, wine, sugar, garlic powder and ginger. Pour over vegetable-shrimp mixture. Cover tightly.

Refrigerate several hours, stirring once or twice. Thread vegetables and shrimp on 6 wooden skewers. Arrange in a 13 x 9-inch microwave-safe dish. Cover with waxed paper. Microwave on 50 percent power (MEDIUM) for 8 minutes.

Rearrange, moving outside skewers to center of dish. Baste; re-cover. Microwave on 50 percent power (MEDIUM) for 8 minutes more, or just until shrimp turn pink and bell pepper is tender. Serves 6. (129 calories per serving)

Skinny Shrimp Scampi

- 2 tablespoons margarine
- 2 tablespoons lemon juice
- 2 garlic cloves, minced
- 1/2 teaspoon butter-flavored salt
- 1/8 teaspoon black pepper
- 1 pound uncooked large shrimp, shelled, deveined (about 18–20)
- 1 tablespoon minced fresh parsley

In a shallow 1 1/2-quart microwave-safe dish, microwave margarine on high for 20 seconds, or until melted. Stir in lemon juice, garlic, butter-flavored salt and pepper. Stir in shrimp. Microwave on high for 1 1/2 minutes. Rearrange, moving outside shrimp to center of dish. Microwave on high for 1 1/2 minutes more, or just until shrimp turn pink. Sprinkle with parsley. Serves 4. (177 calories per serving)

Braised Sirloin Tips Over Rice

- 2 pounds beef sirloin tip, cut into 1-inch cubes
- 1 (10½-ounce) can beef consommé
- ⅓ cup red burgundy *or* cranberry cocktail
- 2 tablespoons soy sauce
- 1 clove garlic, minced
- ½ teaspoon onion powder
- 2 tablespoons cornstarch
- ¼ cup water
- 4 cups hot cooked rice

Brown meat on all sides in a large heavy skillet. Add consommé, wine or cranberry cocktail, soy sauce, garlic and onion powder. Heat to boiling. Reduce heat; cover and simmer for 1 hour, or until meat is tender. Blend cornstarch and water; stir gradually into the stew. Cook, stirring constantly, until gravy thickens and boils. Cook 1 minute more. Serve over rice. Serves 8. (390 calories per serving)

One-Pan Chicken Pizzarella

- 1 pound boneless, skinless chicken breasts, sliced into halves
- ½ teaspoon dried oregano *or* 1½ teaspoons fresh oregano, chopped
- ¼ teaspoon dried basil *or* ¾ teaspoon fresh basil leaves, chopped
- ⅛ teaspoon garlic powder
- ⅛ teaspoon black pepper
- 1 (8-ounce) can plain tomato sauce
- 1 (4-ounce) can mushrooms, undrained
- ½ cup (2 ounces) shredded part-skim mozzarella cheese

Place chicken breasts in a shallow baking dish (11 x 7 inches *or* 12 x 8 inches). Sprinkle oregano, basil, garlic powder and black pepper evenly over cutlets. Pour tomato sauce and mushrooms over chicken. Bake, uncovered, in a preheated 350-degree oven for 35 minutes, or until chicken is fork-tender; sprinkle with cheese and return to oven. Bake 4–5 minutes, or until cheese is melted and bubbly. Serves 4. (195 calories per serving)

Pepper Steak

- 1 pound lean beef (top round *or* flank steak)
- ¾ cup beef bouillon (1 bouillon cube dissolved in ¾ cup hot water)
- 1 tablespoon powdered dry milk
- ½ teaspoon monosodium glutamate
- 2 tablespoons cold water
- 2 green bell peppers
- 1 tablespoon soy sauce
- ¼ teaspoon ginger
- ¼ teaspoon garlic salt
- Salt and pepper to taste

Cut beef into thin strips. Brown on all sides under the broiler for 5 minutes. Remove stems, seeds and membranes from peppers. Wash and cut each pepper in eighths. Place peppers in a 10-inch frying pan, with just enough water to cover peppers; cook over medium heat until softened, about 5 minutes.

Mix soy sauce with ginger, bouillon and garlic salt; add to peppers in frying pan. Salt and pepper to taste. Simmer about 5 minutes. Add beef strips and cook another 5 minutes. Add 2 tablespoons of cold water, the dry milk and monosodium glutamate to beef and peppers. Continue cooking and stirring until sauce thickens slightly. Serves 3. (280 calories per serving)

Sweet & Sour Green Beans

- 1 (10-ounce) package frozen green beans *or*
- 1 pound fresh green beans, cut in 1-inch pieces
- 1 teaspoon margarine
- ½ teaspoon all-purpose flour
- 1 tablespoon water
- 1 tablespoon lemon juice
- 1 tablespoon sugar
- ¼ teaspoon dill seed, optional
- Dash paprika

Cook frozen green beans according to directions on package, omitting salt, or cook fresh green beans in ½ cup unsalted water until tender. Drain and set aside. In separate pan, melt margarine; stir in flour and brown slightly. Stir in remaining ingredients and cook over low heat until thickened. Pour over drained green beans and heat 5 minutes. Serves 4. (40 calories per serving)

Tangy Sauced Turkey Tenderloins

- 3 tablespoons vegetable oil
- 2 teaspoons ground cinnamon
- 6 turkey breast tenderloins
- 8 ounces spinach, coarsely chopped

Dressing

- 1 (8-ounce) carton plain lowfat yogurt
- ¼ cup tomato, peeled, seeded and chopped
- ¼ cup cucumber, peeled, seeded and chopped
- 1 tablespoon chopped parsley
- 1 green onion, finely minced
- 1 teaspoon lemon juice

Combine oil and cinnamon. Brush over 1 side of each tenderloin. Place brushed side up on a broiler pan and broil 6 inches from heat source. Turn tenderloins over; brush top sides with oil and cinnamon. Broil 5 minutes more, or until tenderloins test done. Cut into strips and keep warm.

Combine ingredients for dressing and place in a bowl. Place spinach around edge of serving platter. Arrange tenderloin strips on top of spinach. Set bowl of dressing in center of platter. Serves 6. (260 calories per serving)

Turkey Chili

- 1 pound ground turkey
- 1 cup chopped onion
- ½ cup chopped green bell pepper
- 2 tablespoons chopped pimiento
- 1 (16-ounce) can tomatoes
- 1 teaspoon chili powder
- ½ teaspoon black pepper
- Dash red (cayenne) pepper

In a plastic colander, combine turkey, onion and bell pepper. Set colander in a microwave-safe bowl. Microwave on high for 5–6 minutes, or until meat is no longer pink, stirring several times with fork during cooking. In a medium-size bowl, combine turkey mixture, pimiento, tomatoes with juice, chili powder, black pepper and red pepper. Cover tightly. Adjust power level to medium. Microwave 13 minutes. Let stand 5 minutes. Serves 4. (181 calories per serving.)

Vegetable Bean Soup

1 tablespoon vegetable *or* olive oil
1 cup sliced leeks
1 clove garlic, minced
3 cups water
1 (16-ounce) can vegetarian beans in tomato sauce
1 (8-ounce) can whole-kernel corn
1 cup cubed potatoes
1/2 cup sliced celery
1/2 cup sliced carrots
2 teaspoons Worcestershire sauce
1 bay leaf
1/4 teaspoon dried thyme leaves
1/4 teaspoon salt
1/8 teaspoon pepper

In 3-quart saucepan, sauté leeks and garlic in oil until tender. Add water and remaining ingredients. Bring to a boil. Cover; simmer 30 minutes, or until vegetables are tender. Remove bay leaf before serving. Makes 6 cups. (152 calories per serving)

Dietetic Strawberry Pie

1 3/4 cups cornflakes, crushed
3 tablespoons margarine
Sugar substitute equivalent to 1 tablespoon sugar
2 egg whites
2 cups frozen strawberries, thawed, drained and unsweetened, reserve juice
2/3 cup reserved strawberry juice (add water if needed)
1/3 cup lemon juice
Sugar substitute equivalent to 1/2 cup sugar
1 envelope gelatin

Preheat oven to 375 degrees. Mix together first 3 ingredients; use back of spoon to press into a lined 9-inch pie plate.

Combine strawberry juice and gelatin in small saucepan. Heat, stirring constantly, until gelatin is dissolved. Add lemon juice and sugar substitute. Stir in egg whites.

Refrigerate until thickened to consistency of egg whites; beat at top speed of electric mixer until light and frothy. Add drained berries. Pour in crust and refrigerate at least 3 hours before serving. Serves 8.

Orange-Honey Fish

1 pound fresh *or* frozen orange roughy, grouper, cod or other fish fillets
2 tablespoons finely chopped green onion
1 teaspoon finely shredded orange peel
2 tablespoons orange juice
2 tablespoons honey
1/2 teaspoon paprika
1/4 teaspoon salt
1/8 teaspoon pepper
Orange slices (optional)

Thaw fish, if frozen. Pat dry. Cut into 4 serving-size portions. Measure thickness of fish.

For glaze, in a small bowl stir together onion, orange peel, orange juice, honey, paprika, salt and pepper.

Place fish on the unheated rack of a broiler pan. Brush some of glaze over fish. Broil 4 inches from heat (allow 4–6 minutes per 1/2 inch thickness) until fish just flakes with a fork, brushing occasionally with glaze. Garnish with orange slices, if desired. Serves 4. (127 calories per serving)

Sesame Chicken Salad

3 cups cooked rice
2 cups slivered, cooked chicken breast
1/4 pound fresh snow peas, trimmed and cut into julienne strips
1 medium cucumber, peeled, seeded and cut into 1 1/2 x 1/4-inch strips
1 medium red pepper, cut into 1 1/2 x 1/4-inch strips
1/2 cup sliced green onion, including tops
2 tablespoons sesame seed, toasted (optional)
Sesame Dressing (recipe follows)

Combine all ingredients; stir well. Serve at room temperature or slightly chilled.

Sesame Dressing

1/4 cup chicken broth
1 tablespoon peanut oil
3 tablespoons rice vinegar *or* white-wine vinegar
3 tablespoons soy sauce
1 teaspoon sesame oil

Combine all ingredients in jar; cover tightly and shake vigorously. Makes about 3/4 cup. (261 calories per serving)

Peaches With Lemon Sauce

4 large, firm ripe peaches, cut in half and pitted
1 1/2 tablespoons cornstarch
2/3 cup water
2 tablespoons plus 1 teaspoon lemon juice
1 egg yolk
1 tablespoon reduced-calorie margarine
1 tablespoon sugar
1 teaspoon grated lemon peel
1 teaspoon granulated sugar substitute

Place peach halves with backs together in microwave-safe custard cups. Cook on HIGH for 8 minutes, or until juices come to a boil and begin to cover fruit. Remove from microwave as each 1 boils and turn halves over carefully to prevent bruising. Let stand in juices while preparing sauce.

In 1-quart microwave-safe bowl, stir together cornstarch and water. Stir in lemon juice, egg yolk, margarine, sugar, lemon peel and sugar substitute. Cook, uncovered, on HIGH, 2–3 minutes, or until mixture begins to thicken, stirring gently after 1 minute. Let stand 1 minute; spoon over peaches. Serves 4. (95 calories per serving)

Lemon Parsley Sauce

1/2 cup margarine
Juice of 1 large lemon (about 3 tablespoons)
1 teaspoon grated lemon rind
1 tablespoon chopped parsley

Heat margarine and lemon juice in a saucepan. Add grated lemon rind; stir in chopped parsley. Pour over fish. Makes 3/4 cup. (70 calories per tablespoon)

Christmas Eve Salad

1 (8¼-ounce) can sliced beets
1 (8-ounce) can chunk pineapple, packed in juice
1 medium orange, pared and sectioned
1 pink grapefruit, pared and sectioned
2 bananas, sliced
1 (8-ounce) can water chestnuts, drained and sliced
2 tablespoons lemon juice
1 teaspoon sugar substitute, divided
3 cups shredded lettuce
1 lime, cut into wedges
¼ cup blanched almond slivers
1 tablespoon anise seed

Drain beets and pineapple, reserving liquid. In large bowl, combine beets, pineapple, orange, grapefruit, bananas and water chestnuts. In small bowl, combine reserved beet and pineapple liquids, lemon juice and ½ teaspoon sugar substitute. Pour over fruit.

Let stand 10 minutes; drain. In serving bowl, arrange fruit on shredded lettuce. Garnish with lime wedges and almonds. In cup, combine anise seed and remaining ½ teaspoon sugar substitute; sprinkle over salad. Serves 8. (115 calories per serving)

Tuna in a Pita

1 (6½-ounce) can tuna in water
2 tablespoons choppedonion
1 tablespoon choppedcarrot
1 tablespoon vinegar
2 whole-wheat pita breads, cut in half to form pockets
2 tablespoons alfalfa sprouts
3 leaves Boston lettuce
Non-stick cooking spray

Combine tuna, chopped onion, chopped carrot and vinegar in small bowl. Spray non-stick cooking spray into the bowl for about 3 seconds. Mix well. Toast ½ pita which has been sprayed with non-stick cooking spray for about 1 second. Fill pocket of pita with tuna mixture, alfalfa sprouts and lettuce. Serve immediately. Serves 4. (155 calories per serving)

Breakfast Home Fries

½ teaspoon margarine
¼ cup chopped onion
½ teaspoon browning sauce
½ teaspoon garlic powder
¼ teaspoon dried leaf thyme
½ teaspoon paprika
2 medium (5½-ounce) baking potatoes, peeled and cut in ½-inch cubes

In a 1½-quart casserole, combine margarine, onion, browning sauce, garlic powder, thyme and paprika. Microwave on high for 20 seconds, or until margarine is melted. Coat potatoes in margarine mixture. Microwave on high for 8–9 minutes, or until potatoes are fork-tender, stirring potatoes every 2 minutes during cooking. Serves 4. (83 calories per serving.)

Herbed Fillet of Sole

⅓ cup lemon juice
¼ teaspoon dry mustard
½ teaspoon tarragon
2 tablespoons margarine
1 pound fillet of sole

Combine lemon juice, mustard and tarragon. Spread margarine in flat baking dish and add fish. Brush with seasoned lemon juice. Broil 2–3 inches from heat for 5–8 minutes for thin fillets (10–12 minutes for thicker fillets). Brush once or twice with lemon juice mixture during broiling. Fish is done when it is firm and flakes easily with a fork. Do not overcook. Serves 4. (165 calories per serving)

Cranapple Relish

1 apple
2 cups fresh *or* frozen cranberries
2 packages substitute sugar sweetener
1 navel orange, peeled
½ teaspoon ground coriander

Shred apple in a food processor or with a hand grater. Quarter orange and combine with cranberries in a food processor or food grinder. Process until coarsely chopped. Blend apples, cranberry mixture, coriander and sweetener together. Cover and refrigerate until ready to serve. Serves 6. (39 calories per serving)

Fruit Cocktail With Yogurt or Sour Cream

½ cup fresh *or* frozen strawberries
½ cup fresh pineapple
¼ cup sliced bananas
½ cup yogurt *or* ¼ pint sour cream

Into 4 serving glasses, distribute strawberries; cover with 2 teaspoons yogurt or sour cream in each glass. Next, place a layer of pineapple, a layer of bananas, then another layer of yogurt. Top off with a large strawberry. Serves 4. (164 calories per serving)

Baked Custard

2½ cups sugar
4 egg whites
1 teaspoon vanilla
1 tablespoon table sherry
Few drops yellow food coloring
Dash nutmeg

Mix all ingredients, except nutmeg. Pour into lightly oiled custard cups. Sprinkle with nutmeg. Place custard cups in pan of hot water and bake in a 325-degree oven for 50 minutes, or until knife inserted near center of custard comes out clean. Serves 6. (80 calories per serving)

Velvet Zucchini

2 (7–8-inch) zucchini
2 tablespoons butter *or* margarine
1 small onion, chopped
1 clove garlic
¾ to 1 teaspoon curry powder
½ cup light cream
1 (13¾-ounce) can chicken broth

Sauté zucchini, onion and garlic until soft. Add curry powder; simmer covered for 15 minutes. Blend in blender. Add cream and broth; blend until smooth. Serve hot or cold. Garnish with a dollop of sour cream and fresh parsley. Great with garlic-cheese bread and tossed salad.

Vegetable DELIGHTS

Herbed Corn on the Cob

- ½ cup unsalted butter, room temperature
- 2 tablespoons chopped fresh parsley
- ¼ cup snipped fresh chives
- Salt
- Freshly ground black pepper
- Tabasco
- 4 ears fresh sweet corn

In food processor, combine butter, parsley and chives. Adjust seasonings with salt, black pepper and Tabasco to your taste. Husk and clean corn. Place each ear individually in center of a piece of aluminum foil, shiny side up. Coat the ear with ¼ butter mixture. Wrap foil around corn, making sure ear is well-sealed by foil. Cook corn in a preheated 400-degree oven. Place corn on lower rack of oven, sealed edge up.

Cook until tender, turning frequently, about 10–15 minutes. Remove from oven to a rack to cool slightly. Transport corn in the foil to your destination. Carefully peel foil back to form a trough to hold corn in butter while eating.

Tangy Cheese-Stuffed Potatoes

- 6 large baking potatoes (about 3 pounds)
- 1 (8-ounce) container sour cream dip with toasted onion
- 1 cup (4 ounces) finely shredded sharp cheddar cheese
- ½ cup butter, softened
- ¼ teaspoon pepper
- Paprika

Heat oven to 425 degrees. Pierce potatoes with tines of a fork. Bake for 40–50 minutes, or until tender. Halve potatoes lengthwise. Scoop out insides, reserving shells.

In a large mixer bowl combine hot potato, dip, cheddar cheese, butter and pepper. Beat with an electric mixer on high speed until fluffy. Spoon potato mixture into shells; sprinkle tops with paprika. Place in a 13 x 9 x 2-inch baking dish. Bake for 25 minutes or until heated through.

Microwave directions: Pierce potatoes with tines of fork. Arrange in a circular spoke pattern in microwave oven, leaving a space between each potato. Cook, uncovered, on 100 percent power (HIGH) for 16–17 minutes or until tender, rearranging twice.

Scoop out pulp and make filling as directed above. Arrange half of filled potatoes on a 12-inch microwave-safe pizza plate. Micro-cook, uncovered, on HIGH for 4–5 minutes, or until hot, giving dish a half-turn once. Cover loosely to keep warm. Repeat with remaining potatoes. Serves 12.

Asparagus Cheese Casserole

- 2 cups cooked asparagus (fresh, frozen *or* canned)
- 3 hard-cooked eggs, sliced
- ½ cup buttered bread crumbs
- 1 cup shredded cheddar cheese
- 3 tablespoons butter
- 1 tablespoon chopped onion
- 2 tablespoons flour
- 1 cup milk
- ½ teaspoon salt

Melt butter; add onion and cook until tender. Add flour and blend. Add milk and cook until mixture thickens. Finally, add seasoning and cheese, cooking until well-blended. Alternate layers of cooked asparagus and egg slices with sauce in a buttered baking dish. Top with buttered crumbs. Bake in a moderate oven at 350 degrees for 25 minutes, or until crumb topping is browned and sauce bubbles up through the mixture.

Delicious Herbed Eggplant

- 1 large, firm eggplant, peeled and sliced
- ⅓ cup light cream
- 1¼ cups herb-seasoned stuffing mix, divided in half
- 1 (10¾-ounce) can cream of celery soup, undiluted
- 1 slightly beaten egg
- Salt to taste
- 2 tablespoons butter
- ½ teaspoon oregano

Place eggplant in a 2-quart casserole; cover with plastic wrap. Microwave on HIGH for 7 minutes; drain. While eggplant is cooking, combine cream, egg and ¾ cup stuffing mix, soup, salt and oregano; blend well and stir in drained eggplant. Return mixture to 2-quart casserole.

Combine butter and remaining stuffing mix. Sprinkle over eggplant mixture. Cover with waxed paper. Microwave on HIGH for 7–9 minutes. Let stand, covered, 3–5 minutes. Serves 4.

Spinach Lasagna

- ½ cup chopped onion
- 1 tablespoon oil
- 2 cups tomato sauce
- 2 cups ricotta cheese
- ½ cup Parmesan cheese
- 1 egg
- 2 tablespoons fresh oregano *or* 1 teaspoon dried
- 8 uncooked lasagna noodles
- 3 (10-ounce) packages frozen chopped spinach, defrosted and drained
- 2 cups mozzarella cheese

Place onion and oil in casserole; microwave on HIGH for 1–2 minutes; add tomato sauce and cover. Microwave on HIGH for 4–5 minutes until boiling. In a bowl blend ricotta cheese, half (¼ cup) Parmesan cheese, egg and oregano. Spread 1 cup sauce on bottom of 11 x 8-inch dish. Overlap 4 uncooked noodles over sauce.

Spread on in order: 1 cup ricotta cheese, all of spinach and 1 cup mozzarella cheese.

Spread on in order: 1 cup sauce, 4 overlapping uncooked noodles, remaining ricotta cheese mixture, remaining sauce.

Cover. Microwave on HIGH for 10 minutes; rotate dish if necessary. Microwave on MEDIUM for 22–28 minutes until noodles are tender. Let stand, covered, for 10 minutes. Top with remaining mozzarella and Parmesan cheeses.

Creamy Broccoli Casserole

- 3 cups broccoli, chopped
- 1 cup mayonnaise
- 1 egg, beaten
- ¼ cup onion, minced
- 1 cup grated cheddar cheese
- 1 can cream of chicken soup
- ½ cup seasoned bread crumbs

In boiling water cook broccoli; drain. Place in a greased 2-quart casserole and set aside. Combine mayonnaise, egg and onion. Beat well. Stir in cheddar cheese and chicken soup. Pour over broccoli in casserole and sprinkle with bread crumbs. Bake at 350 degrees for 30 minutes. Enjoy!

Brussels Sprouts & Chestnuts

- 1¼ pounds small brussels sprouts, washed, damaged leaves removed
- 2 cups water
- 4 tablespoons (½ stick) unsalted butter
- 1¼ cups all-purpose flour
- 1 cup chicken broth
- 1 cup half-and-half
- 1 cup shredded Swiss cheese
- 1 (15½-ounce) can chestnuts, drained, rinsed, cut in half
- Salt and freshly ground white pepper

Trim stems of sprouts and cut crosses in them to speed cooking. Boil water in a small skillet. Add brussels sprouts. Cover. Reduce heat and cook 6–7 minutes, or until just tender. Drain.

In the meantime, heat butter in medium saucepan. Add flour. Stir until smooth and lightly golden. Gradually whisk in broth and half-and-half, stirring constantly over low heat until thickened and smooth. Add cheese and stir until melted. Add sprouts and chestnuts; cook, stirring until just heated through. Season with salt and pepper and serve hot.

Broccoli Cheese Stuffed Shells

- 6 ounces jumbo macaroni shells (24 shells)
- 3 quarts boiling water
- 1 (10-ounce) package frozen chopped broccoli, thawed
- 1 cup ricotta cheese
- ½ cup shredded Swiss cheese
- 1 tablespoon shredded onion
- 3 cups canned stewed tomatoes

Add shells to boiling water. Cook, uncovered, stirring and cooking until tender. Drain in colander and rinse. While shells are cooking combine broccoli, ricotta cheese, Swiss cheese and onion. Stir until well-blended.

Pour about 1 cup of tomatoes over bottom of micro-wave safe 13 x 9-inch pan; break up tomatoes with a fork. Spoon about 1 tablespoon of cheese mixture into each shell and place in pan; pour remaining 2 cups of sauce around shells. Cover with plastic wrap and microwave on 70 percent power (MEDIUM HIGH) for 13 minutes.

Irish Potato Casserole

- 2 pounds frozen hash browns, thawed
- 1 teaspoon salt
- ½ cup butter, melted
- 2 tablespoons minced onion
- 1 cup cream of potato soup, undiluted
- ½ cup shredded cheddar cheese
- ½ teaspoon pepper
- ¼ cup parsley
- 2 cups sour cream
- 2 cups cornflakes, crushed

Place potatoes in a greased 9 x 13-inch pan. In bowl, combine all ingredients, except cornflakes, cheese and parsley. Spoon creamed mixture over potatoes. Sprinkle with cheese, parsley and crushed cornflakes. Bake at 350 degrees for 40–60 minutes.

I usually serve this with corned beef or ham. Fantastic!

Vegetable Tacos

- 1 tablespoon butter
- ⅔ cup sliced green onion
- ½ cup chopped green pepper
- 1½ cups cooked corn, drained
- 1 cup kidney beans, drained
- 3 tablespoons chili sauce
- ½ teaspoon chili powder
- ⅛ teaspoon garlic powder
- 1½ cups (6 ounces) shredded Monterey Jack cheese
- 12 prepared taco shells, heated
- 2 cups chopped tomatoes
- 2 cups shredded lettuce
- 1½ cups (6 ounces) shredded cheddar cheese

Preheat oven to 350 degrees. Melt butter in medium-size saucepan. Sauté onion and green pepper until tender, about 5 minutes. Stir in corn, beans, chili sauce and seasonings. Heat over medium heat 5 minutes, stirring occasionally. Remove from heat. Stir in Monterey Jack cheese.

Fill taco shells with cheese-vegetable mixture. Place on cookie sheet. Bake 5–7 minutes or until hot. Remove from oven and top with tomatoes, lettuce and cheddar cheese. Serve immediately. Makes 12.

Spring Vegetable Tart

- **6 slices white bread**
- **2–3 tablespoons margarine *or* butter, melted**
- **4 ripe tomatoes, sliced**
- **2 large sweet onions, sliced and sautéed in butter *or* margarine**
- **2 large white potatoes, cooked and sliced**
- **Pinch of basil and rosemary**
- **Salt and pepper to taste**
- **½ teaspoon sugar**
- **1 package frozen spinach, cooked and well-drained**
- **Margarine, cheese and grated cheese**

Trim bread and cut each slice in half. Completely line a well-buttered 9-inch baking dish with bread, forming a tart shell. Brush well with melted margarine or butter. Sauté tomato until soft, but not mushy. Layer tomato in tart shell. Top with a layer of sautéed onions and sliced potatoes. Dot with bits of margarine and cheese.

Season each layer with basil, rosemary, salt, pepper and sugar. Drain cooked spinach in a colander until completely free of liquid. Place on top layer. Dot with margarine. Sprinkle with grated cheese. Bake in preheated oven at 375 degrees for 25 minutes, until tart is hot and bubbly. Cut into squares and serve.

Cheesy Sliced Baked Potatoes

- **4 medium potatoes**
- **1 teaspoon salt**
- **2–3 tablespoons butter, melted**
- **2–3 tablespoons chopped fresh herbs *or* 2–3 teaspoons dried herbs such as parsley, chives, thyme *or* sage***
- **4 tablespoons grated cheddar cheese**
- **1½ tablespoons grated Parmesan cheese**

Peel potatoes if skin is tough, otherwise, just scrub and rinse. Cut potatoes into thin slices, but not all the way through. Placing potato in a wooden spoon helps cutting. Potato should still be in 1 piece with an accordion-look to sliced part. Put potatoes in a baking dish. Fan slices apart slightly. Sprinkle with salt and drizzle with butter; sprinkle with herbs. Bake at 425 degrees for 50 minutes. Remove from oven. Sprinkle with both cheeses. Bake for another 10–15 minutes until lightly browned, cheeses are melted and potatoes are soft when pierced with fork.

To microwave: Prepare potatoes as recipe indicates, but microwave at high power for 10 minutes, rearranging after 5 minutes. Let rest for 5 minutes. Sprinkle with cheeses and microwave for another 4–6 minutes at high until cheese is melted and potatoes are soft.

Easy to prepare; may be made ahead of time, refrigerated and then baked when needed. Looks very attractive and elegant; goes well with roast beef or ham. Serves 4.

*May use 1½ teaspoons of caraway seeds or cumin in place of herbs.

Apple Butter Sweet Potatoes

- **2½ pounds sweet potatoes**
- **¼ cup (½ stick) unsalted butter**
- **½ cup apple butter**
- **¼ teaspoon salt**
- **1 tablespoon dark brown sugar**
- **⅓ cup pecans, coarsely chopped**

Prepare sweet potatoes; cut into 1-inch cubes. Cook in lightly salted boiling water to cover until tender, about 15 minutes. Drain and let cool. Melt butter in large non-stick skillet over medium heat; mix in apple butter, sugar and salt. Add sweet potatoes. Cook over medium-low heat until heated through, stirring often, gently. Turn into serving bowl. Sprinkle with pecans.

Cream of Broccoli Soup

- **⅓ cup margarine**
- **1 garlic clove, minced**
- **1 medium onion, chopped**
- **⅓ cup flour**
- **1 cup water**
- **1 chicken-flavored bouillon cube**
- **3 cups broccoli florets**
- **1 cup mushrooms, chopped**

Melt margarine; sauté garlic clove and onion. Stir in flour. Add water, bouillon cube, broccoli and mushrooms. Simmer for 20 minutes, stirring constantly.

Main-Dish Eggplant

- **8 ounces ground beef**
- **Salt and pepper to taste**
- **½ small onion**
- **1 small clove garlic**
- **2 tablespoons chopped green pepper**
- **1 (8-ounce) can tomato sauce**
- **2 tablespoons chopped parsley**
- **½ teaspoon dried oregano**
- **1 (8–12-ounce) eggplant**

Shape meat into patties; sprinkle with salt and pepper. Use a large skillet; cook patties over medium heat until almost desired degrees of doneness; remove from pan; discard drippings leaving only a thin film in skillet.

While meat cooks, chop onion; mince garlic; prepare green pepper and parsley; peel eggplant and cut into 1½-inch cubes. Add onion, garlic and green pepper to warm skillet. Cook on low heat about 2 minutes; stir in tomato sauce, parsley and oregano. Arrange eggplant cubes and meat patties on tomato sauce in a single layer.

Cover; cook over medium heat for about 8 minutes. Turn eggplant and meat, spooning on sauce. Cover; cook about 8 minutes longer, or until eggplant is barely tender—be careful not to overcook. Serve with pan sauce. Serves 2.

Variations: This dish is also good made with ground lamb in place of beef and ½ teaspoon rosemary, instead of oregano. A double-quick version of this dish is to sauté thick slices of peeled eggplant; serve topped with heated meat (or meatless) spaghetti sauce and Parmesan cheese.

Lemon Carrots

- **1 (1-pound) can diced carrots,**
- **1 teaspoon sugar**
- **1 teaspoon lemon juice**
- **2 teaspoons butter**
- **½ teaspoon grated lemon peel**

Reserve ¼ cup liquid from carrots. Combine carrot juice, sugar, lemon juice and butter. Heat and stir until hot. Add carrots and heat through. Sprinkle with lemon peel.

Asparagus Mousse

- $1\frac{1}{2}$ pounds asparagus
- 2 cups whipping cream
- 2 egg whites
- 1 package unflavored gelatin
- 2 tablespoons lemon juice
- Salt and pepper to taste
- Nutmeg
- $\frac{1}{2}$ cup freshly chopped watercress
- Watercress sprigs for garnish

Rinse asparagus; cut or break away the woody ends; cook stalks in boiling water for 5 minutes, or until soft but not mushy. Cut off a few tips and reserve for decoration. Purée remaining asparagus in a food mill or food processor. Season well with salt, pepper and nutmeg to taste. Whip cream. In a separate bowl, whip egg whites.

Put gelatin in a small cup with lemon juice. Set the cup into a bowl of hot water and stir gelatin mixture until all the crystals have dissolved. Blend this mixture thoroughly into the asparagus. Stir in whipped cream. Finally, fold in egg whites. Pour mixture into a wide bowl or into custard cups. Allow to sit in a cool place, but do not over-refrigerate so that the mousse gets very cold. Before serving, garnish with reserved tips and watercress sprigs. Serves 8.

Sautéed Potatoes With Garlic

- 4 potatoes (about $1\frac{1}{2}$ pounds)
- Salt to taste
- 2 tablespoons corn, peanut *or* vegetable oil
- 1 tablespoon butter
- 1 teaspoon garlic, finely minced
- 2 tablespoons parsley, finely chopped

Place potatoes in a kettle and add cold water to cover; salt to taste. Bring to a boil and cook about 20 minutes, or until potatoes are tender. Drain. Peel potatoes and cut them crosswise into $\frac{1}{4}$-inch-thick slices. Heat oil in a skillet; when it is hot, add potato slices and garlic. Cook, shaking skillet and stirring gently to redistribute the slices so they brown evenly, for 10 minutes, or until all slices are browned on both sides. Add butter and parsley; toss to blend. Serves 4.

Spinach-Stuffed Onions

- 1 (3-ounce) package cream cheese, softened
- 1 egg
- $\frac{1}{2}$ cup soft bread crumbs
- $\frac{1}{4}$ cup Parmesan cheese, grated
- $\frac{1}{4}$ cup milk
- $\frac{1}{4}$ teaspoon salt. Dash pepper
- 16 ounces chopped spinach, cooked and well-drained
- 1 large onion

Preheat oven to 350 degrees. Beat together cream cheese and egg until light. Add crumbs, cheese, milk, salt and pepper; mix well. Stir in spinach. Peel onion and cut in half crosswise. Separate layers and form shells. Place in shallow $1\frac{1}{2}$-quart baking dish.

Fill base of shells with smaller onion pieces, if necessary. Spoon spinach mixture in onion shells. Cover with foil and bake for 35–40 minutes, or until onion shells are tender and filling is set.

Note: You may use 2 onions for more uniform shells. Serves 4–6.

Fire & Ice Tomatoes

- 6 medium tomatoes, peeled and quartered
- 1 medium onion, sliced
- 1 medium green pepper, cut into strips
- $\frac{1}{4}$ cup water
- 1 tablespoon plus 2 teaspoons white sugar
- $1\frac{1}{2}$ teaspoons celery salt
- $1\frac{1}{2}$ teaspoons mustard seed
- 1 large cucumber, peeled and sliced
- $\frac{3}{4}$ cup cider vinegar
- $\frac{1}{4}$ teaspoon salt
- $\frac{1}{2}$ teaspoon cayenne pepper
- $\frac{1}{8}$ teaspoon black pepper

Combine tomatoes, onion and green pepper in a bowl. Combine vinegar, water, sugar, celery salt, mustard seed, salt and peppers in a large saucepan. Bring to a boil over medium heat. Boil 1 minute. Pour hot mixture over vegetable mixture. Cover and refrigerate 8 hours, or overnight to blend flavors. Serve with a slotted spoon.

Holiday Vegetable Trio

- 6 medium-size potatoes (about 2 pounds)
- 1 (16-ounce) bag carrots
- 4 large parsnips (about 1 pound)
- $\frac{1}{3}$ cup hot milk
- 4 tablespoons ($\frac{1}{2}$ stick) butter *or* margarine
- 1 tablespoon brown sugar
- $1\frac{1}{2}$ teaspoons salt

In 4-quart saucepan over high heat, heat potatoes and enough water to cover to boiling. Reduce heat to low. Cover and simmer 25–30 minutes until potatoes are fork-tender. Drain. Cool potatoes until easy to handle. Peel. Return potatoes to saucepan.

Meanwhile, peel and cut carrots and parsnips into 1-inch chunks. In 3-quart saucepan over high heat, heat carrots, parsnips and $\frac{1}{2}$ inch water to boiling. Reduce heat to low. Cover and simmer 20–30 minutes until carrots and parsnips are tender. Drain.

In saucepan with potatoes, add carrots, parsnips, milk, butter, brown sugar and salt. With potato masher, mash vegetables until almost smooth. Serves 12.

String Beans in Sauce

- 3 slices bacon, fried crisp and crumbled, reserve drippings
- 2 cans string beans
- 1 teaspoon salt
- 4 tablespoons bacon drippings
- 1 large onion, chopped
- $1\frac{1}{2}$ tablespoons flour
- $\frac{1}{2}$ teaspoon pepper
- $1\frac{1}{2}$ teaspoons sugar
- 1 tablespoon vinegar
- $\frac{1}{2}$ cup grated cheese

Cook beans in microwave until hot; drain, reserving $\frac{3}{4}$ cup liquid. Return beans to microwave to keep warm.

In skillet, sauté onion in bacon fat. Stir in flour. Add bean liquid and cook until thickened. Add remaining ingredients, except beans, and cook until cheese melts. Pour sauce over beans and serve hot.

Green Tomato Mincemeat

1 peck green tomatoes (about 75 medium-size tomatoes)
25 apples, peeled, cored and chopped
4 lemons, unpeeled and seeds removed
3 pounds raisins
3 pounds brown sugar
2 tablespoons ground cloves
2 tablespoons cinnamon
1 tablespoon nutmeg
2 tablespoons salt
1 pound butter

Place all fruits through the grinder/processor and finely chop. In large enamel or stainless steel (not aluminum) kettle bring to a boil over medium to low heat. Add spices, salt and butter. Stir with wooden spoon until butter is melted.

Simmer for several hours, stirring occasionally until mixture is thick and rather transparent.

This was always put into sterile jars and canned, but today I prefer freezing after mixture has cooled completely. The aroma, while cooking, is sheer heaven.

Pickled Mushrooms

3 pounds small, fresh button mushrooms
Water
3 tablespoons salt
2 large cloves garlic, chopped
2 onions, finely chopped
25 crushed peppercorns
2 teaspoons dried thyme
3 lemons, juice and rind
6 cups white wine
2 cups cider vinegar
4 bay leaves
2 tablespoons salt
1/2 cup snipped parsley
1 cup olive oil

Cover mushrooms with water containing 3 tablespoons salt. Soak for 10 minutes; drain; add to the marinade (containing all remaining ingredients). Heat. When mixture boils, turn down heat to simmer for 10 minutes, or until mushrooms are tender. Discard lemon rinds and chill.

These may be put into jars for preserving if they are ladled into sterilized jars while boiling hot and sealed with rubber rings.

Stuffed Squash

3 acorn squash, each about 1 1/2 pounds
2 tablespoons butter *or* margarine
1/4 cup chopped onion
1/4 cup chopped celery
1/4 teaspoon salt
1/8 teaspoon pepper
1/2 teaspoon lemon juice
1 apple, pared, cored and diced
1 cup fresh cranberries
2 tablespoons water
1/2 cup sugar

Halve squash; scoop out seeds. Place cut side down in baking pan. Add 3/4-inch of water. Bake in a 400-degree oven for 35 minutes. While squash is cooking, melt butter in saucepan. Add onion and celery; cook until tender.

Add salt, pepper, lemon juice and apple. Cook over low heat until apple is tender. Add cranberries and water. Cook just until berries begin to pop. Add sugar; stir until dissolved. Turn squash over in pan and fill with cranberry mixture. Cover and bake 15 minutes longer. Serves 6.

Southern Eggplant

1 medium-size eggplant
2 medium-size onions, sliced (about 1 cup)
2 tablespoons butter
3 tomatoes, peeled and cut into eighths *or* 2 cups cooked tomatoes
1 1/4 teaspoons salt
1/4 teaspoon white pepper
1 (7-ounce) can shrimp, drained and cut
1/4 cup toasted, buttered bread crumbs

Cook eggplant, covered in 1 inch boiling water until tender, about 25 minutes. Cool, peel and dice. Cook onion in butter until tender; add tomatoes and cook until soft, about 7 minutes. Add seasonings, shrimp and eggplant; mix. Pour into greased 1 1/2-quart casserole; top with buttered crumbs. Bake covered, in a 350-degree oven for about 1/2 hour.

Pearly Carrot Combo

1 cup water
2/3 cup pearl barley
1 1/2 cups milk
5 carrots, grated
1/4 teaspoon salt
1/2 teaspoon honey
1/4 teaspoon nutmeg
2 eggs, beaten
2 tablespoons butter *or* margarine, divided
3 tablespoons bread crumbs

In a saucepan bring water to a boil; add pearl barley; simmer until water is absorbed; cool. Mix next 6 ingredients with pearl barley. Grease a 1 1/2-quart casserole with 1 tablespoon butter; sprinkle bottom of casserole with half the bread crumbs. Pour mixture into baking dish; sprinkle top with remaining bread crumbs; dot with remaining butter. Bake at 375 degrees for 40 minutes, until golden and bubbly. Serves 5.

Lamb in Asparagus Sauce

2 pounds lamb, cubed
2 pounds asparagus
2 onions, chopped
1 tablespoon flour
3 tablespoons butter
1/2 cup cream
Salt
Pepper
Lemon juice to taste

Trim off tough part of the asparagus stem and then boil the asparagus for 8 minutes. Drain, reserving a cup of liquid. Toss meat in flour. Melt butter; sauté meat and chopped onions until brown. Gradually add reserved cooking liquid and simmer meat for 45 minutes, or until tender. Meanwhile cut off tips from asparagus and purée stems. Add cream to purée; season to taste with salt, pepper and lemon juice. When meat is tender, stir in purée. Arrange tips in a serving dish; pour in meat and sauce. Serve with new potatoes.

INDEX

APPETIZERS

BEVERAGES

BREADS

BRUNCH FARE

CAKES

CASSEROLES CREATIVE

INDEX

INDEX

INDEX